THE PREPPER'S WATER MANUAL:

A Resource Guide For Smart Preppers And Owners Of Self-Sufficient And Off-The-Grid Homesteads

Harvest Rainwater - Drill For Water - Drive A Well Point - Dig A Well - Build A Distillation Unit - Design A Filtration System - Manage Your Well - Store Your Water - Avoid Waterborne Disease - Learn Why The Weather Matters

Daniel Schoeman

Art production and Book design by A.D. Schoeman.

Cover design and Ilustration by A.D. Schoeman.

All illustrations done by A.D. Schoeman and the Inkscape Openclipart project.

Note To Readers.
The information provided in this book is designed to provide helpful information on the subjects of water management. This book is a reference guide presented solely for educational and entertainment purposes. The author and publisher are not offering it as professional services advice. While best efforts have been used in preparing this book, the author and publisher make no representations or warranties of any kind and assume no liabilities of any kind with respect to the accuracy or completeness of the contents and specifically disclaim any implied warranties of merchantability or fitness of use for a particular purpose. No warranties or guarantees are expressed or implied by the publisher's choice to include any of the content in this volume. Neither the publisher nor the individual author shall be liable for any physical, psychological, emotional, financial, or commercial damages, including, but not limited to, special, incidental, consequential or other damages. Our views and rights are the same: You are responsible for your own choices, actions, and results.
References are provided for informational purposes only and do not constitute endorsement of any websites or other sources. Readers should be aware that the websites listed in this book may change.

DEDICATION

This book is dedicated to my father, a man honest and wise.

To my mother, whose light shines brightest.

*For When The Well Is Dry, We
Will Know The Worth Of Water.*

-Benjamin Franklin

CONTENTS

Foreword

Welcome to a conversation about water.

Every chapter discusses a certain aspect of water management. The reader will have to adapt the information to his or her real-life environment and individual water-related needs. When dealing with water, don't forget that water is a very simple medium and that it just wants to flow; whether at the bottom of a well or on top of a roof, water needs to flow without being obstructed. Keep this philosophy in mind when drilling, connecting pump lines, dealing with contaminants and when installing filters in a water feed line.
Allow a steady flow of living water.

Initially, I wrote this manual as a guide to assist me during a potential, water-related emergency of my own. Almost two decades of traveling through South East Asia, Australasia and living in Africa for another 25 years, has definitely left me with an awareness of the value of water as a resource for sanitation, medicine, farming and sustaining life. Although very informative and rewarding, the research also revealed that water distribution and weather cycles were starting to cause a scarcity of clean, drinkable water and this was becoming a major topic of discussion, even at government level.
It led me to an alarming conclusion.
At this moment in human history, the probability of us humans running out of potable water is actually very high.

Fear has the capacity to cripple and it is my hope that the information in this book will empower the reader; the aim is to cultivate a strong belief in the individual's own ability, and to motivate each of us to reach out to the community and to bring like-minded people together.

I trust that this knowledge will serve as a tool to give you the peace of mind to, like the camel, weather the storm no matter what nature throws at you.

Water.
Why It's An
Issue.

Growing up in the 70's and 80's, I still remember what a pleasure it was to run into a neighbor's yard and to grab a fistful of strawberries, a peach or even a fig. It wasn't about the thrill of taking something that didn't belong to me, but more about having access to, what I believed to be, the absolute best fruit in the neighborhood. This particular neighbor was well-known in the community and considered quite the innovator, a real "can do" man who had a solution for every problem. He allowed us kids to come and go as we please, pretending not to see, just as long as we didn't do any harm to the network of pipes, pumps and barrels that crisscrossed his yard. His back-yard creations were surely works of art, way ahead of their time, but as kids we were ignorant and unaware of the ingenuity and craftiness that lay before

our eyes. I often think back to those days. At the time, many families owned their own swim-ming pools where neighbors, friends and family congregated over weekends. If you didn't have a pool, there were water holes, rivers and lakes to ex-plore. The greatest convenience was, of course, to grab a glass and fill it up with water straight from the faucet; it tasted good and during the hot summer months I drank at least five glasses per day. As a child, I did not realize that I was living in a world of abundance, a landscape rich in water. Safe to say that I took the whole experience for granted, not realizing that I was part of a generation who still had the peace of mind that there was enough to go around. This abundance was designed and created by a system of common sense and the unselfish aim of serving and providing for the community. Something from those days must have stuck with me, because many years later I became obsessed with self-sufficiency, organic farming and prepping for scenarios where we run out of resources.

The importance of water is realized universally. No matter where in the world, we all envision a life with an abundance of water. Water means growth and it is the foundation of life, found inside the cells of all living organisms and responsible for maintaining health at the cellular level. It is the one commodity we cannot do without. Found in a liquid, solid and gaseous states it plays a vital part in the survival of every species on planet earth. Not a day goes by that we humans don't use gallons of water, whether on ourselves or on our homestead. Water nourishes, replenishes, cleans, and treats; it's a base in our cooking, is used for cleaning and nourishes plants and livestock. Not only is water used for drinking but it is also responsible for sanitation and removal of waste material. Water-born

Not a day goes by that we humans don't use gallons of water, whether on ourselves or on our homestead.

diseases are known to decimate populations and can quickly spread to adjacent areas. An absence of water causes droughts, crops to fail and livestock to perish.

Nowadays, more and more of us are starting to experience new stages of dissatisfaction when it comes to our water quality and source. The situation is dismal in certain parts of the world as weather systems, economic development and the exploitation of water as a resource are all creating conflict and disapproval. Corporations are continuously exploiting our water resources and sadly, sacrificing the well-being of the community has become the norm, all in the quest of making a buck at any cost. In some areas pesticides, chemicals and antibiotics contaminate runoffs and the result

Start to pay attention

Getting serious about water means that you are aware of the issues that face you and your household. To become an in-house activist, start by calculating your family's monthly water consumption. Inspect faucets and pipes for leaks beforehand and start thinking how you can save water, especially in the bathroom.

Hint! Toilets use about 40% of your household water!

is tap water that's not fit for human consumption. Bottled water seemed like a good idea not so long ago, till we calculated the costs and realized that most companies do not deliver "mineral water" but mere tap water. Natural disasters and extreme weather events are on the rise. Earthquakes, hurricanes, tsunamis, flooding and droughts all pose a threat to disrupt water supply lines or to contaminate the water sources that we rely on. Even countries with an abundance of freshwater, take it for granted; they assume that this commodity will just exist indefinitely.

Although water covers about two thirds of the planet, finding it in a fresh and drinkable form is no simple task. Actually, nearly one billion people on this planet still do not have access to it and in some parts of the world people even spend their entire day searching for semi-drinkable water. Recently the UN Deputy Secretary General declared that "The human right to water is a historic, noble, even sacred mission and cause." The problem with finding water is not a simple one and one driving force behind water scarcity is overpopulation. Simply put: More people means that more water is required for waste removal, manufacturing, sanitation, construction, food production, etc. Water treatment infrastructure has to adapt to the needs of the people and more money will

We can safely say that water plays a vital part in the survival of man and to live a self-sufficient lifestyle, we will need to know more than the average man about water.

have to be invested in water research and treatment facilities. The future definitely holds some problematic issues for us humans and the current prediction is, that in the next 20 years, the quantity of fresh water available will decrease by 30%. If this statistic becomes a reality, it has the makings of a catastrophe and it also has the potential to disrupt the daily routines of millions of people. It certainly holds true that we humans have neglected the safeguarding of our water supply, and we have created a mountain of problems out of a resource that should have been free and available to all in the first place.

This book is about water. Whether you live in the inner city, suburbs or out in the country, you can bet that water matters and that it always will. It now makes more sense than ever to secure a water source on your property and to store as much as possible for emergencies. Your water needs must be met, even before you think about owning a homestead, going off-grid or living a

self-sufficient lifestyle. If you are an individual who has stopped taking resources for granted, and if you want to give yourself a decent chance at having access to clean water at all times, then this book is for you. To give ourselves a fair shot at surviving any water crisis, we need to know what we are dealing with. Knowledge can provide us with the know-how to weather this crisis and to survive in comfort. Over the next few chapters we'll discuss the ins and outs of water. We will look at weather patterns and how to locate, collect, treat and store water. There is a "can do" attitude in all of us and this is exactly what's needed to get us back on course again. With some knowledge, a good dose of common sense and the right attitude, you can ride out the storm and be wiser for it. The aim is not to isolate, but to create a community of like-minded people who are passionate about survival and who want to educate themselves for the greater good of man.
Let's take a look at the various topics covered in this book.

• Understanding water. If we want to be prepared for whatever disaster situation, we will have to become highly knowledgeable about water. This means understanding how the water cycle works and how it influences our environment. Extreme weather events need to be investigated to avoid becoming a victim.

• Storage. Knowing how to store water is very important. The container you use must be suitable for long-term storage.

• Rainwater Harvesting. This is where you start saving on your water bill and where you can fill tanks for the long emergency.

• Cleaning water. Water filtration and purifying is essential. If you are able to clean water, no matter the source, you stand a much better chance at having potable water.

• Wells and boreholes. Having a well in your backyard just takes a big load off your shoulders. It is a precious resource that needs careful management.

• Testing your water. When, how and where to test is an issue, especially after floods or suspected contamination.

Start to figure things out

There is no substitute for water. You cannot rely on soda, juice or sports drinks for nourishment. All liquids are not the same when it comes to water absorption. A liquid with sugars and additives have to be processed in the body before the actual water is extracted and absorbed. This means that your body has to work harder and use more energy for this task. Water is the real deal.

New Projects and Common sense

• Safety is everything! Whether you dig, install, buy, modify or remove, remember to use your common sense and to put safety first. Safety applies not just to you, but to children, visitors, workers, livestock, pets and wild animals.

• Follow local laws and regulations and avoid unwanted attention. Keep everything legal and obtain permits where needed. You have enough on your plate as it is.

• Buy quality. If it sounds too cheap, it probably is. Avoid tanks, filters and pumps imported from countries known for their cheap prices. Why take a chance on something that's function is to keep you alive? Example: Use Schedule 40 PVC pipe and avoid the thinner, cheaper selections.

• Every storage container, no matter how big or small, must be food grade quality or have a food grade liner on the inside. Don't use any container that was previously used for chemical storage.

• Know how to repair and maintain all systems related to water on your property. Keep spare parts.

• Always have a backup plan. Groundwater does not last indefinitely and wells run dry. Pumps use electricity. What will you do when there's no power? Be prepared for any worst-case scenario.

• Test your water! Whether from a lake, river, well or rooftop, always have it tested. If unsure about the presence of pathogens, boil it. Never assume anything. Always have a water test kit at hand. They are reliable, inexpensive and simple to use. When in doubt, test first!

• Make nice with your neighbors. Communities create a network of trust and cooperation. Try to find like-minded people in the community and reach out to them. This is not just about getting, but also about giving.

• Research. Don't take resources for granted. Use the websites provided by government agencies that are responsible for environmental protection, disease control and water management.

Understanding The Origins Of Water

The blue planet. As seen from space, our planet is an attractive blue ball, wrapped in water and covered in a web of clouds. It is easy to become mesmerized by the appeal that the oceans, rivers and lakes have, for those are the very places where humans chose to settle and to start civilizations. Innately, every human being is aware of the possibilities that water can create; it is the very source of life that we have come to depend and to rely on. For billions of years, tiny drops have been migrating in an endless cycle round and round the earth. Minute little molecules have traveled as droplets, from the oceans to the clouds, across the land, and down into rivers and lakes and into the ground. This constant movement of droplets, from solid to liquid to gaseous states, is what's known as the Water Cycle. Our fauna and flora have come to depend on these droplets that circulate the planet, to the extend that nothing on earth can survive without it. When we look at the water cycle, we quickly realize something very important. Water, or its absence, represents the absolute most important resource known to man, and it has been a part of our planet from the beginning of time. The water in my glass, has been traveling nonstop, since before the age of the dinosaurs. It's fallen as a drop of rain in the Sahara, as a torrential monsoon in India, a flash-flood in Arizona or become part of a glacier in Canada. It has never ceased to exist; it has merely taken on a different state of existence. Water cycles exist in a state of balance and provide us with the fundamental basics that we need to understand droughts, floods and extreme weather patterns. As land-owners, we have to become experts at understanding the inner workings of the water cycle on our planet. If there is one thing that space exploration has taught us, it's that a planet without water is completely uninhabitable.

When we look at our planet we have to ask ourselves, why do only some planets have water and where does this water come from? Currently there are two theories related to the origins of water on planet Earth. The older and more established theory states that water was possibly carried all the way across the universe through comets and meteorites. A newer, and also very plausible theory states that water has been a part of this planet from the beginning. Whatever the case, it is correct to assume that the vast majority of the water on planet earth has been here for millions of years. Of concern for Preppers, and owners of self-sufficient homesteads, is making sure that we understand the "water cycle" and how it applies to us and our

Water Cycle

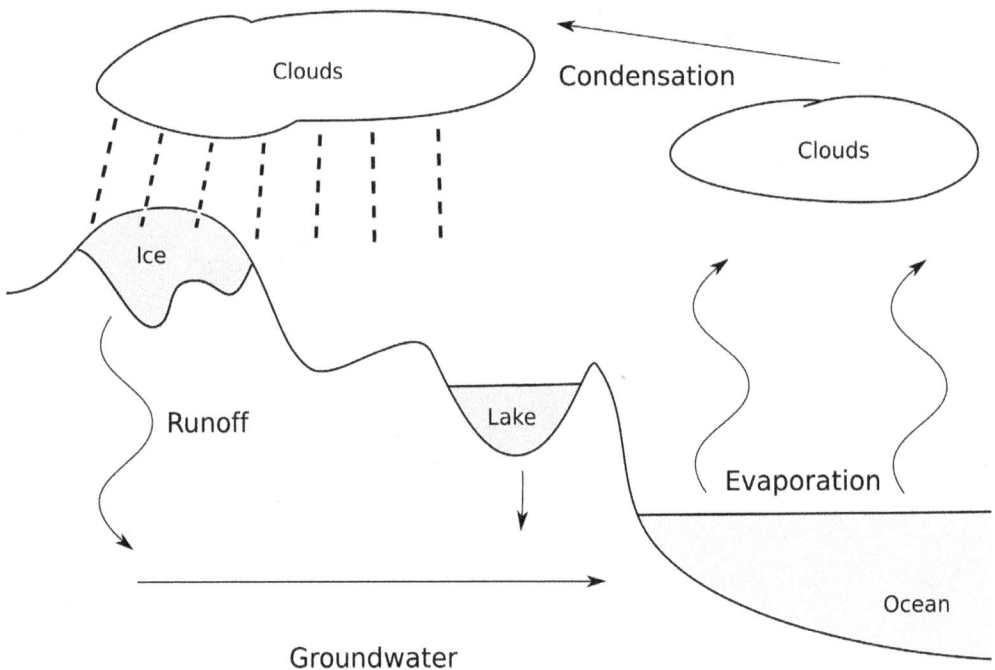

Liquid water > Evaporation > Condensation > Precipitation > Runoff/ flow back to the original state

Understanding The Origins Of Water

immediate environment.

The Water Cycle

We are all familiar with the classic water cycle (a.k.a. the hydrological cycle) that we learned about as youngsters.

1. The cycle starts with the evaporation of water from the surface of the ocean.

2. The moist air rises up and it starts to cool down.

3. This water vapor condenses and it forms clouds.

4. Clouds filled with moisture are moved all around the globe and the moisture returns to the surface as precipitation (rain). Not only does the rain form lakes and rivers, but the rain also replenishes groundwater deep inside the earth.

(Take note that this is the very system that we mimic in water distillation and filtration systems.)

What makes the water cycle really interesting is the fact that we call this a "closed hydrological system". It is a closed system, because the amount of water on the planet does not fluctuate. Yes, it can be broken down and reformed through various chemical processes, but there is no significant input or output of water to or from the planet. Where does it go, you

Global Water Crisis

- Droughts caused by extreme weather events are destroying agriculture and displacing people. Waves of migrants are fleeing areas ravaged by droughts.

- Population growth has increased the need for water and also released more contaminants into existing groundwater sources.

- The demand for more food is putting stress on groundwater reserves.

- Weak infrastructure is not able to cope with the demand and most countries are in dire need of new technology to solve the water crisis.

might ask, in times of drought? The simple answer is:

Somewhere else.

In theory, when there is a drought in one part of the world, there will be floods in other parts. Abundance over yonder, means scarcity over here. It is a balanced system that is in constant flux. Water does not disappear, it just moves with the weather systems and returns as precipitation when conditions permit.

Let's look at a breakdown of where, and in what forms, water is found:

- 96% of water accumulates on the earth's crust. This is the water present in reservoirs like the oceans, lakes, seas and rivers.

- 2% is found in a solid state in the ice caps, glaciers and mountain caps.

- 1.7% is found as groundwater inside the crust.

- 0.001% is found in the atmosphere and air around us as clouds, falling rain and water vapor.

At first glance, the above-mentioned statistics might seem pretty decent. The percentage (96%) of water found on the surface crust seems to favor man's chances of survival. But how much of this water is actually potable freshwater?

The answer is quite disturbing. Only about 2.5% of this water is freshwater. Add to that the fact that most of this freshwater is frozen as ice, and suddenly we are looking at a figure of only 0.65 %, which represents the earth's total water supply that is neither salty nor frozen.

The moral of the story?

Right now, water is absolutely the most precious resource on earth!

The tiny percentage of 0.65, represents the possibility of life on our planet and we hu-

The aggressive pumping of our groundwater supply is putting stress on aquifers which can have catastrophic consequences.

mans are scrambling to safeguard ourselves from running out. The National Geographic Society calls it " Water Wars" and states that underground water is pumped so aggressively around the globe that land is sinking, civil wars are being waged and agriculture is being transformed. Right now, the city of Beijing is sinking at a rate of 4 inches per year, due to the depletion of the groundwater underneath.

The water cycle teaches us that we cannot pump water from wells more rapidly than they can be replenished. We rely on precipitation runoff to replenish our groundwater. This is a very important aspect of the water cycle, since more than 30% of the planet's fresh water (in liquid form) is groundwater. We all want to share in this resource, but first we will have to familiarize ourselves with the location, depth and quality of groundwater in our area. Water is not an infinite resource and to avoid complications, we will have to learn how to manage and conserve this resource. You might need X *amount* of water for your

Understanding The Origins Of Water

land, but if every neighbor in your area is extracting water from the same aquifer, things can take a turn for the worse. Imagine a bottle with 15 straws in it. The bottle will be empty in seconds. If, during one summer, we have fewer rain events that usual, that groundwater aquifer will not be replenished and we could potentially sit with a dry well.

This is the reality as more and more people are drilling wells and extracting groundwater.

Conservation

There is a good chance, that you have very good water just a few feet underneath your land and if so, you will be eager to drill a well. That's your right to do so, but be aware that besides just drilling a well, you also might have to change your lifestyle and your opinions about sustainability. Traditionally, homestead owners have always required large quantities of water for irrigation and livestock. If we look at the present

Water and Droughts

Surface water is freshwater found above ground that accumulates in nature through precipitation. Once this water penetrates the soil, it gets filtered down into aquifers that store groundwater. A large portion of the freshwater on earth is lost through runoff to the oceans. When a period of abnormally dry weather endures in a region, it can create an imbalance that causes a drought.

We can identify four typical drought scenarios.

• **Rain events** - When there is a shortage in local precipitation.

• **Moisture content of soil** - If conditions arise that causes the soil to lack the moisture necessary to sustain a particular crop.

• **Water levels** - When the surface water and groundwater levels are both below normal.

• **Supply** - When the demand for water cannot be met through the supply infrastructure.

evidence as seen through the water cycle, we quickly start to realize that the perceived abundance of water is an illusion. In certain areas the situation is deteriorating rapidly and we will have to adapt and evolve with it. This could mean that some of us will have to start thinking about scaling down. If the supply cannot cover the demand, we will have to change on our end. This is already happening all over the world in many first world countries. Farmers are looking at alternative agriculture practices that can still secure a high yield, but that utilize less land and less water. This is definitely possible and actually recommended by the experts. Make the right decision and start thinking about water conservation on your property.

Consider some of the following options:

- Scaling down on irrigation. Drip irrigation reduces evaporation and saves huge amounts of water. Timers can schedule irrigation for the cooler parts of the day.
- Create a water-rich vegetation with low water needs.
- Recycle your house's grey water. This is something that every human on the planet should be doing. Why waste water that can feed your garden?
- Go organic. Organic methods help retain soil moisture and have a higher yield.

Before considering a well or bore-hole, design a system for water conservation that will make you less reliant on the groundwater.

- Harvest, capture and store water. Rainwater is naturally captured and stored in ponds. Using rainwater for livestock and irrigation is a great way to lessen the impact on the local groundwater.
- Retain the moisture of the soil by using compost and mulch. Extreme weather events are causing a definite rise in temperatures in certain parts of the world. By using compost and mulch, you can retain some of the moisture and reduce water evaporation.
- Educate yourself about anything water conservation related. How to rotate crops, how to protect crops, increase yield, grow local indigenous crops, etc.

The water-related problems of the day, affect not just the individual, but the whole community of land owners. We have to investigate and part of the process is to look at the problem from all angles. A major component of the water cycle is the weather. We'll discuss that in the next chapter.

Saving Means More

Saving water is very rewarding in the long run. It means that you will put less stress on your water supply and stored water will last longer. Some simple measures to save water and minimize waste:

• When brushing your teeth, turn off the tap. You can save up to 1.5 gal (6L) of water a minute.

• Take shorter showers. You can easily save more than 1.5 gal (6L) a minute. Showers are more water-efficient than bathing.

• Check and double-check all pipes, shower heads and faucets for leaks.

• Replace older toilets, shower-heads and faucets with efficient "water-saving" products.

• Place a water displacement device in your toilet tank. This reduces water usage with every flush.

• Design and implement a grey water system. Shower and washing machine runoff can be reused.

• Create a water-smart garden or no-waste irrigation set-up for crops.

• For small gardens, use a watering can instead of a hose.

• Educate your family about awareness. Wash dishes by hand, don't flush every time, plug the tub when you shower, etc.

• Install a water meter. The evidence of water fees will encourage saving.

Try to calculate your household's water consumption to see where you can save.

A typical domestic water consumption graph:

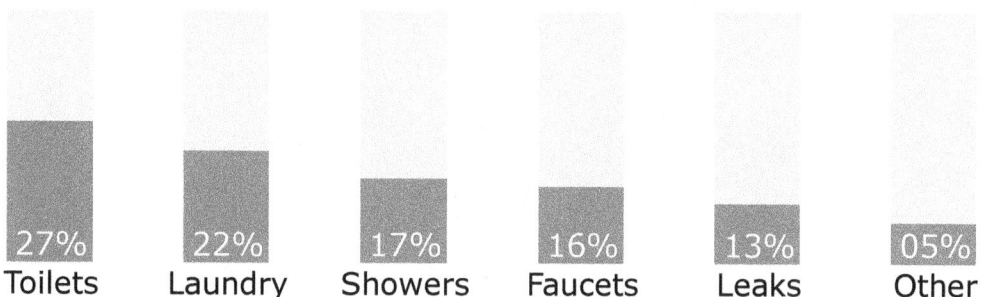

27%	22%	17%	16%	13%	05%
Toilets	Laundry	Showers	Faucets	Leaks	Other

Weather Patterns And Systems

Rain in the dry season is a sight to behold. When you live close to the land, you very quickly become aware of nature, its inner-workings and how it affects your homestead. Land owners instinctively know when to expect the winds to change and when the rains will come. It is obvious, that both people and animals, look to rain events as the prime provider of water and the giver of life. The rain comes and goes with the seasons and historically we have always been able to predict these patterns. This is the very thing that allows us to plant our seeds well before the rain starts to fall. Long periods of stable weather is optimum for landowners with livestock and vegetation. Stable weather means predictable weather patterns and that means a happy homestead that provides with abundance.

Unfortunately, we are currently living in a period of human history where stable weather patterns have become a thing of the past. We are constantly reminded of the abnormal weather conditions that are causing problems all over the planet. We see spring blossoms in the middle of the winter, snow in Egypt, record highs in the arctic and cold fronts in the tropics. We call these extreme weather events and speculation abounds as to what's causing it all. We can speculate all we want, but that doesn't solve anything, because the fact of the matter is that these systems are here to stay and there is nothing we can do about them. The safest thing to do is to be prepared and to be aware of what every weather pattern represents and how it will influence local rainfall expectations in your area.

The Two Main Patterns

Let's look at the facts and what we do know about weather patterns that contribute to abnormal weather conditions. Take note that these are abnormal conditions that do not come around every year.

Currently, our civilization is confronted with two specific fronts. They have been identified as El Nino and La Nina. Both El Nino and La Nina are generated in the Pacific ocean and both conditions affect the weather all over the world.

El Nino

When taking a closer look at the El Nino phenomenon we know that it causes the tradewinds to weaken and warm water is carried to the east (the west coast of the Americas). This is a "warm phase" that, on average, comes around every five years. It results in the following conditions:

North America
This area experiences warmer-than-normal winters in the Northern US and Canada. Expect above average rainfall in the Southern United States. It is very wet between Jan. and April in California and also very wet in the Southeast to the Atlantic coast between Nov. and the following April. Expect drier than normal conditions from Dec. to the following March in the Ohio and Tennessee valleys and From Nov. to the following March in the Pacific Northwest.

El Nino

El Nino Rainfall

South America

Heavy rains along the West coast from June to Sept. and on the East coast from Sept. and into the following Jan. On islands nearby in the Pacific Ocean, expect above average rainfall from Jan. to May.

Indonesia and the Philippines

Very dry conditions in Indonesia, and the Philippines from June to the following Jan.

Australia

This area truly feels the effects of his system. Very dry conditions in central Australia from July to Nov. Very dry conditions in Eastern Australia from July to following Jan. Very dry conditions in Northern Australia from July to following March.

Africa

Expect droughts in Northern Africa from July-Sept. and further droughts in Southern Africa from Nov. to following March. Heavy rain is expected in East Africa from Oct. to the following Jan.

India

India will experience droughts From June to Sept. Heavy rains is expected in the far South from Oct. to Dec.

Northern Middle East

The areas Northwest of India and covering the Northern Middle-east region, is wet from Jan. to April.

Conclusion

Start to become more aware of the change in weather conditions. When an El Nino pattern is predicted, analyze how it will affect your local area. If you expect higher precipitation numbers than usual, take measures to harvest more water for times of need. Drier weather will require action as well. Get involved with water management in your community and make sure the majority of landowners are aware of the dangers posed by abnormal weather patterns that cause droughts. Share and discuss the El Nino related information with your local governmnet office to contribute to an emergency response system.

El Nino Field Notes
My area and rain events

Expected Weather:

Preparedness:

La Nina Rainfall

La Nina

La Niña is considered the "cool phase". During this event the trade winds are stronger that normal and more warm water is carried to Asia and upwelling increases. It usually follows immediately after an El Nino event and can last anything from 9-12 months. The El Nino event can be strong or weak, just depends on mother nature. This pattern is also characterized by a shift in rainfall patterns in many parts of the world:

South America

Drier than normal conditions can be expected along the West coast of South America from June to Sept. The East coast will also be drier than normal be-tween Aug. and Dec. The nearby islands of the Pacific Ocean will be drier than normal between June and the following April.

Australia

Wetter than normal conditions over Northern Australia from Sept. to the following Jan. Southern Australia will receive more rain from May to the following Feb. Central Australia will experience above average rainfall between Sept. and the following Jan. Tasmania will have more rain from Aug. to Dec.

Indonesia, Malaysia and Philippines

Above-average precipitation to be expected between June and Dec. More tropical cyclones in the Western Pacific ocean.

USA

Expect above-average precipitation across the Northern Midwest USA from Dec. to the following March. Generally, expect below average rainfall to the South, southern and central parts of the Rockies and Great Plains and Florida. More specifically: In the Southeast from Oct. to the following April, and in the Southwest from Jan. to April.

Africa

Wetter than normal conditions are also observed over Southeastern Africa during Nov. to the following April. Northern Sub-Saharan Africa will be experiencing more rainfall from July to Sept. East Africa to the interior will be drier than normal between Nov. to the following March.

India

From June to Sept. expect the Indian monsoon rainfall to be greater than normal, especially in Northwest India. The South will be drier than usual from Oct. to Dec.

Northern Middle-East

Expect drier than average conditions from Jan. to May.

Conclusion

Be aware and expect a possible change in weather conditions when a La Nina event is predicted. Do your own research for your geographical area and analyze how much such an event will affect your homestead (if at all). If you expect higher precipitation numbers than usual, take measures to harvest more water for times of need and to arrange storage. Do this out of principle and be prepared to help other people in your community. Drier weather will require action as well and here you might need government assistance. As mentioned before, the consciousness that arises from being prepared should be contagious and should affect all members of the community all the way up to your local government office. This means a reliable infrastructure of trust and dependency that can save lives in the long run.

La Nina Field Notes
My area and rain events

Expected Weather:

Preparedness:

Finding A Water Source For Your Land

It's only when we try to find water ourselves, that we realize just how hard it can be. When looking at buying rural land, finding a dependable water source should be your first concern. In looking for water, you have three basic options:

Public or municipal water is water that's provided by the government in service to the people. Certain rural areas may not be serviced by a municipal water system.

Surface water includes water from a river, stream, lake, or spring.

Groundwater is water pumped from a well.

Do not even think about buying a property if your water source is not guaranteed. Don't let emotion get the better of you. Make sure you do your research, for in certain areas potable water is scarce and to make it work, you'll have to become an expert at wa-

ter management. I'll go so far as to say that, when buying a property, finding water is not an afterthought, it is the decider. Factors like surface water, groundwater, depth of the water table, local rainfall and community preparedness, all have to be taken into account. You also have to consider the possibility of contamination through runoff from adjacent properties. Living downhill from a farm that uses harmful pesticides means that during a rain event your property will be affected adversely. Areas prone to flooding are more susceptible to pathogen contamination due to stagnant water formation that causes microbe proliferation. This can cause a myriad of problems down the line. If you want to avoid these issues, you will have to make a thorough assessment of the water situation not only on your land, but also in the surrounding

A Water Source Must Be Found

Having access to water, whether from a public municipal line or from a well or spring, will define your property. Everything that you learn about the process of attaining water rights will be helpful in the long run. It will provide you with the knowledge to secure your water rights, and with he peace of mind that comes with it.

communities. This also applies to current landowners who might be dissatisfied with their water situation, for whatever reason. Unfortunately, in many areas you will need government approval, in the form of permits and licenses, before you can drill a well, harvest rain from the roof or develop a spring running through your property. No matter which direction you choose, the first and most obvious step will be to examine the information provided by your local government. You can go downtown to the department of water management or to a water utility office. Alternatively, you can also view the information provided online, by various government agencies. Let's take a look at the different options.

Public Water

Having access to the public water supply is considered a great benefit, since you are almost always guaranteed a steady flow from the faucet. When buying a new property, this kind of information will be provided by the seller, sales agent or on a government provided land listing. It should clearly state whether the land is served by a public water supply line. On paper this sounds wonderful, but the reality is that your water has a long way to travel between source and faucet, which means that many variables can influence the quality of the water before it flows out your kitchen faucet. It will be worth your while to investigate the potability of your water and if contaminants are found to be present, to be aware of the options at your disposal. You will have to do some investigation yourself to determine what forms of water sources are available. A property that's within the city limits will definitely have access to a public main water line. This is provided through a network of pipes that's managed by the government or a government appointed entity. Many rural properties are also connected to the public water line. In some areas the water is supplied by a local community well. This is also considered a form of "public water" and similarly you will have to apply for the right to join this well. There are of course properties without public water or community wells. This means that you will have to improvise to find an alternative source of water.

The Main Water Line

Find out where the main water line is located and where the original source is located. Inquire as to the quality of the source and also about the water pipes and if asbestos cement pipes are still in circulation. You want to avoid contaminants, or at the very least, be aware of them. Concerning connecting to the main water line, make sure that you get comprehensive answers concerning the following:

- Be legal
Make sure you know which permits and legal documentation are required to connect to this main water line.

- Fees
Check the fees to connect to the main water line. In certain countries the government will connect your water free of charge. Check with the local government office to inquire after fees and whether you need a water meter or not. Water meters are very expensive.

- Regulations
Make sure that you get answers regarding the following:

- What regulations will affect your usage of the water?
- Who should install the connection line?
- Does the installation require government inspection or regulation?

Local Community Water

In more remote areas it's not uncommon for the local communities to pool their resourc-

Before buying

- Investigate extreme weather patterns in the area and the probability of droughts and floods.
- Research regulations concerning rainwater harvesting and having a well.
- Find the expected annual rainfall for the area.
- Talk to neighbors about their experiences.
- Check the depth of the local water table.
- Investigate all surface water souces.

es together and to create a local water well. These wells are operated and maintained by the community members themselves and are considered a "public" water source for the local area. When inquiring about a local community water source, make sure about the following:

- The water quality
Since no government agencies are involved you have to make sure that the water is 100% potable. Take a sample and have it tested at a government-certified laboratory. If your situation is more urgent, and you need an immediate answer, test the water yourself with a DIY water test kit. These kits are simple to use and very reliable.

- Life expectancy
How long is the water source (well) expected to produce water? This is not a simple question. Understand that the groundwater is dependent on precipitation. If the community extracts water more rapidly than it can be naturally replenished, then you will end up with a dry well. This is where extreme weather events can destroy communities with unexpected droughts.

- Hidden costs
What are the hidden costs, maintenance, infrastructure, etc. Can you access the water line and how much does it cost? Do you need a water meter (expensive)? What are the local rates.

Finding water relies on you becoming an expert at everything related to water. This means research and prepping.

Alternative Sources

Having a community or government provided water source is obviously a great option. You should still look into finding an alternative water source on your land. If you live in a real remote area, this might be your only option. Using surface water from a spring or lake, or groundwater from a well, are both great options to reduce your water bill and to provide you with water in a time of need. To prospective land owners, this means that you will have to make a thorough assessment of your land.

• Step 1. Walk your land
Get a general feel for the vegetation and wildlife present. Try to locate areas with lush vegetation compared to their surroundings. Shallow groundwater can be found by knowing the landscape. Vegetation with water-loving plants, like willows and aspen trees will be an indicator of groundwater at shallow depths. Conditions for large quantities of shallow groundwater are more favorable under

valleys than under hills. Areas where water is at the surface in a depression as springs, seeps, or swamps reflect the presence of groundwater, although not necessarily in large quantities or of usable quality. Make notes of all surface water present or evidence of past. If you find a tiny rivulet or stream flowing on your land, track it back to its source. A spring can be a great source of water. Start celebrating if the source provides a year-round, steady flow of clean water, and if it is located within your property boundaries. Call in an expert to help with capping the spring.

• Step 2. Talk to the locals
Finding water and knowing about water is something every landowner is willing to discuss and to offer advice about. Questions you should be asking:

a. How deep is the water table and are there springs in the area?
b. What's the water quality like?
c. Does the ground consist of clay, rock or sand?
d. What's the expected yearly local precipitation and which are the wettest months of the year?

• Step3. Test for presence of water
If you are completely on your own, in the boonies, then you need to lower a pipe and look for groundwater yourself. This

Spring Water

Springs are usually fed by shallow groundwater. Some springs seep out of banks, slopes or hills and typically groundwater emerges from one defined discharge in the earth's surface. This is called a concentrated spring. Others "seep" from the ground over a large area and has no defined discharge point. This is a seepage spring.

• Determine if it's year-round water. Look for signs like plant growth with roots growing towards the water source. Is there a worn-out channel for water to flow, indicating flow over a long period of time? Check the temperature of the water throughout the day. A constant temperature indicates consistent flow; the water should be slightly cooler than the air.

• Take a sample and have it tested.

• Determine the flow rate. Take a pipe and see how long it takes to fill a bucket (E.g. measure 5 gallons). Best to do it during the dry season, when the water table is at it lowest. Springs used for drinking water supplies should yield at least 2 gallons per minute throughout the entire year.

• Call an expert to cap your spring, or in an emergency, place a black flexible PVC pipe with a screen filter inside the source and secure and cover it without disrupting the original flow channel. Store the water in a holding tank.

is why you have to do research first. If the locals provided you with hope that there is groundwater at drill-able depth or if you saw unusual lush growth in one area of your land, then you will have to test. Consult an expert to assist you.

• Step 4. Secure your water rights

You have to secure the rights to your land. This means, depending on where you live, a visit to your local water office. Your

Questions to ask a licensed well driller:

- The cost per depth drilled?

- What local regulations apply to drilled wells?

- What permits are required?

- The probability of finding water and the expected depth?

- The soil conditions in the area. Rock, clay, sand or gravel?

- Once you've struck water, what is the life expectancy of the well?

- How will weather cycles like El Nino and La Nina affect the water table and the yield of the well?

- For future scenarios, what could possible contamination causes be?

water rights consist of the right to use, a reasonable quantity of public water, for a certain period of time, as it occurs on your property.

• Step 5. Research

Use the Internet, the local library or visit a local government office. You must be aware of the water cycles and of the weather systems that affect precipitation in your area. This will give you a fairly clear indication of what to expect over the coming months. Once you are familiar with a certain area, you can use a system of deduction to figure out what is causing a water scarcity or drought. Lakes are fed through rivers, which run down from the mountains. The mountains depend on rain. It is crucial for any Prepper to know the topography and environment that he or she lives in.

• Step 6. Talk to a licensed well driller or to a hydrologist

Get a hydrologist to obtain information on the wells in the target area. The locations, depth to water, amount of water pumped, and types of rocks penetrated by wells also provide information on groundwater.
Licensed well drillers will not only inform you about drilling for surface water, but also about how to use submersible pumps to extract water from springs and lakes.

In general, your water right consists of the right to use:

1. a reasonable quantity of public water,

2. for a certain period of time,

3. occurring at a certain place.

Governments enforce legislation that's designed to protect the use and enjoyment of water that travels in streams, rivers, lakes, and ponds, gathers on the surface of the earth, or collects underground. If you have the right to divert water from a river, stream, lake, or spring, you have a surface water right. If you have the right to pump water from your well, then you have a groundwater right.
In areas with an abundance of surface water, these rights are mostly accepted, as insisted by the landowner.
In areas prone to droughts and water shortages, things can get more complicated because of competition, and you will have to apply for a permit before you can utilize the water resource.

When applying for water rights, the office with jurisdiction will consider the following:

• The protection of the environment.

• Preventing waste of precious water resources.

• The fair distribution of water resources.

The main focus is to ensure that the public interest is served.

Note that you do not own the water, you just own the rights to the use of it.

Chapter 4

Storing Water For An Emergency

Storing drinking water is essential for daily use and also for emergency situations. The supply and quality of water to your house can be disrupted by the following:

- A natural disaster like a hurricane, typhoon, earthquake, tsunami or even by a solar flare.

- These days extreme weather events are causing a multitude of water related problems like droughts, floods and unwanted algal blooms in lakes.

- Man-made disasters like chemical spills can bring communities to their knees.

- Wells that feed the community or your property can simply run dry.

Any of the above mentioned emergencies can cause serious problems for your homestead.

When this happens, you will possibly have to deal with the following:

- The disruption of water supply lines could mean that you and your family are without water, till maintenance crews come to the rescue. You still have to perform your daily duties. A grown man or woman working all day without enough water can lead to dehydration, heat stroke or heat cramps.

- The resulting water restrictions can be very hard on homesteads and can cause serious damage to crops and death to livestock.

- When panic sets in, the masses will besiege Asupermarkets and convenience stores. Water will be the first thing on everyone's minds. History has shown us that this is true; it's happened before and it will happen again.

Water in containers

Water can be stored in various containers and select locations. Prepare storage in and around your home for sitting out an emergency. Also prepare containers for when you go mobile in a hurricane scenario. If you are prepping for future scenarios, plan carefully and make decisions concerning quantities, container material, types of containers and storage location.

- When electricity to your home is disrupted, the water pumps stop working and this means that water stops flowing out of the faucets. Do you have backup generators for your pumps? Are you prepared for a solar flare that can render all electrical appliances useless?

Nothing is guaranteed anymore and instead of waiting for things to change, why not take the initiative and start prepping. If you live on a homestead out in the country you must have water stored away for a time of need. The question that always comes up is, "Just how much water do you need?".

Take note of the following:

1. An average family of four needs around 400 gallons (380 liters) of water per day to perform their daily activities.
2. On a more serious note, just for drinking purposes in a dire emergency, a healthy person needs a gallon per day.
3. Children, sick people, pregnant women and people living in tropical zones will require more water.
4. Pets require around 1 gallon of water every three days.

To give yourself a decent chance of surviving a disaster, you should store at least 3 months' worth of water. To put it into perspective:

You will need to store large quantities of water!

Get your thinking cap on and consider every possible scenario that might affect your water supply. To get started, we will look at ways to store water in and around the house. Make sure that whatever product or container you buy, that it is a quality product that will not let you down.

Various Options

When using storage containers found in and around the house consider the following:

• **Glass** is a safe container that's easy to sterilize.

Glass must be kept away from

sunlight at all costs. If not, you will sit with algal growth in your water.

Glass breaks, so store containers carefully and do not stack them. Glass should not be used in areas prone to earthquakes.

• Foodgrade **Stainless Steel** containers are safe to use. They are easy to clean, do not break and do not leach chemicals.

• Foodgrade **Plastic** Containers are really not the best option, but are by far the most convenient. Remember that any translucent container will attract algal growth when exposed to sunlight.

Avoid any container with **Bisphenol A** and **Phthalates**. The recycling numbers found at the bottom of containers mean the following:

1. PET/ PETE. These are safe when new, but (if you have a choice) remember not to re-use water and soda bottles.
2. HDPE. Considered safe.
3. Vinyl (PVC). Unsafe. Absolutely unsafe! Avoid at all costs.
4. LDPE. Considered safe
5. Polypropylene (PP). Considered safe.
6. Polystyrene. Absolutely unsafe!
7. Various unmarked plastics. Absolutely unsafe!

Remember that all stored water, no matter the container, should

Store your water in a cool, dry and dark place. Don't expose plastic bottles to sunlight or to any heat source like a water heater or generator.

---

be rotated at least once every six months. This is not just for quality, but also for taste.

Depending on size, a container filled with water can be very heavy. If you are not young anymore and if you live on your own, then moving big containers will be problematic. Make sure you select containers that suit your needs and also your physical ability to move them around. **A small platform on wheels, like a dolly or pushcart, can be used for hauling heavy containers filled with water.**

Before using any container for water storage:

1. Wash the container inside out with dish washing soap and rinse throughly with water.
2. Mix one teaspoon of unscented household bleach with a ¼ gallon (0.95 Liter) of water.
3. Shake the container and thoroughly expose it to the bleach.
4. Wash around the opening where lids and screw on

caps are used. Also wash the caps or lids.

5. Rinse thoroughly and spray clean with a pressured hose.

Once your containers are clean, you can fill them up with water. If your budget allows, get some water preserver concentrate to add to your water. This should especially be considered for untreated well-, spring- or rain-water. This will extend the life of your water to at least 5 years. Write the date on the container and replace the water every six months from then on out.

Besides containers, you also have to think about location. Try to store your water in a cool, dark place. It's also not a good idea to store all of your water in one location. A natural disaster can cause a building to collapse, a fire to start or simply just render one part of your property inaccessible. Consider the following locations:

— Garage
— Barn or Shed
— Any secondary structure on your dwelling.
— Basement
— Attic or loft
— Under the stars, under protective covering.
— Storage rooms and storage containers.
— Closets and cupboards.
— Under beds.
— Cars, trucks and trailers. Being mobile with a supply

A family of four require around 100 gallons (380 liters) of water per day to perform their daily activities.

of water in the back greatly increases your chances of survival.

— Secret location for dire emergencies. If, for whatever reason, you feel that there is a need to hide a cache of water underground, in a tree house, a cave or on a different property, then make arrangements to do so. This will be a practical option in a flight scenario.

Depending on your level of alertness, you will do well to be prepared for both a "sit and wait" and a "get out of Dodge" scenario. You can never be too prepared!

Bottled water

Keeping a supply of bottled water is a simple option and very practical. Ready-to-drink water will come in very handy in case of an emergency.

• Always keep bottled water at hand. Leave it in the back of your car, in the kitchen, or at the front door, and make sure that all family members are aware of the location. Bottled water is easy to transport, fairly cheap and readily available.

• Bottled water come in all sizes. Small bottles are light and fit into small spaces. They are great for storing all around the house and in vehicles. Larger containers like water dispensers can also come in handy. A five gallon water dispenser is great for everyday use, but the jugs can also be used in an emergency. Again, make sure that you are physically able to move these containers and if not, scale down and select smaller containers.

• It is best to check the brand before you buy. Government approved and commercially produced water is best. Avoid water with added "nutrients", ions, flavorings, fluoride or with the so-called "perfect Ph". Basically just stick to plain old water and a brand that you are familiar with. The aim is to store it indefinitely and chemical additives will just shorten the shelf-life of the water.

• Store your bottled water in a cool, dry and dark place. Don't expose plastic bottles to sunlight or to any heat source like a water heater or generator. Sunlight encourages bacterial growth and that is the last thing you want in your water.

• Don't stack your bottles too high. Water is heavy. Plastic is not indestructible and cracks and leaks can occur.

• Concrete floors are not suitable for storage of plastic water containers. Make shelves

Some helpful hints

• Most of the mentioned products come with water treatment tablets. These tablets purify the water and also improve the taste.

• Large, heavy containers become mobile with a dolly or pushcart. Water is heavy. Don't wait till the tank is filled up before attempting to move it!

• Do not reuse soda, juice or milk bottles for water storage. These containers are for one-time use and by reusing them you risk chemicals leaching into your water. Water with suspected chemicals should not be given to humans or animals!

• Don't just plan for your family, but plan for your pets and livestock. Water from rainwater tanks, ponds, storm water runoff, wells, and rivers can be used for animals in time of need. Animals can handle pathogens far better than humans.

• Common sense dictates that all of the mentioned methods have to be scrutinized for drinking safety. Use your purifiers and filters to clean your water first. Boil if you suspect pathogens. When in doubt, use your test kit and test the water before drinking.

for your storage containers and keep them off the ground to avoid exposure to flooding, spilling and other domestic accidents.

• Rotate your bottled water often.

Boxed bladders

You can also store your water in boxed bladders. This is a great option if you expect to be on the move during an emergency. They fit easily into trucks, cars and trailers.

• These bladders do come in different sizes, but the 5 gal (19L) ones are the most popular.

• They are food grade quality and BPA-free.

• The boxes are structurally strong and they keep the bladders in position which makes transportation easy.

• Look for ones with a fill hose and quality faucet. You do not want the container to leak after just a month in storage.

• They should come with a water preserver concentrate.

As an alternative, some people recommend using the bladders found in boxed wine containers. These are obviously not designed for water storage and also not structurally strong or durable enough to be transported. However, if in a true emergency, and you need to fill up a container with water, then consider this as an option.

Stackable containers

Similar to the boxed bladders, having stackable containers is a great option if you expect to be mobile during an emergency. These are basically just quality containers that are convenient to move, refill and stack.

• Typically, these containers come in 5 gal (19L) sizes, but they are stacked as an "8 pack". That means 40 gal of stacked

---

The CDC recommends the following after a natural disaster has occurred in your area.

To clean clear tap water:

• Use unscented household liquid bleach.

• Add ⅛ teaspoon (0.75 ml) of bleach to 1 gallon (3.79L) of water.

• Mix well and wait 30 minutes or more before drinking.

To clean cloudy tap water

• Use unscented household liquid bleach.

• Add ¼ teaspoon (1.5 ml) of bleach to 1 gallon (3.79L) of water.

• Mix well and wait 30 minutes or more before drinking.

(1 Gallon = 16 cups)

---

water.

• They are made of high density Polyethylene (HDPE), food grade quality and BPA-free.

• They are structurally strong and are very easy to stack. This makes moving your containers around, a simple task.

• They come with handles which simplifies transportation.

• Included is a fill hose and faucet. Make sure that the quality of the faucet is up to standard.

These containers are very practical and they will provide a very realistic solution to your storage needs.

Water bricks

Similar to stackable containers, water bricks are easy to move, stack and store.

• They typically come in 3.5 gal (13.2L) bricks and are also stacked as an "8 pack", which gives you 28 gal (106L) of stored water. Smaller 1.5 gal (5.7L) bricks are also available.

• What makes them unique is that they come with ridges that "lock" the bricks together and provide a very stable platform for water storage.

• They are made of high density Polyethylene (HDPE), food grade quality and BPA-free.

• Due to their design, they are great space-savers.

• They are considered very convenient due to the sturdy carry grips.

• Some brands have a wide opening which means that besides water, they can also be used for food storage or to keep items dry.

Water barrels

These days you can buy 55 gallon (208L) barrels that are specifically designed for emergency water storage.

Before you consider using one of these, make sure that it is clean on the inside and that the "plastic smell" has been washed away. You can use a bit of bleach, or simply wash it out with vinegar and baking soda.

Typically, expect to find:

• The barrels are made of high density Polyethylene (HDPE), food grade quality and BPA-free.

• These containers come with treatment solutions, a hand pump and a siphon.

The barrels are heavy when full, so put a dolly underneath for transportation before filling it up. Avoid storing these barrels on concrete and prepare a little platform made out of wood or cardboard just to be on the safe side. You can run the water through a charcoal filter before drinking it.

Having six of these barrels will be enough water for a family of four, for a three month emergency.

They can be placed all around your property and are not as big

Typical Symptoms Of Mild Dehydration

- Dizziness and weakness.
- Dry, sticky mouth. Swollen tongue.
- Thirst.
- Few or no tears when crying.
- Dry skin. Inability to sweat.
- Headache.
- Little or no urine. Especially from infants.
- Muscle cramps.
- Constipation.

Typical Symptoms Of Severe Dehydration

- Fever and confusion.
- Darkened urine color. Little or no urination.
- No tears when crying.
- Rapid breathing and heartbeat.
- Extreme thirst.
- Low blood pressure.
- Unconsciousness.
- Sunken eyes.
- Dry skin that doesn't bounce back when pinched into a fold. It's lost its elasticity.

and cumbersome as large, traditional rainwater tanks.

Storage tanks

You can also look at larger options for in-house storage. High-capacity water storage tanks are becoming more and more popular. They are very similar to the standard water tanks that are used for rainwater harvesting.

• They are made of high density Polyethylene (HDPE), food grade quality and BPA-free.

• They come in a variety of sizes from 150-600 gallons (567-2270L).

• Some brands offer small, 150gal (567L) tanks that are stackable and that fit through a standard doorway.

• They also come with spigots, inlets and outlets that make rotation of water a simple process. Try to get a brand with a spigot that connects to a standard garden hose. This makes draining and rotation a very simple process.

• They come with a water preserver concentrate.

Some of the larger models are very heavy once full, so plan carefully where you want to place them.

Water liners for bathtubs

If you are aware of an impending disaster in your area and you haven't had time to put emergency measures into place, then an "emergency water pod" might be the answer. Water pods are plastic liners that you put in the bathtub and fill with water from the faucet before the emergency strikes. You can buy them in different sizes and each bladder-like pod comes with a siphon. They are perfect for hurricane, earthquake or tsunami scares.

• They are made from food grade quality material and BPA-free.

• These are for absolute emergencies only. They can be used just once and are disposable.

• They can keep water fresh for up to 4 months.

• The normal size allows storage of up to 100 gal (378.5L) of water.

• They come with a pump that can be used to empty the pod.

If you do not have a liner prepared, you can still fill every bath and basin in the house with water. This water can be used for many chores like washing clothes, bathing, flushing toilets and general sanitation.

Dehydration

Be prepared and therefore, be aware of the symptoms of dehydration. If you find yourself in a hot environment with a shortage of water, then you should already be on the lookout for signs of dehydration.

Sweating, urination and breathing all cause the body to loose fluids. Everybody is susceptible to dehydration, but children, the elderly and sick people are especially at risk. Dehydration can also lead to heat stroke and cramps which can be absolutely life threatening.

When the body overheats, we get muscle cramps. This is not a serious problem and getting out of the sun and hydrating with water will take care of it.

When the body starts to overheat, and show signs of confusion, nausea and vomiting, headache, or high temperature, then we are dealing with heat exhaustion. This is still not a life-threatening condition, but if no action is taken to lower the person's core body temperature, then we have the potential for heat stroke. Typical symptoms of heat stroke:

- Headache. (Don't administer any headache medicine.)

- Rapid pulse.

- Confusion.

- Temperature elevation of up to 105 F (40.5 C) or more.

- Nausea and vomiting.

- The skin can turn red due to the blood vessels trying to expel the heat.

- Rapid breathing.

- Possible loss of consciousness.

- Seizures.

- The person's skin might be cool, but the core temperature

will be high.

<u>When a person suffers from heat stroke, immediately take action:</u>

1. Bring the person indoors, out of the sun.

2. Remove the person's clothing and use ice or cold water to lower their body temperature. If water is scarce and an issue, wet a towel and use it to wipe the victim's body down.

3. Use a fan (hand or electric) to help with cooling the body of the victim.

4. Replace lost fluids through hydration. Get electrolytes back into the system.

5. Elevate the person's feet. It should be elevated higher than the victim's heart.

6. Place icepacks wrapped in towels in the groin area, under armpits and behind the neck. Speaking from personal experience, this is a very effective method of lowering the body's temperature.

The key message concerning heat stroke:

If you stay hydrated, you will most likely not get heat stroke.

This is where I have to reiterate:

You must store more water than what you think you will need in an emergency.

Running out of water should not be an option.

Conclusion

These days when it comes to water storage, there are plenty of options to choose from. There is of course no perfect solution that will fit everybody's needs. When selecting the right option for you and your family take into account that you might be mobile in a "get out of Dodge" scenario, or that you might be stuck in a "sit and wait" scenario. It is definitely best to be prepared for both types of scenarios. In addition, you will do well to buy a portable, emergency water filter for every family member. A convenient, lightweight option is the straw-type, that filters everything you drink from. They weigh about 50 grams and should be perfect for a group on the move. Keep it within reach if a disaster strikes, for if you have to flee your home this will be a life-saver. Make sure that all your storage vessels are easily accessible. Your water should be located where you can quickly reach it in an emergency. Find a good balance between using large and small storage containers and arrange them in and around the house. Make sure that you have access to all container valves and openings and rotate your water frequently.

The latest research is pointing at some contradicting evidence concerning the safety of plastics. BPA (Bisphenol A) is a chemical agent added as a hardener to plastics. A common replacement for BPA is to use BPS (Bisphenol S). Once thought to be safe, it now seems that BPS also causes health problems of its own. If you are one of the growing amount of people who are totally against the use of plastics, then you have to consider stainless steel, ceramic, clay or glass.

Unfortunately, these materials are all heavy and they are not always considered convenient for emergency storage. It will come down to creating a system that works for you and your family. Make sure that every family member is taken care of and also that they are informed about water conservation and the basics thereof.

Hidden Water Sources

Unknown to some people, you are already storing water in various appliances in your house. In an absolute emergency and as a very last option, pay attention to the following:

• Your water heater. It has a hot water tank that stores water. Turn off the gas or electricity feed beforehand.

• Some homes rely on pumps with pressure tanks. These tanks are reservoirs filled with clean water.

• Melt ice cubes in your freezer and take advantage of the ice buildup at the back.

• The house pipelines are filled with water. Drain them by opening the highest faucet first and then go to the lowest faucet to drain the pipes. You might have to close off the main valve first.

• Toilet top tanks also store water. Boil and filter first.

• Swimming pools usually have chlorinated water. In an emergency, act quickly and fill every container you can find with water from your pool. Filter and boil it before drinking. The water in your pool will become contaminated very quickly if it's not treated and after a few days it will be like drinking swamp water.

• Aquariums have water. Filter and boil the water before you think about consuming it. This is contaminated water, so only consider this option as a last resort.

Take care to still boil or filter water obtained from these locations. If you suspect any form of chemical contamination then discard the water immediately.

Collection And Storage Of Rainwater

Collecting rainwater makes sense on so many levels and it is an obvious choice whether you live in the city or out in the country. A big benefit of rainwater is the fact that it's free of minerals and salts that cause corrosion in appliances. This is the very reason we sometimes refer to it as "soft" water. Moving outdoors, we see that gardens thrive under rainwater for it contains nitrates and has a nearly neutral (slightly acidic) pH. To benefit from this method and to join the long line of rain harvesters before us, we simply have to look up to the sky, to our roofs. Most roofs are already fitted with gutters and spouts which make them perfect for water harvesting. Take a walk around your house and other structures on your property. Examine the roof and gutters, checking for type of material used, the condition they are in and making notes of where your gutter downspouts are. If you are not familiar with the workings of pipes, fittings, pumps and water flow, consult a local plumber in your area to assist or, at the very least, to discuss your options with. Learning about plumbing is fun and it is also a very rewarding skill that you will use many times over. Inspect the ground around your house for stability and make sure that areas under downspouts are clear and level. Locate your storm-water drain and determine how overflow from tanks will reach the drain. Make a list of all the areas on your land that you want to supply with rainwater.

Be creative, but also be realistic. A simple system is less likely to break down and requires less maintenance.

Collection Of Rainwater

Rainwater is free, easy to collect and useful for various purposes. Under the right conditions it can provide enough water for a small household or garden. It is however, dependent on weather cycles and therefore it is generally not enough for large-scale irrigation.

Boiling of rainwater gets rid of pathogens. Filtration gets rid of chemicals, dirt and mold.

When dealing with rainwater we will identify three components that deserve our attention.

The collection area. The roof functions as the collection area and basically the larger the roof area, the more water you can harvest.

The conveyance system. The gutters, downspouts and piping function as the conveyance system.

Storage facilities. Water barrels and tanks function as your storage facilities. Remember that all water collected should still first be treated before consumption.

Plan First

Collecting rainwater means that you are taking a step closer towards self-sufficiency. An obvious incentive for you to collect rainwater is that it's free and that it reduces your water bill. Dry areas with depleted groundwater sources are perfect for rainwater harvesting; even if you live in a water-rich environment, you can conserve water through rain-harvesting. By not collecting rainwater, you are allowing this precious resource to go to waste and to flow into the ground or down the road into the storm-water drains. Not only can we use rainwater for showering, washing, cleaning and watering the garden, but it

Plumbing Glossary

Aerobic zone. Area with clean water in tank.

Anaerobic zone. Area with sediment-filled water of poor quality.

Catchment area. The collection surface from which the rainfall runs off.

Cistern. A water storage tank.

Downspout. A pipe used to carry water from a roof to ground level.

First Flush Diverter. A chamber (pipe) that diverts the first flush of contaminated water, flowing from the gutter, away from the tank.

Gutter. A shallow trough fixed beneath the edge of the roof for channeling of rainwater.

can also be used for your water heater, swimming pool or for fire fighting. Back in the day we were able to use rainwater for drinking, but these days it is advisable to test a few samples first. Depending on where you live, the two main issues with rainwater are contaminants and water quality. The rain droplets move with the clouds through our atmosphere and cover great distances. On this journey, they come into contact with various chemicals and pollutants. Chemicals can be simple particles coming from chemical plants, paper mills, incinerators, power plants or even more seriously, radioactive particles from nuclear plants. Sadly, the day has come that acid rain, a scenario typical of science fiction movies, has become a reality of daily life. Besides our atmosphere, the rain also has to fall and collect on various surfaces. These surfaces (normally rooftops) can be coated in chemicals or might simply just be dirty from bird droppings, chimney runoff,

Questions to ponder before installing a rainwater tank:

• How will you use the harvested water?

• Do you require a pump?

• What size tank do you require?

• What type of tank do you require?

• Where will you put your tank?

• Does the tank require approval from local government?

• Can all installation requirements be met?

• Can you maintain your rainwater tank on your own?

• What are the rainfall expectations in your area?

mold, etc.

Water quality has become more of an issue of late. Whenever we discuss rainwater, the argument comes up that, in a perfect world, potable water should contain natural minerals, which are beneficial to human health. The main concern with rainwater is that it's basically "too clean"

Plumbing Glossary

Hard water. Water with high mineral content. It is typically formed when water percolates through deposits of limestone and chalk, and is made up of calcium and magnesium.

Roof. The structure forming the upper covering of a house. For rainwater harvesting purposes, the roof should be sloped and made of smooth,

hard, non-absorbent material.

Soft water. Water that contains low concentrations of ions and in particular low levels of calcium and magnesium.

Storm-water. Surface water flowing in unusual quantity resulting from heavy rainfall.

and void of minerals since it accumulated through evaporation as part of the earth's water cycle. If you happen to live in an area with an abundance of clean rainwater, experts advocate that ideally it should not be consumed for long periods of time. When it comes to this argument, every landowner can make the decision for him- or herself. Many farmers swear by rainwater and have been drinking it for 20-30 years without any issues. Some people recommend supplementing your diet with minerals. Others recommend leaving the "soft water" in a clay

Roof Surfaces for Harvesting rain

- **Metal** is the best texture because it is smooth and facilitates the efficient flow of water. Consider steel (galvanized or stainless) and similarly tin, aluminum or copper. Galvanized roofs are coated in zinc and you'll have to check the manufacturer's specs to see if the levels are within acceptable limits. Similarly, old tin roofs consisted of a sheet of metal that is covered in lead and tin. You don't want lead in your water. Modern tin roofs use a combination of tin and zinc. Make sure the material you are using is safe to use.

- **Clay/ Concrete Tiles** are porous but still very good for harvesting potable water. Make sure the clay tiles are glazed and well-fired to improve the runoff coefficient. Clay tiles are prone to moss and algae growth so be sure to clean them often (yearly).

- **Asphalt shingles** are very common and the well-known brands are generally considered fine for harvesting water. The older shingles were made of asbestos and should be avoided Check with the manufacturer first. Nowadays many shingles are imported from China where they are using a faster and cheaper manufacturing process. Look at the manufacturer's specs to see which materials are used and if they can potentially leach contaminants, and also if they release grit. The adhesives that are used during the installation process present a potential hazard and it is recommended to wait two to three years before you use new shingles for rainwater harvesting (time to off-gas).

- **Slate.** Slate is suitable for potable water, provided it's not coated with toxins/ chemicals.

(Don't use treated timber, asbestos or a surface with exposed lead flashings.)

pot that naturally adds minerals from the clay to the water. These are theories that have not been tested properly and I cannot recommend or reject them. When there are no alternatives, make the best decision for you and your family.

As a self-sufficient homeowner, determine how you will use the harvested water. A rainwater harvesting system has six main functions:

— To collect water from the roof.
— To transport the water through downspouts and piping.
— To remove debris and to clean the water before it enters the tank.
— To store the water in a tank or cistern.
— To add pressure (pump) to the water for use.
— To treat the water for human or animal consumption.

This is where you can start to get creative. Visualize your dwelling as your water harvesting system feeds different parts of the house and land. Use your senses to determine what will work and what not. Start small and make sure that you can build, repair and maintain the whole system. Set small goals at first and become master of your creation. Be conscious of waste and try to conserve as much water possible. For gardening and irrigation, allow water to flow gently and to infiltrate the soil. Avoid erosion by having an overflow route for water in heavy downpours and try to utilize the overflow as a resource. Use the water as a means to create a living area of growth; this is a resource from which you can harvest food, feed livestock and also produce other resources. The yearly mean average of rainfall will give you an estimate of how reliable rain-harvesting in your area will be. Determine if the rainwater in your geographical area is affected by contaminants and if it needs purification or not.

Collecting Water

Common sense dictates that we can collect water by simply placing containers outside. More containers will equal more water. Although this can be quite laborious and time consuming, it is doable when the situation demands it. Makeshift structures with tarps can also be used to collect rainwater and this is often done in tropical zones.

A better option is to harvest the water straight from the top of your house with the help of a **conveyance system**. This system consists of the roof which acts as the catchment area and which allows rainwater to flow down into gutters and downspouts. Houses are perfect for rain harvesting. Depending on

Water from roof

Clean water to tank

Ball seals
chamber off

The ball floats
up with the
dirty water

Dirty water flows
into the chamber

As it rains, water builds up in the gutters. Often gutters are filled with debris containing animal droppings, insects or dead animals like mice or lizards. This means that the first flush of water can be contaminated with unwanted microbes that you do not want in your tank.

The solution to this dilemma is the First Flush Diverter. This system consists of a chamber (pipe) with a ball float on the inside. As the water flows from the gutter towards the tank, it is diverted into the chamber. Once the chamber is full, the ball float rests on a seat at the top of the chamber and thus it seals off the top of the chamber. This prevents the new water from entering the diverter. Now the rest of the water can flow towards the tank.

It is advisable to fit the longest length chamber possible. Fit a diverter at every pipe that supplies water to a tank. You can install the chamber below the rainhead filter.

Allow enough space underneath the chamber to allow opening of the release valve.

These diverters come in kits and are very easy to assemble.

the location, a house with a large roof of 2000 ft² (190m²) can provide about 50,000 gallons (190 000 Liters) per year. Let's take a closer look at the conveyance system.

Gutters should be fitted to the edge of the roof area of all structures on the dwelling. Gutters come in different sizes. Surprisingly, gutter sizing is not as simple or straightforward as you would think. If it's an option, consult an expert about local plumbing codes to determine the appropriate gutter size for your area and your specific roof. Plumbing codes usually use the vertically projected roof area when calculating for drainage design. It also depends on the rain patterns and how often your area experiences rainstorms and of what intensity. The slope and size of the roof will also factor in.

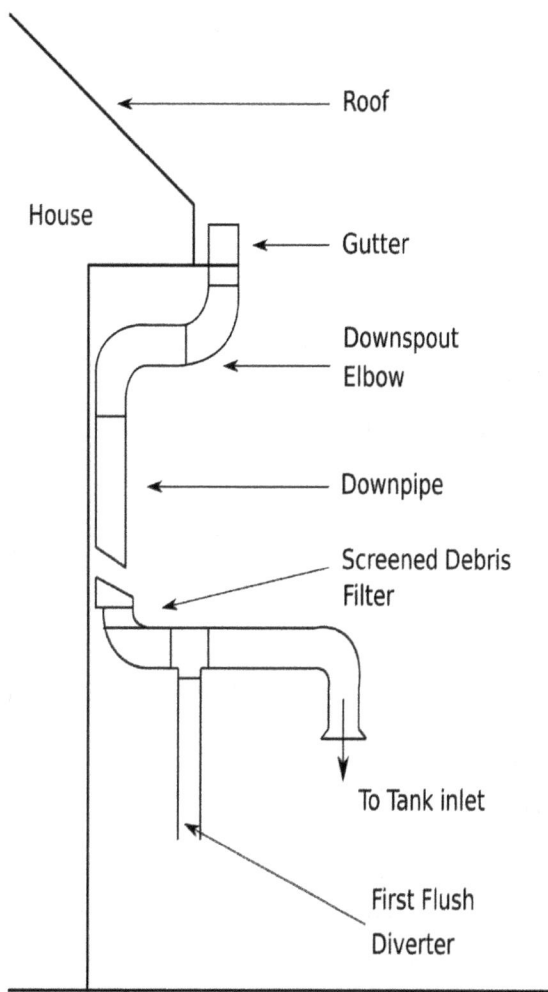

House

Roof

Gutter

Downspout
Elbow

Downpipe

Screened Debris
Filter

To Tank inlet

First Flush
Diverter

Gutters and Installation

- To drain, gutters need to be sloped towards the downspout at an angle. Having a 1" to 2" slope over 40 feet is sufficient.

- Provide gutter supports for every 3 feet of gutter length. In areas with heavy snow, you need a support for every foot.

- Rounded-bottom gutters are easier to clean and limit debris buildup.

- To prevent UV sunlight breakdown, you can paint PVC gutters and pipes.

- Common house gutters should be at least 5" (13cm) wide. For large homes, a 6" (15.2cm) wide gutter will do.

Keep the basics in mind:

- As a general rule, gutters should be at least 5 inches (13 cm) wide.
- Gutter length should not exceed 50 ft. (15.2m).
- Gutter supports (also called hangers) should be able to carry the weight of a full gutter with water or ice.
- The gutter outlet capacity should suit the downspout capacity. It cannot exceed the bottom width of the gutter. The size of the downspout should be constant throughout its length. As a general rule, provide one square inch of downspout area for every 100 square feet of roof area.

There are a range of gutter protection options out there to keep gutters clear of leaves and debris. You can fit a First Flush Diverter, which diverts the first flush of contaminated water into a downpipe or chamber

Gutter Styles

K-Style Gutter

Half-round Gutter

As a general rule, you can expect every 1″ (2.5cm) of rain on 1,000 square feet (93 square meters) of roof area to collect more than 600 gallons (2275 liters) of water!

and away from your tank. This diverter should be cleaned regularly. **Roofs with steep slopes** require commercial grade gutters to cope with accelerated runoff speed. Steep slopes lead to water loss due to acceleration. Most countries have local government websites with "Roof area catchment calculators" and gutter and downspout sizing tables. Make use of these resources as they can provide you with valuable information about rainfall in your geographical area. As a general rule, you can expect every 1″ (2.5cm) of rain on 1,000 square feet (93 square meters) of roof area to collect more than 600 gallons (2,275 liters) of water! There it is. A great reason to invest in a rainwater harvesting system. Use this number as an estimate to calculate the potential of your roof catchment area (see p.68).

Once you have a conveyance system in place, you can move on to the next phase, which is storage of the rainwater.

Storage Tanks

From the conveyance system, the water goes into a storage container. Rain barrels are very handy and you can spread them out by connecting one to every downspout, overflow pipe (or basically anywhere around the dwelling) to collect extra water. These collection vessels can provide water for wildlife, pets, livestock or landscaping. They are aesthetically pleasing and very useful, but for the more serious rain harvester, you will need a tank.

Tanks are large storage vessels that are fed through gutters and pipes. Tanks are incredibly important and an essential part of the homestead. Not only are they used for rain harvesting, but they can also be used to store water from springs and wells. If, for this reason, your tank is located in a remote location on your property, make sure that you have a clear access road to it. In an emergency, it might be your only source of water.

Before we continue, understand that tanks are huge, wide containers filled with potentially thousands of gallons of water. Make absolutely sure that the catchment system is secure to prevent animals and children from accessing the tank!

When discussing tanks, we have to remember that tanks provide water storage for both dry and wet systems.

The Dry System

Good:
- Very simple and fairly cheap.
- Pipes are easily accesible to maintain.

Bad:
- Pipes are exposed to elements.

The **Dry System** is a form of conveyance system. When looking at the pipes, we notice that this system's **main characteristic** is that all pipes are "dry", until it rains. The pipes do not hold water after the rain stops. The dry system is the simplest and cheapest setup to implement. All pipes are above ground which means that they are visible, reachable and thus easy to maintain. The pipe system runs directly from the gutter of the roof into the tank. Water flows from the highest point to the lowest and when the rain stops, the pipes are "dry" and do not hold any water. This inexpensive system allows you to store a large amount of rainwater and is great for climates with infrequent, larger storm events. This system is generally found on structures with only a couple of downspouts. The collection tank is usually located right next to the catchment area, so there's no need to run piping underground. With the pipes located above ground, gravity assists in pulling every drop of water down into your tank.

The Wet System

Gutters and pipes are dry once rain event stops

Good:

- Aesthetically pleasing.
- Practical solution when tanks are far away from house.

Bad:

- Vulnerable to mosquito infestations.
- Prone to anaerobic fermentation.
- More expensive, more work.
- Pipes should be drained between rainfall events.
- Pipes are prone to cracking infreezing conditions.

The **Wet System** is a bit more complicated and expensive to implement. Its **main characteristic** is that the water rests in the pipes, until the next rain event. The pipes are connected to multiple downspouts with different gutters. They continue down along the wall and along (or under) the ground and then run up against the tank and into the tank inlet. The pipes are always charged or filled with water and that is why we call it a "wet or charged" system.

The elevation of the tank inlet must be below the lowest gutter on the house. A benefit of this system is that it allows you to locate the tank away from the house.

In areas with **mosquitoes**, special care should be taken to insect-proof the buried pipes and all connections and fittings must be absolutely watertight. Stagnant water in pipes can create a potential breeding habitat

Downpipes · **Gutter** · Tank inlet lower than gutter · **House**

for mosquitoes to lay their eggs. This system should be installed with the help of a professional. Pipes in the ground are susceptible to cracking in freezing conditions.

Tank Types

Let's take a look at typical tanks available at hardware stores all over the world. Whatever your needs, rest assured that you have plenty of options to choose from. Tanks come in all shapes and sizes and every year we see new designs with better design characteristics. When buying a water storage tank, consider the following:

— **Location.** Underground or above ground? Under decks or in basements? Consider piping distance from house to tank required.

— **Size and design.** Consider what size and design will suit your installation location. How much space is available to place the tank? Larger tanks suit colder climates with freezing conditions.

— **Tank material.** Will it survive the environment you intend to use it in? Consider climate, temperatures (especially freezing temperatures), and conditions like the occurrence of wildfires. How long is your tank guaranteed to last?

— **Water quality.** Does the tank material affect the taste and quality of the water?

— **Cost.** Consider that delivery, installation and setup charges will all affect the price.

Talk to the tank distributor and make sure that you get the right tank for your needs. If a tank does not fit into the designated space provided, you can look for a "slim tank" or go smaller and use two or three appropriately sized tanks. There are also modular tanks on the market that form a linkable "wall" where you can store your water. Do not use a translucent plastic tank for water storage! These tanks allow sunlight into the tank and this causes the water to grow algae.

Fewer tanks generally means less maintenance. For most households one large tank will suffice.

A small roof with a small tank is good for toilet flushing and washing. A large roof with a large tank allows for a variety of options, both inside and outside the house.

Let's look at the different storage options. Make sure that your tank meets or exceeds NSF 61 standards. You should gather as much information as possible before buying a tank. Typical tanks to consider:

Plastic (polyethylene), fiberglass, wood, metal, stainless steel, bladder type, or concrete.

● Polyethylene

Material: Plastic (Polyethylene)

Size: Wide range
Price: Affordable
Convenience: They are light and come with plumber's fittings that are easy to fit and assemble. Available at most hardware stores.
Characteristics: These are very popular tanks. Polyethylene tanks are tough and lightweight. They are UV and rust resistant. Painting these tanks is not advised since most paints don't stick to plastic and will flake in the elements. Buy pre-painted and remember that dark colored tanks absorb heat. Place them in the shade where possible. When placed outside, they will last for a long time. Placing them inside, in the shade, can increase their lifespan to much longer. They are normally placed above ground. For buried installation, you need a specially reinforced tank. Buried tanks are more expensive because the tank has to be reinforced and the excavation required is costly. Don't put a tank in ground with high clay content, for the clay expands and contracts and this can potentially damage the tank.

These tanks are definitely not to be used in areas prone to wildfires.

Get product specs when buying from your distributor. Make sure that your tank is government approved and that it meets all industry standards.

On a side note, it's worth mentioning that we are still dealing with a plastic container that you are using for water storage. Plastic brings an element of toxicity to the table and this can be a turn-off for some buyers. Make sure you do thorough research on this subject, to give you the peace of mind that you require for you and your family's wellbeing.

● Fiberglass

Material: Layered fiberglass and resin
Size: Wide range
Price: Affordable
Convenience: Light, tough and easy to transport.
Characteristics: Fiberglass tanks are also tough and lightweight. Years ago they were mostly used above ground, but these days you can find excellent underground fiberglass tanks. Tanks come in a wide range of colors and sizes and they are resistant to heat, rust and chemical erosion and won't degrade. The tank fittings are built into the tank and therefore you are guaranteed few issues with leaks. These are long-lasting tanks and they are actually reasonably priced for what you get. These tanks should be opaque to prevent algal growth and there should be a liner on the inside of the tank that's approved for storage of drinking water for human consumption. Get product specs when buying from a distributor. Make sure that your tank is government approved and that it meets all

industry standards.
Worthy of consideration is the fact that most fiberglass tanks are not recyclable and will most likely end up as landfill. They contain polyester resin and other toxic substances, which are released into the environment when they degrade.

● Metal

Material: Galvanized sheet metal or corrugated steel
Size: Wide range
Price: Affordable
Convenience: Light, easy to transport, and be custom made on site.
Characteristics: Metal tanks are tough, strong and lightweight. They provide a great solution for household uses, irrigation and fire protection. Depending on brand and manufacturer, they can be used above or below ground. These tanks should be considered in areas prone to wildfires. They also do not crack in sub-zero conditions. There should be a food-grade liner or epoxy coating on the inside of the tank that's approved for storage of drinking water for human consumption. Get product specs when buying from a distributor. Make sure that your tank is government approved and that it meets all industry standards. These tanks have a typical lifespan of 30 - 35 years.

● Stainless Steel

Material: Stainless Steel

Size: Wide range
Price: Expensive
Convenience: Strong, durable and easy to transport.
Characteristics: These are very good tanks. Stainless steel tanks are superior in the categories of strength, durability, and hygiene. They are mostly used above ground, except where the manufacturer specifically states that it is to be used below ground. Certain metals do add the possibility of rust, but stainless steel will not readily rust or discharge in water. These tanks should be considered in areas prone to wildfires and they can easily last 50 years or more. When buying, make sure that the manufacturer provides information and a guarantee specifically for the seals, especially where the floor meets the wall of the tank.

• Concrete/ Ferrocement

Material: Concrete with or without rebar
Size: Large sizes
Price: Fairly expensive
Convenience: Are usually manufactured on site. Durable and strong.
Characteristics: Concrete tanks are tough, permanent structures and can be custom made. These tanks can be poured in place or they can be prefabricated off-site. Some manufacturers also provide underground holding tanks.

These are structurally strong tanks that last a long time. The concrete keep the water temperature low and stable, which also prevents algal growth. They are perfect for areas prone to wildfires. Make sure that the inside of the tank is plastered with material that is suitable for drinking water. These tanks have an advantage in that the concrete dissolves calcium into the water (due to the acidic nature of rainwater), which provides a pleasant taste. These days you can buy waterproof plaster to fix cracks and leaks.

• Wood

Material: Redwood, Pine, Cedar
Size: Wide range
Price: Expensive
Convenience: Looks great, all natural and no contaminants.
Characteristics: Wood tanks are still available, but they have become more expensive and therefore less popular. They used to be made of redwood, but you can also find tanks made of pine, cypress or cedar. They are custom built by skilled technicians who wrap the wood with steel cables under tension. The natural qualities of redwood is very appealing since it contains no resin and the tannins in the wood function as a natural preservative which keeps boring insects at bay. They are not to be used in very dry climates for they tend to shrink and to leak. Used above ground only.

A food-grade liner is placed on the inside for potable use. Wood tanks will outlast any of the alternatives.

• Bladders/Pillows

Material: Typically flexible reinforced Material (Polymer Alloy, PVC, Polyurethane)
Size: Wide range
Price: Fairly expensive
Convenience: Fits under decks and between walls. Out of sight.
Characteristics: Bladder or Pillow tanks are manufactured from a flexible material. This type of tank rises and expands as you fill it with liquid. These bladders are very convenient in that they can fit into tight storage spaces and thus they are ideal for storage under decks, in basements or in between walls. For potable water storage make sure that the bladder comes with a food-grade liner. It connects easily to downspouts, pipes and pumps and is manufactured from a high strength fabric. These bladders come in sizes ranging from 25-5,000 gallons (94-10,000 liters).

These are the most popular and widely available storage options. There are still other kinds of tanks available out there. In each case a professional should first be consulted. No matter which option best suits your needs, always make sure that your water does not come into contact with any unwanted chemicals or pollutants and that where necessary, a food-grade liner is placed on the inside of the tank. Make sure that the fabric used is NSF 61 rated.

Safety of plastics

When it comes to storing water for human consumption, you might want to consider the following information. Most of these tanks use plastics, liners made of plastic, resins or coatings, that will come into contact with your water. Although they are all, for the most part, gov-

Safety precautions

• While under construction, close all holes and containers when the work site is abandoned.

• Make sure the inlets to all water tanks are child proof or locked.

• Keep all electrical wires (pumps) contained and out of reach.

• Access to all wells are for adults only. This is not a play area for kids.

• Protect your resources. Don't allow criminal elements to access your pumps, tanks, pipes, well or outside water faucets. Use locks on inlets and pump casings if needed.

Basic Tank Setup

Roof

Gutter

Tank Inlet

Inspection Port

Overflow

Aerobic Zone

Drainage Outlet

Tank Outlet

Anaerobic Zone

Water travels from the roof into the **gutter** and from there it travels down the **downspout** and into the tank.

Not all rainwater systems have a first flush diverter for contaminated water. If you inherited a system without a diverter, just make sure that you drain the sludge from your tank more often. Invest in a good filter screen at the inlet area and also add a filter at the outlet.

The **tank inlet** is where the water enters and it can be modified to suit your needs. It can be attached to the tank or you can leave an open space between tank and downspout. Just remember that all tank openings should be closed or fitted with screens or strainer baskets to keep bugs and critters out.

The **anaerobic zone** is where the unwanted water rich in sediment settles. The **tank outlet** is raised to avoid the sediment from the anaerobic zone. It should be the same size as the tank inlet.

The **aerobic zone** is where the clear water void of heavy particles is found. If a rain event delivered too much rain, the overflow will allow excess water to escape. This pipe can be connected to the stormwater runoff or even to other tanks or pools. The **inspection port** must be closed at all times. Remember to do inspections often to ensure longevity of your system.

Advanced Tank Setup

Roof

Gutter

First Flush Diverter

Tank Inlet and screen

Inspection Port

Overflow

Floating Pick-up

Aerobic Zone

Drainage Outlet

Anaerobic Zone

Tank Outlet

The **First flush diverter system**. These days most conveyance systems use the first flush diverter system. This takes care of the initial flow of contaminated water.

Inlet areas. Some inlets are connected to the tank to prevent mosquitoes and debris from entering. Others have a space between the downpipe and tank. These tanks use tank screens and all water must pass through this screen before entering the tank.

Calming inlets are specially designed to prevent the stirring up of sediment in the tank.

Floating Pick-up. Inside the tank, the heavier sediment will settle at the bottom or anaerobic zone of the tank. The lighter particles float at the top. As the name suggests, a floating pick-up floats in the calm, clear water in the middle of the tank. This intake avoids the heavy sediment at the bottom of the tank and lets the best quality water in and also filters floating debris. You'll find the best quality water in your tank around 6-8 inches from the surface. Ensure that your pick-up is collecting water within this range.

The floating pick-up connects to the pipe outlet, typically near the very bottom, where water is drawn for household and irrigation use.

Your overflow outlet can have a flap or cover to keep critters out.

ernment approved, you will do well to do some of your own research to decide if plastics (made out of oil) or similar, is something you want your water to be stored in. This might the deciding factor when purchasing a new water tank for your home.

Preparations

Whether you are using a rain barrel (50 gal/ 200 L) or an actual water tank, you still have to prepare the ground underneath the tank, install tank components and distribute the water for "end use".

Step 1. Start at the top since water flows downhill. Locate the downspout of the gutter. The downspout is the pipe used to guide water from the gutter, down to the ground. Gutters are angled to allow drainage of water and the exit point is the downspout.

Step 2. Remove any overhanging branches and prepare the ground by making sure that it's level. The position of the tank will be determined by its size, shape and type.

- Your tank must be placed at least 3 feet away from the house and on solid, compacted ground or on a hard surface.

- Relying on gravity for sufficient flow rate for irrigation requires you to elevate your tank onto a raised platform. For every 10 feet of elevation, you can expect to achieve 4.3 psi of water pres-

sure.

- Soft sandy areas will need reinforcement. Flatten the area and use a support structure with wide wooden beams or stone slabs to make a flat, sturdy level for the tank to rest on. Use wood that can resist flooding and does not become water-logged.

- There should be ample drainage underneath and if not, consider creating a layer of pea gravel to remedy the situation. Dig about a hand's width into the ground and create a clean, sunken rectangular area. Fill it with gravel and make sure it drains away from the house. Prepare a level layer of bricks, concrete blocks or thick wooden beams on top. The tank can rest on top of this structure.

For a concrete slab, you just have to make sure that the area is level. Pour more cement if necessary, but make sure it drains away from the house to the storm-water drain.

- If the ground is not suitable, you can raise the tank onto a structure made of metal or wood. This must be a very solid structure capable of holding the weight of a full tank. Get advice from your supplier about elevation of the specific tank.

- The main thing to remember is to have your tank at the level position, and in a suitable location. Plan ahead, for tanks are heavy, really heavy when full. A full tank cannot be moved with-

Collection And Storage Of Rainwater

out draining it first.

- You do not want a leaking tank to drain into any structure and therefore you have to provide a barrier between your tank and the building. Concrete is best for this.

Step 3. Next, you need to decide if you need one, two or more tanks.

A house with one downspout deserves one tank/ barrel.

Houses with two or three downspouts are slightly more complicated. You have two options:

a. Place a tank underneath each downspout. This means two or three tanks around the house.

b. Alternatively, you can connect gutter spouts from one side of the house, to connect with spouts from another side, to all flow into one tank. This involves a bit more work, but the end result is worth it.

Step 4. You can hire an expert to take care of the assembly and construction components, or you can just do it yourself. Doing it yourself brings you closer to the project and means that you can maintain, repair and replace everything yourself when necessary. Go to your local hardware store and make sure you get local advice about rainfall, gutter sizes, tank types and sizes, pumps, etc.

Tank Setup

Once you've done your research, you can buy your tank or barrel. New is best, but a good second hand tank will also do. Make sure that it is completely clean and remove all coats of paint, solvents or chemicals. If unsure, do not use it! New tanks should come with plumber's fittings and a warranty. Translucent tanks and pipes should be avoided because they will encourage algal growth. Ask about options concerning a water level indicator. This is a very useful accessory to have.

1. Place your water tank in the area that you have prepared. Visualize the full effect that it will have on your dwelling (irrigation, household, water heating systems, general use, car washing, swimming pools, fire fighting) and prepare accordingly. Connect fittings provided for the inlet, outlet, overflow and drainage outlets. If you are using two or more tanks, do not stack them. Normal tanks are not designed to withstand that kind of pressure.

2. Check your roof surface. Make sure there are no chemicals, paint or paint flakes or mold. Chimneys cause smoke residue that gets washed down into gutters. You want a clean roof, preferably metal, asphalt shingles or tile. Asbestos roofs and roofs with flashings that contain lead are not suitable. If you live in an area where farmers spray pesticides overhead, then your rainwater can really only be used for irrigation. Clear overhanging branches from gutters.

3. Place guards or screens over the gutter holes. These screens are also called rainheads and they will keep debris and leaves from clogging your downspouts. (You can make your own by cutting heavy duty screen material and fastening them over openings with a radiator clamp.)

4. Connect the downpipe. At the top, the downpipe connects to the downspout under the gutter. At the bottom, the downpipe connects to a downspout elbow that connects to the tank. Use PVC cement and primer to connect these joints.

It keeps insects and debris out.

Tank

Some tanks have a unique design in that the downpipe does not enter the tank itself; it stops a few inches above the tank. The tank inlet is then covered with a screen guard that keeps debris and mosquitoes out.

Downpipes should be uniform in size. Make sure you have the correct size and fittings. The fittings come with the tank and

Tank with inletscreen, to keep insects and debris out.

you should check if they have O-rings.

All downpipes must be secured to the building structure. Avoid random "flying" pipes that run from the roof to the tank.

5. First Flush Diverter. Install the diverter between the downspout and the tank. Every downpipe that flows into the tank should have a diverter. Leave enough space at the bottom of the diverter chamber to be able to open and close the release valve by hand. Try not to waste the water, since you can still use the contaminated water from the diverter for irrigation.

6. Check the overflow outlet. The tank must have an overflow outlet. This is where you can get creative. You have the option of letting the overflow pipe drain straight into the storm-water system. You can also connect your overflow to a lower lying tank that can be utilized for secondary water needs. You can also connect your overflow to flow into a pool, pond or cistern for livestock or firefighting needs.

Get smart, consider your needs

and don't waste your water. Be wary of letting water flow directly onto the ground. Not only does it cause erosion and loss of soil, but it can potentially also damage structure foundations.

7. Drainage outlet. The water of poorest quality is located in the anaerobic zone at the bottom of the tank. The tank must have a drainage outlet. Flushing out sludge is part of the maintenance required and should be done biannually.

8. Tank Accessories. The main purpose of tank accessories is to give you access to cleaner water.

- Modern tanks come with a floating pick-up (extractor) that floats at the top of the water's surface. This is to guarantee the best water gets used and not the water at the bottom rich in sediment.

- Overflow siphons act as skimmers and when the tank overflows, they skim the pollen and dust from the water's surface. This means cleaner water.

- Calmed inlets prevent the disturbance of water and sediment when rainwater enters the tank. This means cleaner water.

9. Water outlet. If your outlet drains from the bottom of the tank, make sure that it is at least 4 inches from the bottom, to avoid using the dirty sediment-containing water. This is the anaerobic zone of the tank. From here, the water flows to your irrigation system in your garden. Remember to prepare fittings for secondary applications like fire fighting equipment, pond/ pool systems, etc. A well laid out rain harvesting system can rely on gravity for irrigation, but if your water flow is not strong enough for domestic use, it's time to invest in a pump.

Pumps And Filters

Pumps are used to supply the house or irrigation system with pressured water. If you have a simple irrigation system that relies on gravity (tank is elevated), then a pump is not necessary. When selecting a water pump for your home or garden you need to consider:

- The distance the water needs to travel between your tank and end use. A longer distance requires a more powerful pump.

- Your water pressure requirements.

- The noise made by the pump.

- The energy usage.

Pump suppliers can advise you on the correct pump for your application and they will calculate the flow rate per indoor appliance.

Pumps are traditionally placed in a position that is lower than the pump outlet on the tank, for they are better at pushing than pulling water (This also helps with priming in older pumps).

In a basic setup, the water flows from the tank, into the pump, which pushes it out towards the end use. Make sure that you have stop valves on entry and exit points of the pump. This allows you to clean, maintain or change the pump.

You will expect great flow rate from your pump. For a standard water pump (centrifugal pump), the inlet size is slightly larger than the outlet size. This is built into the pump casing and you have to use the correct size piping to ensure optimum pump efficiency. Avoid chaotic pipe structures. Plan ahead and keep piping in straight lines and as simple as possible. Pressure in the system causes leaks and the less joints and connections the better.

Modern pumps (on-demand pumps) come with a pressure sensor that senses a drop in pressure when you open a faucet/ tap and they turn on automatically to compensate for the loss of water pressure. This type of pump is very low on power usage.

Filters can be very beneficial to a rainwater harvesting system. Filter size is measured in microns or mesh. A micron unit is about one millionth of a meter or 0.001 mm. A wire mesh system indicates how many openings there are in one inch of screen.

The first group of filters in a system are cartridge sediment filters and they are used in a series that typically range from large pore size to small.

Example: In a traditional set-up, you will use a 20 micron filter followed immediately by a 5 micron filter and later by a 1 micron filter.

A small filter (5 micron) is more thorough at eliminating particles, but works at a slower flow rate and it's also more expensive.

A large filter is less effective and only removes large particles, but works at a faster flow rate.

A large micron sediment pre-filter should be placed in-line before the water reaches the pump. This filter will remove large unwanted particles from the system, while still allowing great flow rate to the pump. Filter selection will depend on the end use of the system. If you are simply using your rainwater for irrigation purposes, then a large sediment pre-filter, installed before the pump, is all that you will need. If you want to make the water potable for human consumption, then you will need a more elaborate system. (See p. 132)

Besides a pump, you can also add a **pressure tank** if your water is intended for indoor use. From the pump, the water goes into a regular pressure tank, which keeps the water under pressure for indoor use. A pressure tank has the capacity to store a certain amount of water under pressure that can be used throughout the day. This means that the pump is used less often and it also allows you to save on electricity and increases the life of the pump.

As we continue along the water line, from the pressure tank you can consider sending your water through a purification system like a reverse osmosis system followed by a UV light. This is a very effective system that will rid the water of almost all unwanted contaminants, pathogens and chemicals. Concerning water treatment options, there are various methods available for ridding your water of contaminants. Some are more effective than others, but they also differ in price-range. We discuss a wide variety of water treatment options in Chapter 9. Having a water meter at this point in the system is a great idea to measure the water usage of the household. Be conservation minded and keep an eye on consumption per person, and number of water-using appliances.

Having a backup pump in case of emergency is a must. If you lose power, you should have a backup plan. Can your tank setup rely on gravity alone? You should know how to assemble, service and install the pump. These days solar pumps are very efficient and affordable. A solar pump combined with a pressure tank can provide an

Pump Basics

• Use a pre-filter to clear sediment before the water flows into the pump.

• Keep suction piping leading to pump, as short as possible. This ensures good flow, uniform velocity and good pressure.

• Eliminate elbows mounted close to the pump inlet. This causes "loading" and puts strain on the pump. A straight run of pipe is best.

• Eliminate trapped air from system by keeping water levels high and avoiding unnecessary "high bends" in pipes, which can cause air pockets.

• Don't put any weight on your pump. Your piping arrangement should not put any weight or stress on the pump casing.

• Make sure your pump has a cover to protect it from the elements and to keep all electrical wires contained.

• Make sure your pump is secure and if needed, create a casing that allows you to lock the pump in place.

• Remember:
Long pipe, high friction, low flow.
Short pipe, low friction, high flow.

effective solution for your water pressure needs.

CAUTION! Keep children away from your pump and pipes; it's not a play area and leaking pipes can ruin a rain event for the serious harvester, especially when you live in a remote area.

Control The Flow Of Water

Once you have a tank filled with rainwater, you will quickly realize that you have different options concerning the usage of this resource. To use your water effectively and to maximize usage, you will have to switch between municipal (mains) water and your tank water. Since the water from your tank is free, you will obviously have to use it first. Once the water level in the tank becomes too low, you can switch to the public water supply. This can be done either manually or with an electronic switch-over device. The benefit of using this setup is that you will mostly be draining the "free" water from the tank and thus your tank will have space for the next rain event, and it will save you money on your water bill.

• The manual way is very reliable and cheap, but it means that you have to be physically available to go outside to open/close the line.

• Using an automatic switch-

Pump pipe dimensions. A typical setup has a pipe, leading from the tank, of ¾ inch and the discharge pipe , towards the house, smaller at ½ inch. This adds more pressure to the charged system of the house.

over device is a bit more expensive and it uses electricity. It is however very convenient and provides a smooth flow of water.

Make sure you check the local government regulations in your area on whether it is required to have a device installed or not.

Maintenance

Maintenance and cleaning is an essential part of the upkeep of the system. You should know your system inside out and be able to repair, replace or service any of the components at work.

Regular inspection of your collection system is a must.

Every three months:

• Clean gutters and check screens and guards.

• Remove any algal growth if present.

• You must have an access hole to see into the tank. Keep the lid of the access hole clean.

Every six months:

- Inspect integrity of tank, pipes and the pump system.
- Clear overhanging branches and other vegetation.
- All tanks must have a drainage outlet to wash sludge and heavy sediment out.

Avoid exposure to sunlight and also to contaminants like external water sources.

Contamination

If you do suspect biological contamination like dangerous pathogens (water smells bad and the color is off), you will have to act quickly.

- Get rid of the source of contamination. Obviously you should investigate what's causing the contamination (dead bird or rodent).
- Estimate how long the water has been exposed to contaminants.
- Consider draining the tank, especially if the water has been exposed to contaminants for an extended period of time.
- In case of an emergency, where draining is not an option, you will have to consider boiling and filtering the water or treating the water with chlorine. Chemicals like Chlorine are only to be used in an emergency. There are different options available and best to buy a product that's been tried and tested in your community.

A standard measure involves using household bleach (with 5% Chlorine) and adding about 1½ teaspoon (8ml) to every 45 gal (200 L) of water.

Adding bleach provides a solution of 2 parts per million of chlorine (0.0002%)

Use Your Water

Once your tank is filled with rainwater, you will find that using the harvested water is just an absolute pleasure. It is a great relief knowing that you have water stored for a time of need and that nature provided it for free.

- If you want to use the water indoors, then you will have to test it first. Rather safe than sorry. Make sure that you have a reliable filtration system that takes care of pathogens and chemical contaminants.
- One of the most common uses of harvested rainwater is for landscape irrigation. It is suitable for irrigation since the water does not have to be treated first and because all minerals have been removed which is good for root health. Remember that the soil adds minerals back for the roots to absorb. Drip irrigation is an efficient way to water plants without wasting water. Don't flood your garden with water. Think how much water your plants need and what is the best delivery system.
- Rainwater is also a good way to attract wildlife. Lush areas create an abundance of birds and insects, which in turn increases pollination and regen-

eration of the land. Man-made ponds attract wildlife and can be a supplemental source of water for these animals.

• Livestock can also benefit from rainwater.

• Having water at hand means that you can create a system for fire protection. Quality of water does not play a role when fighting fires.

In areas where the local government or municipality does not provide main, municipal water or where water is just scarce, rainwater can provide an alternative option. Through careful planning and maintenance you can access remote areas on your land by utilizing pumps and cisterns.

Overflow and storm-water management is very important. When the precipitation rate is higher than the absorption rate (ground) it creates water runoff that eventually ends up in the rivers, lakes and oceans. Avoid erosion of your soil by creating an intelligent overflow system that allows the excess water to flow where it can be absorbed, channeled or stored (ponds).

Colder Climates

Harvesting rainwater in cold climates with snow and ice is no simple task. Although the fundamental basics are the same, the ice factor definitely complicates things.

Freezing temperatures can be destructive to a rainwater har-

vesting system if water in the pump and pipes are allowed to freeze.

For freshly fallen snow, 14 inches of snow will equal 1 inch of water. When the snow is compacted, expect 4 inches of snow to equal 1 inch of water.

Some important points to consider:

• **Ice is heavy.** All weight-bearing supports will have to be designed to withstand heavier loads. This includes gutter supports, tank stands and roof supports.

• **Roof design.** Using snow guards is essential for gutter protection.

• **Ice contracts and melts.** Prepare for fluctuation of water levels in your tank. A simple, clean tank without complicated internal fittings will make things a lot easier.

• **Tank type and dimensions.** A large, round tank is best simply because of the round curves and the space it provides. More water means that it will take longer to freeze over. Get a tank that is guaranteed (by manufacturer) not to crack in sub-zero temperatures. In areas with heavy snowfall, get a tank that can withstand heavier loads and with a steep-angled roof (for snow to slide off). If you want to put your tank in the ground, follow the manufacturer's instructions.

• **Use insulation.** Check with your local hardware store what works in your area. Spray on

Collection And Storage Of Rainwater

polyurethane foam provides good insulation for tanks, and valves and pumps can be placed in insulation boxes.

- **Pipes.** Pipes are prone to cracking in freezing conditions. Pipes should be drained when not in use and can also be insulated. Bury your pipes below the freeze line when drained of water. Use pipes that are suitable to the conditions in your area. Standard PVC pipes are not recommended. Valves should be placed in insulation boxes.
- **Trace heating.** There are a few ways that you can prevent pipes from freezing over. Trace heating involves taping a heated element to the side of the pipe. The tape used is insulated and can be used for gutters as well.
- **Extras.** To prevent the water in the tank from freezing over, you can consider an aerator that keeps the water moving in the tank, or even a heat pump that recirculates hot water through the system.

Conclusion

New tanks are constantly introduced to the market. Manufacturing techniques and materials evolve, and every year we see a wider variety of tanks to choose from.

The thinner "slim" tanks are perfect for small spaces and are very popular within city limits and for smaller homesteads.

If you want to hide your tanks, for whatever reason, you can consider a camouflage color, paint it yourself or hide it behind walls, decks or screens. There are also new modular tanks on the market that allow you to link them together and to form a "wall" that should blend in nicely with any building structure.

A reminder that tanks can also be used with wells. The water is pumped from the well to the holding tank, from where it continues either to the house for domestic use, or on to the fields for agricultural purposes.

My Checklist

√ I have determined the use of the harvested water.

√ I selected the correct size tank for my needs.

√ I selected the correct type tank for my needs.

√ My tank is at the perfect location.

√ I checked with local government.

√ I double-checked all installation requirements.

√ I know how to maintain my rainwater harvesting system.

√ All entrances have covers to prevent mosquitoes and other critters from entering.

√ I am collecting as much water as possible.

√ My water quality is very good.

√ I have considered all worst-case scenarios. I have a backup plan.

Rainwater Calculations

To accurately calculate the rainwater harvesting potential of a dwelling, we use the following formula: **V = A x R x C x 0.623***

V = Volume of available water, measured in gallons (gal) or liters (L).

A = Roof catchment area measured in square feet (ft²) or square meters (m²).

Length x Width = Catchment area. (No matter roof is flat or pitched.)

R = Monthly rainfall, measured in inches or millimeters (mm).

C = Collection surface efficiency: 0.8 is an average. (Meaning the percentage of precipitation that appears as runoff. Smooth material like metal has a high efficiency, clay has a low efficiency.)

*The value of 0.623 is a conversion factor that converts inches of rainfall over a square foot area, to total volume of gallons rainwater.

Collection calculation (per month):
V = Catchment area (ft²) x Rain (inches per month) x **0.8** x 0.623

Example (Imperial system):
V = 1000 ft² x 2 inches (month) x **0.8** x 0.623 = 996.8 gallons (month)

Example (Metric system):

V (Liters) = A (m²) x R (mm) x C

V = 90 m² x 50 mm x 0.8 = 3 600 Liters (month)

(There is no conversion factor necessary for the metric system.)

(Note that you can make a yearly calculation with the same formula.)

Extracting Water From The Ground

For thousands of years, man has been digging into the ground, to look for water. Even today, in many developing countries, digging a well is the only way to have access to a potable water source.

For the modern landowner, having a well means independence. It's basically like striking the jackpot of self-sufficiency, for having access to clean, drinkable water takes care of a multitude of land-related problems. By definition, and according to the Oxford Dictionary, a well is "a shaft sunk into the ground to obtain water." When we dig a little bit deeper, we see that wells are fed by natural aquifers of water that are found underground. These aquifers are pockets of water that are located under the layers of ground that we walk on. The ground, which consists of layers of sand, clay, gravel and rock, acts as a natural filtration system. Not only does it filter, but it also adds vital minerals and ions to the water as it seeps through. This is a classic example of the Earth providing and catering to our needs. Once this water has traveled down through all these layers, it accumulates in areas with sand, gravel or rock formations.

In theory, the deeper you have to go to reach the water, the cleaner it should be. Note that this deep water can also be contaminated with natural occurring chemicals that seep into the groundwater. Fortunately, we don't have to go too deep to find water. Professional drill teams often go down to 400-500 feet, but in general, most water is found no deeper than 250 feet down. When we look at domestic drill set-ups, we find that most landowners find their water at less than 50 feet.

Most of it is used for irrigation and livestock, but with a bit of luck, you can get quality water from right underneath your feet. This is great news for the self-sufficient homeowner who is willing to try his hand at well drilling or digging. Having access to a well is something that must be on the minds of all people who want to live close to the land. The water in the cities is transported from reservoirs, rivers, dams and lakes and it is exposed to various pollutants and contaminants. On top of that, it has to be treated for human consumption and that's where (gasp!) even more chemicals are added. Whether unhappy with your current water quality, looking for an independent water source, or if your water bill is starting to hurt your pocket, then get moving, for it's time to get yourself a water well.

Well basics

First, realize that this is a fairly ambitious project and that you need to plan your well very carefully. Let's look at the different methods used to extract water from the ground. Remember that both soil type and depth of the water table will determine which option is best for you.

Self drilling a well

Suitable water table depth: Up to 35 feet
Soil: Mostly sand and gravel

This might seem a fairly simple method, but it does involve building and designing a drill from scratch using PVC pipe. The drilling is done by sinking a drill-bit into the ground and creating a hole. As the drill-bit cuts the ground material, the cuttings are flushed out with water pressure. Avoid drilling in rock, but dealing with thin layers of clay in between should be no problem.

Digging your own well

Suitable water table depth: Up to 25 feet
Soil: Sand, clay and gravel

This method involves simple

Well Drilling Glossary

Aquifer. A geological formation that contains or conducts groundwater, especially one that supplies water for wells and springs.

Auger. A hand-held tool consisting of a twisted rod of metal (drill bit) attached to a handle, used for making holes in the soil.

Groundwater. The water that collects/ flows beneath the earth's surface, like porous spaces in soil, sediment and rock.

Standing Water Level. SWL refers to the level of the water in a well, in a normal rest position when undisturbed and under no-pumping conditions.

tools and physically digging till you reach water. Dug wells are mostly found in areas where the water table is known to be located at a shallow depth. Personally, I would not recommend digging deeper than 25 feet. This is a time-consuming and very dangerous excavation technique. Shafts often cave-in and there is also the danger of asphyxia. You will need an expert and helpers to assist you with this job. This is not a recommended method!

Using an auger to dig your well

Suitable water table depth:
Up to 20 feet
Soil: Sand and gravel

An auger is a tool used to cut into the ground and once deep enough, you simply extract it to haul the dirt out. You can add extensions as you move along. Once you reach the water table, you lower a well screen to filter out the sediment. It is a safe and simple method, used in soft soil.

Driving a well point

Suitable water table depth:
Up to 25 feet
Soil: Sand and gravel

This method involves the use of a sledge hammer and driving a well point into the ground. As you go deeper, you add extensions to your drill pipe. The well point has a well screen that filters the water as it enters the well.

Hire a professional

When your water table is located under 50 feet, you can use one, or a combination of the above mentioned methods. If you discover that your water table is deeper, then there is only one option available. Get a local well driller to come over and to give you a quote. Expect it to be fairly expensive. These days people pay around US$4,000-10,000 for a well. You are charged by the foot, so the deeper they go, the higher the costs.

The Soil

Well Drilling Glossary

Water table. The upper level of an underground surface in which the soil or rocks are permanently saturated with water.

Well screen. A filtering device, placed at the bottom of the well, that allows water to enter from the aquifer, but prevents sediment from entering the well.

Well point. A well screen with a forged-steel point and a threaded pipe shank at the top end. Usually 1.25-2" thick. Driven into the ground with a sledgehammer.

Well casing. A tubular casing made of plastic or metal and placed inside a well bore-hole to maintain the well opening.

You will have to take a good look at the type of soil in your area. The dry area of soil above the water table is called the unsaturated zone. This is an area where the soil particles are filled with air and where water droplets are just passing through on their way down to the water table. Very little water is found in this area. The possibility of digging or drilling through this area depends on the layers of soil present.

Sand. On paper, having fine, white sand sounds like a good type of soil to explore for water, but the fact of the matter is that this kind of sand is just packed too loosely. It will collapse on the well pipe and it will do it often. This makes it an extremely complicated medium to drill through. Coarse, yellow sand with large granules and gravel in between is best. (Finding the odd layer of fine sand is not a problem and you can simply go through it.)

Gravel. Drilling through gravel, or a combination of gravel and sand, is the way to go. These layers are filled with air and are thus easy to "push" around. Gravel is very permeable and good for drilling and finding water.

Clay. Clay particles are tightly packed and do not hold much water. Thick layers of clay is very hard to drill through. Your drill instrument will get stuck in the clay and it can turn into a

Shallow water wells go down to about 35 feet and are best drilled in soil with layers of sand and gravel.

nightmare very quickly. Drilling or digging through the odd layer of clay is not a problem; it all depends on how much clay is found in your area.

Rock. Finding layers of rock can be a problem. If it's solid and thick rock, you will have to start a new well. If it's a thin layer with broken rock, then you can try to break it up and to remove or to push through it with your drill.

The Water Table

The area just below the water table is called the saturated zone and this is where we find the wet soil. This is where the water comes to rest and where the best quality water is found. All the way at the bottom of the saturated zone, we find the bedrock area which is where fractured rock is found with rock aquifers.

When drilling or digging your own well you must realize that these are "shallow" wells that we find at the Standing Water Level (SWL). A shallow well will not reach all the way into the rock aquifer.

Consider the big picture when thinking about wells and water.

Sand. Coarse sand is absolutely perfect for finding water. Normally, this sand will be slightly yellow in color. Water moves easily through this type of sand and when you hit a combination of sand and gravel, it's even better.

Gravel. Gravel is very much the same as sand in that the air in between the pieces allows the water to flow easily. Gravel is coarse and does not cake together. It is very permeable, just like sand and thus perfect for finding water.

Fractured Rock. Water found in porous rock with fissures can be of very good quality. You will be very lucky to find this type of water. Most of the time, you need to drill very deep to reach these rock aquifers and to do this you will need to consult a professional.

Clay. Clay particles are very small. They are also sticky and "cake" together to form solid layers that are impermeable and that the water cannot penetrate. If the soil in your area is know for its clay content don't waste your time. Consult an expert to get a definitive answer.

The groundwater is fed through precipitation. Once you have a well up and running, you should take care not to pump it dry. The groundwater relies on precipitation during the wet seasons to maintain its level. Pumping your own well dry can possibly affect your neighbor, since you might both be using the same groundwater. This means that you should gather as much info about the local water table as possible. Make sure you are familiar with the local pre-cipitation patterns in your area. That will require some research on your end.

Top Soil

Sand and Gravel

Clay Layer

Static Water Level

Dry Sand and Gravel

Water Table Level

Saturated Sand and Gravel

Bedrock

Well Depth

Planning

Step1. Research

• Do your research and read up as much as you can about your local environment. Ask the locals. They know what's been tried and tested in the area. Looking at other wells means that you can get a clear indica-tion how deep the water table lies. Other well owners can also provide valuable information concerning rock and sand for-mations in your local area. Make sure that you know what your land was used for in the past. Contaminants remain in the soil for a long time.

• Look at geological survey re-cords that indicate the location of the local water table. These records are quite informative and they will highlight other wells in the area. Aquifers are also indicated on these surveys and can be found at the same depth as the water table. If the local water table is deeper than 50 feet, you will have to ask a professional contractor to drill a well for you.

• Look at topographic maps. These maps indicate the topog-raphy of the land and as a rule of thumb, the lower the eleva-tion, the easier to find water. Look at the slopes in your area and on your property. Will the runoff from rain contaminate your well? Avoid putting a well near a slope and look for a flat area with minimum risk of flood-water contamination.

• In selecting a suitable location, you will have to look at your im-mediate environment.

a.) Be sensible and avoid areas with enclosed livestock, septic tanks, fuel tanks, waste disposal or anything that can seep into the ground and contaminate your well. A good rule of thumb is to stay uphill of these areas and at least 150 ft/ 50m away. Your local health department will have guidelines concerning this.

b.) Stay at least 30 feet (10m) from streams and ponds.

c.) In addition, wells should not be located in extremely wet areas with water-logged soil.

• If you have the means, hire a professional consultant. They will do an analysis of the area and provide you with the relevant information.

Step 2. Get Legal

Deal with the local government. In most areas the government requires permits and permissions. Once your well is up and running, you do not want some government representative to come round and rain on your parade.
Make sure that all boxes are ticked and that you are legal and complying with local laws.

Step3. Plan the type of well you want

Once you've done your research, established the depth of the local water table and checked with your local government office, you can decide which kind of well will suit you. Shallow water wells can be drilled yourself where the distance to the water

Dry Unsaturated Zone

Static Water Level

Water Table Level

Groundwater

Wet Saturated Zone

Well Depth

Bedrock

table is no more than 35 ft./ 10.5m. Some home drillers are able to go considerably deeper, but that takes experience and know-how.
A shallow water well can only be used for drinking once it's been tested and deemed safe for human consumption. Water coming from a shallow water table only traveled a few feet through the soil and it has not been filtered properly. This is information that is not to be ignored. People tend to get excited when they see the clear liquid gushing out of the ground, but keep in mind that there are various natural occurring chemicals in the ground that can affect the quality of your water.
A deep groundwater well must be drilled by a professional. It can easily be 250 ft./ 76m deep and, in theory, the water can be of very good quality (not a guarantee).

How To Drill And Construct A Well Using PVC Pipe

Once you've determined the size and location of the local water table, you can consider building a drill. This will be used to drill through the dry, unsaturated zone which consists of multiple layers of soil. We will find water once we reach the wet, saturated zone. This is where we can extract water from the water-bearing sand.

Manual Drilling

Shallow water wells are the only wells that can be drilled manually using a DIY method. Generally speaking, **shallow water wells are not considered safe for human consumption**. This should not dissuade you from drilling for water. Manual drilling is cheap compared to a machine-drilled well and the water is ideal for irrigation and other domestic applications. Depending on your location, it is possible to find potable water, but that will depend on the quality and depth of the water table.

We will look at a tried and tested method of simple PVC pipe drilling. This method is also called "jetting" of a well. Expect to spend at least of 20-25 hours on this project. These days you can buy a PVC home drill kit online or at select hardware stores. They include parts, fittings and instructions on how to drill for water. The following setup is based on this method and will give you an idea how to approach basic drilling for water. If you prefer to do things yourself, know that with some basic DIY skills you can build and design your own drill, drill bit and well casing. It is a relatively easy and inexpensive project to take on by yourself. The soil that you are drilling in must be drill-friendly. Soil differs from region to region. As a general rule, expect to drill through layers of top soil, dry sand, clay, rock, water bearing sand and gravel. You will be aiming to strike water in the layers with sand, gravel or even rock (seldom). Ground with coarse sand and gravel is considered best for the DIY driller attempting a shallow water well. **CAUTION.** Take note that you will exert yourself physically. It's hard, manual labor, so wear the right clothes and shoes and take a rest when needed. It's noteworthy to mention that if you have any health issues, you should first check with your doctor.

Let's take a look at the basics of well drilling and the different materials that can be used. Note that this is a project that should be started early in the morning. Once you start "drilling" and have water flowing you cannot remove the drill since the inside of the hole will collapse and if you leave it in the hole, the drill pipe will get stuck. Plan carefully and prepare material and equipment in advance. This is preferably a two man job. When looking at the diagram we can see the basic drilling method in action. Water is pushed through a PVC pipe with a drill bit at the bottom. This pipe initially functions as the drill pipe and later it will be used as the well casing pipe. The water is forced down the drill pipe to soften the ground at the bottom, and as the drill tip cuts away at the soil, the water flushes all the cuttings up to the top along the outside of the drill pipe. The action is flush, cut, flush and it is repeated continuously. This PVC pipe will also prevent the ground, surrounding it, from caving in and therefore we can also call it the well casing. Once the hole is deep enough

Drilling Method

Rotate left and right

Water Hose

Water is forced down the PVC pipe and it flushes the cuttings back to the surface level.

Drill pipe

Drill tip

Well hole

and you've reached the water table, you can insert a well screen all the way to the bottom of the well. A well screen consists of two parts. The longest part consists of pieces of PVC pipe glued together with inside PVC slip couplings (long). At the end of this PVC pipe you connect the well screen that is 4-6 feet long. A well screen can filter the sand particles and allow the water to enter the well pipe. This complete well screen is just as long as your well casing.

The use of well water

• Once filtered, it can be used indoors for washing, bathing and cleaning.
• For drinking purposes, get it tested to see if it is actually safe to drink.
• Outdoors it can be used for pools, ponds and recreation.
• Can be used for fire fighting.

• Perfect for irrigation.
• Good for livestock.
• It is perfect for small scale mining and manufacturing.
• Having a well means that you don't need to store millions of gallons of water for an emergency.

Well Drilling Basics

1. Start the hole by rotating the drill left and right. Allow the water to flow and to saturate the soil.

The water, flowing from the two hose pipes, is softening the ground and flushing the cuttings to the surface level.

3. Remove the drill top and leave the drill pipe inside the hole. This pipe now acts as the well casing.

2. Drill down through all the layers of soil till you reach the water table. Add PVC pipe (with couplings) as you go deeper.

Add sections of PVC pipe as you drill deeper. The drill pipe must be long enough to reach the water table.

Water table

4. Prepare your well screen by adding sections of PVC pipe (or to cut one long piece) till it's just as long as the well casing.

Well casing   Well screen

Well Drilling Basics

5. Slide the well screen into the well casing. The well screen should reach inside the water-bearing sand at the bottom.

Well screen is inside the well casing.

Water table with water-bearing sand.

7. Pour pea gravel down the side of the well casing. It should cover the length of the well screen.

Add gravel to the hole to cover the well screen.

Gravel keeps sediment out and allows clean water to enter the well.

6. Pull the well casing up till it's above the well screen. This is a simple method to expose the slits in the well screen to the water-bearing sand.

Pull up the well casing to expose the well screen to the water-bearing sand.

Water table with water-bearing sand.

8. Leave the well casing in place; this is your well. You can also pull out the well casing and fill the annular space around the well pipe with sand.

Add sand and gravel to fill space around well pipe.

Pea gravel to cover the well screen.

Once the well screen is in place, you can slowly pull the well casing pipe up to expose the slits of the screen. You want the water-bearing sand to collapse around the well screen, because that is where the water will enter your well. You now have two options. You can leave the well casing in place, to maintain the structure of the well. You can also remove it completely, but then you'll have to fill the open area around the well pipe with sand and gravel. You can add a hand pump or electrical pump to extract water from your well. These are the fundamental basics of the whole drilling process.

Construct Your Drill

Step 1. The Drill Top

Before you can drill into the ground to make a bore-hole, you will need to construct a "drill". You have an option of buying a PVC home drill kit online or from select hardware stores. These kits come with instructions and the assembly is pretty straightforward. Some provide you with the complete setup and others just provide the drill T-top. The best option is to make your own, by using PVC pipe and plumber's fittings. We will be discussing a simple DIY option, perfected by Mike Willis.

Let's start at the top of the drill and work our way down. This section requires some knowl-

Drill T-Top

PVC pipe
PVC Valve
PVC pipe (X2)
Hose connectors
Reducer Bushings (X2)
PVC Cross Tee
Flexible coupling
PVC Drill Pipe
Hose ()

edge of joining plumber's fittings. Remember to use PVC cement on all joints. Be creative and adapt to your situation. If you cannot find the exact part or fitting, then you have to improvise. Remember to use Schedule 40 PVC pipe; you can use 2", 3" or even 4" PVC pipe. The larger the diameter, the more flushing power you will require from the hose pipes.

Starting with 2" is a good safe size for your first attempt at drilling. If your drill pipe is 2" you can adjust all fittings to accommodate this size. Make sure that the water from the hoses flow freely and without obstruction. You need as much flushing power possible. Before you start, make sure you look at all the material you will need on page 81.

Extracting Water From The Ground

To construct a drill, you will need the following:

- **PVC cement and primer.** To join all fittings and PVC pipes together.
- **Hosepipes x 2.** To flush the hole and to push the cuttings to the top.
- **PVC Cross tee x 1.** This is where water, flowing from the two hoses, are redirected into the main drill pipe. (2" recommended)
- **PVC valve x 1.** The PVC valve allows for air and water (under pressure)to be released from the drill. Also adds the option of connecting a mud pump. (2" recommended)
- **PVC pipe pieces x 2.** To connect hose connectors to reducer bushings. (¾" recommended)
- **PVC reducer bushing x 2.** These connect the hose connectors to the PVC Cross tee. (2" reduced to ¾" recommended)
- **Hose connectors x 2.** They connect the reducer bushings to the hose pipes. (¾" recommended)
- **Flexible coupling x 1.** Rubber tubing with radiator clamps will also do. (2" recommended)
- **PVC pipe piece x 1.** Connects to the bottom of the PVC Cross tee. See next page. (2" diameter and 5" long recommended)
- **Drill pipe handle bar.** Made of wood. It allows you to control the drill.
- **PVC drill pipes 8-10 feet in length.** With bell- or plain ends.
  Once joined, they will be the drill pipe and well casing. (2" recommended)
- **PVC well pipes.** They connect to the well screen. Your well pipe can be one long pipe, or sections joined together.
  This pipe will be connected to your well screen. (1¼ " recommended)
- **Well screen.** This is where the water enters the well.
- **PVC Couplings.** These connect the long drill pipes and the well pipes. Use outer couplings for the drill pipes and inner couplings for the well pipes. (2" recommended)
- **Pump.** Once finished, you'll need a pump to extract water from the well. The pump connects to the top of the well pipe.

The Drill

PVC
Drill
Pipe

PVC Coupling

- **The PVC Cross Tee** acts as the main facilitator that allows water into the drill pipe. The bottom of the Cross Tee connects with the drill pipe. If your drill pipe is 2", then use a similar sized cross tee of 2". Remember that as you drill deeper, you will have to remove the drill-top to add more pipe to the drill. This means that the design must be practical enough to allow the top to be removed and replaced. The top of the Cross tee connects to the PVC valve. The two sides of the Cross tee connect to the reducer bushings and then to the two hose pipes.

- **The PVC Valve** that goes into the top part of the Cross tee allows you to release air or water from the chamber when needed. You can also connect it to a pump at a later stage. It is a handy option to have. Depending on the fittings you use (threaded or not), you might need a piece of PVC pipe to join the valve and the Cross Tee.

- **Reducer bushings** (x 2) are used to reduce the size of the PVC Cross tee down to the size of the hose connectors.

- **Hose connectors** (x 2) will allow water to flow from the hose pipes through your reducer bushings. Make sure they fit your hosepipe connectors before you buy. To join the hose connectors to the reducer bushings, you will need two short pieces of

Extracting Water From The Ground

¾" PVC pipe.

• **Hose pipes** (x 2) that will comfortably reach your drill hole location and at least 15 feet of extra clearing for when the drill pipe is raised. Check the water pressure from faucets. You might have to consult a neighbor to lend you a hose with water pressure coming from his side. The combined water pressure will be great for flushing the hole. The hose pipes connect with the hose connectors.

• **Flexible coupling** (x 1). If you cannot find a flexible coupling, you can improvise with some rubber tubing and radiator clamps. This coupling connects the drill head to the drill pipe. As you drill deeper, you will reach the end of the first drill pipe's length. This means that you have to remove the drill head from the drill pipe. The next step is to connect another drill pipe to the one in the hole. After you have connected the drill pipe in the hole to the new one, you will reconnect the drill T-top to the top of the new pipe. The flexible coupling will allow you to do all of this.

• **PVC pipe** (x 1) cut 5" long. Your drill pipe and your PVC Cross tee are both the same diameter. To join them together, you will use this section.

• **Use PVC cement with PVC cement** primer to join the fittings. Look for a brand that sets within a fairly short period of time. (Later you will use

The Flexible Coupling

1. The Cross Tee is to be joined to the piece of PVC (grey color). Line the 2 pieces up and add PVC cement and primer. This combined unit forms the top of the drill that will connect to the drill pipe.

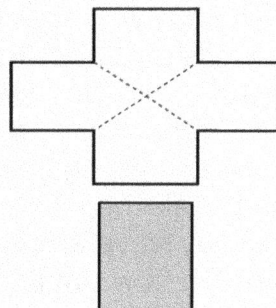

2. Join the 2 pieces. Later the other end of the PVC pipe will slide into your drill pipe.

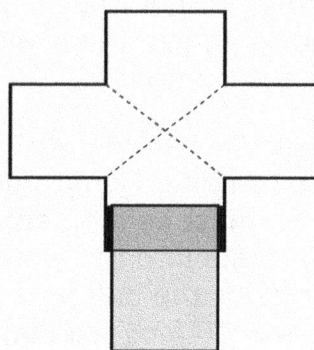

3. The flexible coupling joins the drill top and drill pipe. To change drill pipes, loosen the bottom screw of the flexible coupling and add a new pipe section. No cement needed there, because you have multiple pieces of drill pipe to add later.

Coupling

PVC
DRILL
PIPE

the PVC cement to add drill pipe during the drilling process.)

Make sure that when you assemble the parts (before using the PVC cement), that they all fit snuggly and that there are no loose air gaps. You can get creative with the design of your drill T-top. When picking up your plumber's fittings know that you can tweak the design as you like, but leave ample space for water to flow unobstructed and smoothly through the fittings. If you find that some of your fittings do not have a threaded end, then join them with PVC pipe and cement.

Step 2. The Drill Pipes

The combined length of drill pipes must be long enough to penetrate into the water table. Typically, the drill pipe is made from 8-10 foot sections of 2 inch PVC pipe. The wider the pipe the stronger the flushing power required to flush the cuttings. You can use standard PVC pipes or the ones with the bell endings (which means you can join them without couplings).

To join the drill pipes you will need:

• PVC cement with PVC cement primer.

• Long outer couplings to join pipes together.

• 2" PVC drill pipes cut to 8-10 feet in length. The combined length of these pipes should reach into the water table.

Calculate the maximum depth

you are willing to go by looking at the local water table in your area. You will need at least 3 or 4 pieces of pipe.

Draw lines, measured in feet, on every pipe to indicate the drilling depth.

You can add a setting screw on every coupling if you feel all the twisting and turning might loosen the pipes.

Step 3. The Drill Bit

The drill bit is the part that breaks up the dirt at the bottom of the hole. It scrapes the dirt away, breaks it up and then the water flushes it to the top of the hole. To make your drill bit you have three options.

• The first option is to simply cut teeth into the lead PVC drill pipe. Serrated edges are best and you can manage this with an electric grinder or manually with a hacksaw. You can use this option for soft shallow drilling. It is not a recommended option and the teeth will wear down easily.

• The second option is to make a replaceable bit from a PVC coupling. Just connect the coupling with PVC cement and once dry use a saw to cut the triangular teeth for the drill bit. This can be an effective drill bit in soft soil, but as you go deeper the teeth will undoubtedly wear out.

• The third option is the best option. Get a piece of galvanized plumbing pipe. Serrated edges are best and you can manage

Extracting Water From The Ground

this with an electric grinder or manually with a hacksaw. This drill bit will allow you to cut more effectively through sediment, roots and debris. You can add a short screw to set this drill bit in place since the constant turning of the drill pipe will loosen the drill bit.

Step 4. The Drill Handle Bar

You can make a handle for your drill from wood. A piece of wood fastened with hose clamps will work just fine. Remember that this handle must be moved up the drill as you add your PVC drill pipe extensions. The hose clamps are easy to unscrew and when adding pipe, it will allow you to place the handle around the new piece of PVC drill pipe.

Preparations

Before you start drilling, lay out the individual pieces and make sure all equipment and tools are ready. Check that hoses are the correct length, fitted with correct connections, and will provide enough water pressure. Double-check your T-top and make sure you have a screwdriver ready for later when needed to loosen the hose clamps. Your drill pipes should be 8-10 feet long with lines drawn to indicate drilling depth and a mark where you will refasten the grip handle. This saves time for when you have to add pipe and reposition the grip handle. If you are connect-

If you run out of daylight, pull up the pipe and start again the next day. A pipe left overnight will get stuck.

ing your pipes with couplings, then a coupling should be fitted to each extra length of pipe beforehand. When dealing with pipes this long, you need strong couplings with long connections. Get a crate or platform to stand on to make things easier. A ladder is not a stable platform. **Do not stand on a ladder when drilling.**

How To

When everything is ready, you can start to drill. You should know your water table depth, to give you an indication as to how deep to drill. You do need a fair amount of luck on your side to hit the water table with your first try. Make sure that you have a helper since drilling is very hard to do on your own. Be prepared to dig quite a few holes. Do not prepare the well drilling site by digging any large diameter holes beforehand. Remember that water will be flushed out of the hole for an extended period of time and if not careful you'll soon be standing in a lake of water. Just focus on the hole made by the drill head in front of you and make sure water can drain away from the hole.

1. Start the hole

This is physical, hard labor. You must be in good shape and fairly fit. To start the hole, put your drill pipe down and start twisting it side to side.

Rotate left and right

Start the well hole by rotating your drill left and right.

Allow the water from the two hoses to flow into the hole and to saturate the soil.

Turn the water on slowly. Leave the top valve of the drill head slightly open, just enough for air pressure buildup to escape. Rock the pipe side to side and twist it sideways with the aim of making the hole wider. Make sure that there is ample flow of water.

2. Drill deeper

Once you've progressed to about two feet down, you can start to move the drill up and down to flush the hole with water. This is very important. This action, combined with water flow, is essential to keep the pipe from getting stuck. Constantly keep your eyes on the water coming from the hole. Look for the cuttings and pay attention to the color of the water. Be patient. Do not rush

Move the drill up and down. Rotate it left and right

Allow the water to flow into the hole and to saturate the soil.

anything. You will be drilling for a few hours, so settle in and commit to the task at hand.

3. Add extra pipe

Add more lengths of PVC pipe as you move along. You should have the pipes prepared (with their couplings if necessary) beforehand. This is where a second person will come in very handy. Try to change pipes as quickly as possible. You do not want to stop the flow of water down the well. The whole process should look like this:

1st Section of PVC pipe

2nd Section of PVC pipe

1. Turn off the water.
2. Take off the T-top.
3. Take off the handle grip and fit it to the new pipe.

Extracting Water From The Ground

4. Apply PVC primer and cement.

5. Connect the new pipe.

6. Reattach the T-top and turn on the water.

Make sure that the new connection is secure and that the PVC cement is dry. You can add a short screw to every coupling if you feel the need.

4. Add more pipe

Continue drilling and add more lengths of pipe as you go deeper. When you hit a depth of 10 feet, slow down and make sure

Section of PVC pipe →

Add the PVC pipe sections with couplings as you drill deeper. →

that the water is flowing steadily. You should pay extra attention to the up and down movement of the drill. This is where the ground becomes harder and you want to make sure you don't get your pipe stuck. Be patient and proceed slowly while making sure the ground stays saturated with water.

5. How will you know when you've hit water?

It's not easy to tell when you've hit water. The cuttings and wa-

ter are constantly flowing out of the hole and this can create confusion. Look for sand. Water bearing sand is coarse and light in color. You will recognize this sand when you see it. Don't stop. Let it flow and go a few feet deeper till you find the coarser sand. Expect to find it at the water table depth that you have researched for your area. Let go of the handle and watch your drill "settle" in the hole. It should sink deeper onto the hole all on its own, indicating that you have reached the water table.

6. Drill deeper

Continue to drill deeper. You want your well to penetrate nice and deep into the water table and to be surrounded by the coarse, yellow sand. Work that drill up and down and side to side and try to make the hole as

When your pipe gets stuck

1. One option is to use a mechanical instrument like a winch or a hydrolic jack

2. Try designing a lever with a long handle that rests on a fulcrum. Move the fulcrum as close possible to the pipe. The lever should push up against the drill pipe handle, which should be reinforced with extra clamps.

3. As a last resort, you can try to sink a smaller diameter pipe (½ or ¾ inch) right alongside your drill pipe to get the soil liquefied again and to loosen it.

big as possible. Your drill pipe should feel very loose inside the hole. Go as deep as you can while still in the coarse, yellow sand. If you can still go 8-10 feet deeper, then do so.

You should try to be well under the Standing Water Level (SWL) as used by professional drillers. The SWL refers to the level of the water in a well, in a normal rest position when undisturbed and under no-pumping conditions. Once you start pumping the water from the top, the water level will drop. When you turn off the pump, the water will return to the SWL level. Your well screen top should be 8-10 feet under the SWL.

7. The well screen

A well screen is 4-6 feet long, has a pointy tip and hundreds of tiny slits all along the side. These slits keep the sand out and allow the water to flow into your well.

The well screen is placed inside the drill pipe.

Drill Pipe

Well screen with well pipe extensions.

The well screen with PVC pipe extensions form your well. The drill pipe forms your well casing.

This is the point of entry, where water enters your well. You can buy your well screen from certain hardware stores or from an online merchant.

Your actual well pipe (that you will stick inside the well casing pipe) can be prepared in advance.

If you are using sections of 1¼" well pipe (instead of one long well pipe), then join them together with long inside couplings. This will prevent the pipe from getting stuck inside the 2" well casing.

This well pipe connects to the well screen. If you used a 2" well pipe to drill with, then your well consists of a piece (or pieces) of 1¼" PVC pipe with a 1¼" well screen connected at the bottom. The total length of your well pipe should be approximately just as long as the well casing pipe.

Once you've joined the well screen and the well pipe, your well is almost done. At this stage the water is still running. When ready, turn off the water and take off the T-top.

Slide your well pipe with the well screen attached all the way down the well casing pipe. Make sure it has reached the bottom. If your well pipe is the

Extracting Water From The Ground

The well screen is placed inside the drill pipe.

Water Table

Groundwater

Drill Pipe

same length as your well casing pipe, then just a small section of well pipe should stick out the top.

Now comes the pullback of the well casing pipe. You have two options.

a.) You can pull the total length of well casing pipe from the hole and then fill the space around your well pipe with sand and gravel. The sand and gravel will allow the water to pass through,

Concrete apron

Add sand and gravel to fill space around well pipe.

Add pea gravel to the hole to cover the well screen.

Drilling's hard work. Wear the right clothes and if you have any health issues, check first with your physician.

but it is coarse enough not to clog your well screen.

b.) An easier and better option is to pull it up just far enough for the total length of well screen to be exposed to the water-bearing sand. It will feel strange to pull your well casing back up the hole, but it has to be done. If you leave it in place, you will not get any water from the well.

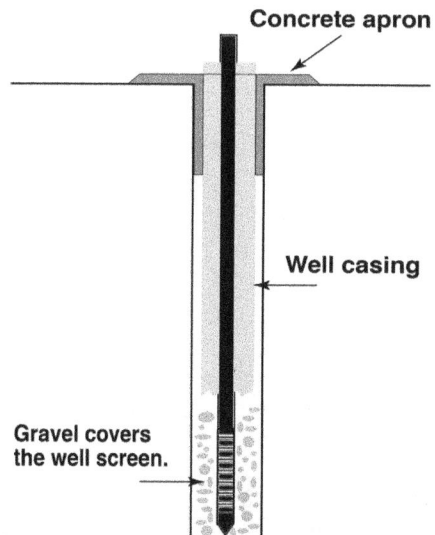

Concrete apron

Well casing

Gravel covers the well screen.

Make sure you are not pulling the well pipe up as well. That's why we suggested inside couplings to be used on the well pipe, so as to not obstruct the well casing pipe when removed. The well screen should be surrounded by coarse sand.

Hopefully the sand has completely covered the well screen. If not sure, you can still pour some sand down the hole. Sand is what you want. It is coarse and prevents plenty of space for water to flow in between and it won't enter your well screen. Pour some cement all around the top of the well to prevent debris and runoff to contaminate your well. Cut the well casing pipe (that's sticking out the top) shorter.

8. The Pump

Install a hand-pump at the top of your well. Use this pump to develop the well and to remove the sediment from the bottom. This could take a while. Remember that off-the-shelf hand-pumps are mostly used for depths up to 20-25 feet. These pumps have to be primed to get the water from 20 feet down all the way up into the pump. If you cannot or don't want to prime your pump, then you will need to install a check valve. It is a one-way valve that allows water to go up towards the pump, but not down and out. Having a check valve means that you don't constantly have to prime the hand pump. The result is that you always have water at the ready in the pump. If you are close to an electrical source then you have an option of installing a simple jet pump.

Conclusion

When drilling for water, just keep in mind that you are simply extracting water from the water table. Keep things simple as possible and remember to focus on longevity. You want the whole structure to last for as long as possible and therefore you have to use quality material (Schedule 40 PVC) and make sure that all fittings are sealed and tight. Examine the process of drilling and see if your own expertise will allow you to come up with an even better solution. Safety should always be a priority and do not take any short cuts.

Keep animals and people (children) away from the area.

Fill, cover and seal the well opening if you decide to abandon it.

If you have any health issues, you should first check with your doctor before starting this project.

Concrete apron

The well pipe functions as well casing and keeps contaminants out.

Gravel covers the well screen.

How to pour pea gravel around the well screen?

- The drill pipe is a 2 inch PVC pipe and once the well is finished, it becomes the well casing.
- The well pipe is the 1¼ inch PVC pipe that we connect the well screen to.
- Eventually, the well pipe is placed inside the drill pipe (well casing).

1. If you are using 2" drill pipe, drill down to the desired depth. Example: 25 feet.

2. Move your drill pipe from side to side, up and down, to widen the hole. The bottom of the hole should be considerably wider than your 2" drill pipe. Having a wider bottom space means that we can fill it with plenty of pea gravel.

3. Prepare your 1¼ inch well pipe, with well screen, in advance. Remember that both your well pipe, and drill pipe, should be more or less the same length (in this case, 25'). When you add the 3 foot long well screen, the well pipe will be around 28' long. The 28 foot long well pipe, all glued together, will later be placed inside the drill pipe.

4. Once you feel that the bottom of the hole is wide enough, you can stop the water and remove the T-top. We are working with a 3 foot long well screen, so take some pea gravel and pour 3 feet of gravel down the drill pipe. As you pour the gravel, work the pipe up and down. The gravel will fill the space underneath the pipe and gradually, as you pour, the pipe will move up. When your drill pipe is three feet higher than it was, it means that you have three feet of gravel inside your hole.

5. This is where the pointed tip of the well screen comes in handy. Slide the whole 1¼ inch well pipe down the 2 inch drill pipe. The well screen will hit bottom (the gravel). Both pipes will be at the same depth in the well. Start to turn and twist the well point and try to work it deeper into the gravel layer. The pointed tip will help in getting it through the pieces of gravel. It will take some time, but you will manage.

6. Once the 28 foot long well pipe and the 25 foot long drill pipe is sticking out at the same level, then you can stop. This means that you have three feet of well screen exposed to the pea gravel at the bottom of your well.

(For a 3" drill pipe, first slide the 1¼" well pipe down inside. Pour the pea gravel down the annular space between the 3" and 1¼" inch pipes. Unlike a 2" pipe, the space between a 3" and 1¼" pipe is enough.)

How To Dig And Construct A Well Using An Auger

In suitable soil conditions, using an auger can be a straightforward method used for water extraction. With the auger you "scoop" out the soil till you reach the water table. Place a well screen in the hole and use a pump to extract your water.

Auger Drilling

Another very simple method to extract water is to use an auger post-hole digger for drilling.

Augers can be used in sand and gravel or a combination of both. You'll have less success in clay and absolutely no success in rock. A 6-8 inch auger should be enough. This is basically a fan-cy drill bit with a handle and it slowly bores into the ground as you turn it. A T-handle will give you more leverage and grip, especially when you get past 10 feet.

Once the auger is filled with dirt, you have to lift it out of the hole and empty it out. You can add extension rods to the auger as you go deeper. This method is obviously useful for digging shallow wells with appropriate soil conditions.

With an auger, expect to drill to a maximum depth of around 20 feet. It will be a slow and energy sapping process. Once you have reached the desired depth, you can fit a PVC well screen inside the hole. The well screen allows clean water to enter your well.

Seal your well and add a hand-pump or centrifugal pump.

How To

1. Get started. Put the auger in the ground. Start drilling by turning the auger in a clockwise direction. This will ensure that

You will need:

- An Auger, post-hole digger.
- Metal extension rods (20-25 feet).
- PVC pipe.
- A PVC well screen.
- PVC cement and primer.
- A length of rope and PVC bailer.
- A pump to bail water.
- A hacksaw.

Extracting Water From The Ground

you are drilling straight down.

Do this throughout the process of drilling. Take your time and be patient. This is time-consuming and hard work.

2. Soil. When full, pull it up and empty it. Repeat.

Go as deep as the auger will allow you. Keep the extracted dirt in a heap nearby. You can use it later to seal your well.

3. Extensions. Add extensions when necessary. Make sure that they are tightened securely. Be patient. It will become harder and harder to turn the auger. Get a second person to assist. As you go deeper and deeper,

keep an eye on the depth that you have drilled. Once you bring up more water than dirt, you've hit the water table. You should know the depth of the water table in your area beforehand.

4. Water table. Once you reach the water table, you still have to go deeper.

Don't get over-excited. You need to be nice and deep inside the water table to have a working well with steady water flow. Measure the depth and aim to go at least another 8 feet deeper.

5. Water. Bail the well when water seeps in. You can try to do it manually, but it's always more effective to use a pump.

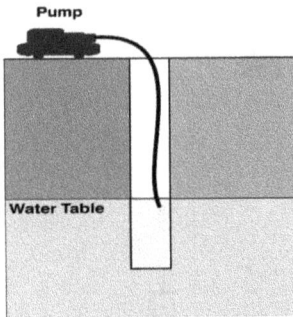
Pump

Water Table

If you do it manually, you will need a PVC bailer tied to a rope.

6. Well screen. Well screens are used for sand or gravel aquifers where we want to prevent particles from entering the well. Once connected, it functions as part of the well pipe and it works like a sieve that extends into the water table and that lets the water into the well pipe while filtering out sand and debris.

Well Screen

Water Table

You can buy a well screen on-line or make your own from PVC pipe. (See page 96.) For a standard well dug with an 8" auger you can use a 4-6" well screen casing. Cap the bottom of you well casing pipe with PVC primer and PVC cement. Make sure it's a perfect seal, nice and tight. Fill the annular space around

the well screen with pea gravel. This will help to keep sediment and silt from clogging the well screen slits. The area above the well screen can be filled with the dirt that you excavated earlier. Pack it in nice and tight. Fill the

Well Screen

Water Table

Pea Gravel

top three feet with concrete and make a nice apron all around your well.

7. Pump. Install a hand-pump at the top of your well, about 3 feet above ground level (to protect your water from flooding). Remember that off-the-shelf hand-pumps are mostly used for depths up to 20-25 feet. These pumps have to be primed to get the water from 20 feet down all the way up into the pump. Not priming the pump will cause damage to the leather cup on the inside. If your water is deeper than 8' down, consider installing a foot valve. This is an inlet valve, connected to the well pipe, that is positioned about 6" from the bottom of the well. It is a one-way valve that allows water to go up to the pump, but not down and out. Having a foot valve means that u don't constantly have to prime the hand pump, since the line is filled and you have water at the ready in the pump.

Well pipe

Foot valve

Well screen

CAUTION! Note that in cold weather, the water in the pipe will freeze and expand. This can split your pipe or foot valve. Consider removing the pump or foot valve in freezing temperatures, or draining the pump and suction line.

For deeper wells, a deep well hand pump will work. If close to an electrical source consider installing a jet pump. See the section on pumps (Chapter 7). If you have any health issues, you should first check with your doctor before starting this project.

Make a PVC bail bucket:

Mechanics: You will need a long cylindrical bucket, with an opening at the bottom. A simple ball check-valve assembly allows the water to flow into the pipe; when full the ball seats against the reducer and seals it.

Material:
• A 2-3 feet PVC pipe to fit inside the well hole. A 4" diameter pipe should fit most holes. This is your bucket.

• A PVC pipe coupling glued to the bottom of the bucket.

• A reducer bushing (4" x 2").

• A solid rubber ball that seats against the reducer.

• A stainless steel bolt.

• A rope long enough to reach the bottom of the well.

Directions:
1. Use PVC cement to attach the coupling to the bottom of the PVC pipe.

2. Glue the reducer bushing to the bottom of the coupling. The ball seats against the reducer opening.

4. Drill two holes about 6" from the bottom and put the stainless steel bolt through. This prevents the ball from going all the way up.

6. Attach the rope to the top for hauling water.

2-3 feet

Bolt

Coupling

Ball seats on bushing

How to make a well screen

The well screen will be used to keep particles and debris out of your well water. It is constructed from PVC pipe and should be an inch or two in diameter smaller than the well hole. **This PVC well screen pipe will also function as the well casing.**
For a 6-8 inch hole, use a 4 inch pipe as your well screen and remember that once you are done, to fill the annular space, around the well screen pipe, with pea gravel.
Make the well screen length 4-6 feet long. This means that you should be at least 8-12 feet into your water table. The deeper you can go the better.
You will need a hacksaw to saw slits into the PVC pipe. Use a new, thin blade. You can choose how you want to group the slits together. The main thing is not to compromise the structural integrity of the pipe, by placing the rows of slits too close to one another. For a large diameter pipe, use a grouping of four lines of slits around the length of the pipe. For a thinner pipe, you can use a grouping of three. You can space them out evenly all along the length of the pipe. You can also experiment with your own design.

CAUTION!

Use common sense when making the slits. Their function is to keep debris and small particles out and they should be positioned and grouped to do just that.
Do not cut through the pipe!
Don't group your slits too close together!

Material needed:

- PVC pipe, as required

- PVC cement and primer

- Hacksaw with new, thin blade

- Measuring tape

- Calculator

- Permanent marker

1. Cap the bottom of the pipe. Use PVC cement and primer and make sure it's a secure fit.

Bottom

2. Start the well screen around 4-6 inches (10-15cm) from the bottom of the pipe. Use the marker to mark the slits.

4-6 inches

3. Cut the slits into the pipe with a hacksaw. You can group them together in short sections with 3-4 slits.

4-6 feet

4. You can also space them out into longer sections with 9 or 10 slits each.

4-6 feet

5. If you have the patience for it, you can cut a continuous line of slits all along the length of the pipe.

4-6 feet

6. For smaller diameter pipes, cut 3 sections of slits all around the pipe.

1.5 inches
For structural support

7. For larger diameter pipes, you can try to get 4 sections of slits in.

1.5 inches

8. For calculating the length of the slits, you need the circumference of the pipe.

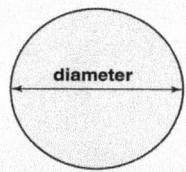

diameter

4" diameter = 12.566" circumference
5" diameter = 15.708" circumference
6" diameter = 18.850" circumference
7" diameter = 21.991" circumference
8" diameter = 25.133" circumference

How To Dig And Construct A Well Using A Well Point

Finding water doesn't have to be a complicated process. The invention of the "well point" certainly simplified the process of extracting water for shallow water wells. These days many shallow water tables are susceptible to pollution and the water obtained should really only be considered for irrigation and household chores. Have your water tested before you use it.

Point Wells

Driving a well point is the act of hitting a screened well point into the earth with a sledgehammer. Once you reach the water table, the well point acts as the well screen and it allows clean water to enter the well and to be pumped to the top. It is a really simple technique for water extraction and it works quite well when the soil conditions permit.

• This method is predominantly used in soil that's rich in thick sand or gravel. Don't use it in soil that consists of hard, red clay or rock.

• It is suitable for areas where the water table is 10-25 feet below the surface.

These well points can be driven 30+ feet into the ground if needed, but that's no easy feat. Check with locals and your local water office to compare the success rate for this method in your area.
It will all come down to soil conditions and depth of water table.

Something to keep in mind is that areas with shallow water tables are more susceptible to contamination from land use. Contaminants can easily seep through the soft, sandy soil into your well, even from distances far away. When planning a "point well" it is best to be at least 150 feet away from potential sources of contamination. These include septic tanks, livestock yards, ponds, sewers, etc. Check with your local government office to get the exact code specifics for your area. Make sure you test your water before consuming it.

How To

Start by collecting all the material that you will need. You can purchase complete well point kits from hardware stores or from an online merchant. When looking at the materials used, you will notice that all the components are made of metal. This makes galvanized steel

You will need:

- **A well point**, also called a "Sand point". The well point is a heavy spear-like object that is around 3-5 feet long and 1¼" to 2" in diameter. It has a metal screen on the outside to prevent larger particles from entering your well and also a fine screen on the inside for smaller particles.

  If you are planning to go down less than 25 feet, then you can use a 1¼" well point with metal piping and a shallow-well pump.

  If you want to go deeper, you will need a 2" well point with metal piping and a deep-well pump installation.

- Galvanized steel **pipe extensions** around 5 feet long. (1¼" or 2" in diameter)

- **Threaded metal couplings.** Try to get long couplings with extra thread.

- **Metal drive cap.** If the drive cap is threaded, the it must be the same diameter as the pipe extensions. Some setups come with a galvanized nipple which is first threaded into the coupling. The drive cap is placed on top of the nipple. Make sure you follow the manufacturer's instructions.

- **Pipe Wrenches** x 2

- **Carpenter's level or Plumb bob**

- **Plumber's tape/ Teflon tape.** Wrap it clockwise, with the thread!

- **Sledgehammer**

- **Auger or post hole digger**

- **Garden hose**

- **A long wooden pole** (or similar) for surging the well hole.

- **Pump.** A Pitcher pump is suitable for a 1¼" pipe and depth of 25 feet.
  A Jet pump is suitable for a 2" pipe and depth of 25-45 feet.

- **An extra pair of hands.** This is a two-man job.

your best option. Quality material will not bend, break or rust.
When selecting your well point,
remember that a well point of
1¼" will suit most wells down to
25 feet.

1. Start by making a hole in the
ground with an auger or post
hole digger. Go down a few feet
just to get you started.

Take the well point and rub a
bar of soap over the openings.
The soap will clog the holes and
prevent debris from entering.
Later, the soap will dissolve
when you strike water. The soap
also makes it easier to drive the
point into the ground.

**2. Place your well point in
the hole.**

You will need to add a coupling
and pipe extension from the
start. Clean the thread first and
remember to use Teflon tape
(clockwise) and to lock the coupling in place. Use one wrench
to hold the pipe in place and the
other to tighten the coupling.
This is a two-man job.

**3. Place the drive cap on the
pipe.** Use the level or plumb
bob to make sure that the pipe
is vertically lined up in the hole.
Drive it into the ground with
your sledgehammer.

Drive Cap

90°

The drive cap protects the pipe
threads on the well point and
provides a better striking surface. Make sure you strike it
evenly. It's best to have a helper
to help with keeping the pipe
perpendicular.

**4. Keep on driving the well
point,** with pipe extension, into
the ground. At first, it will be
smooth and easy. When there's
about ½ foot (15cm) of pipe left
sticking out the ground, you can

stop to add another section of extension pipe. Repeat this sequence as you go deeper.

Pour water at regular intervals down the pipe. Wet soil is easier to penetrate.

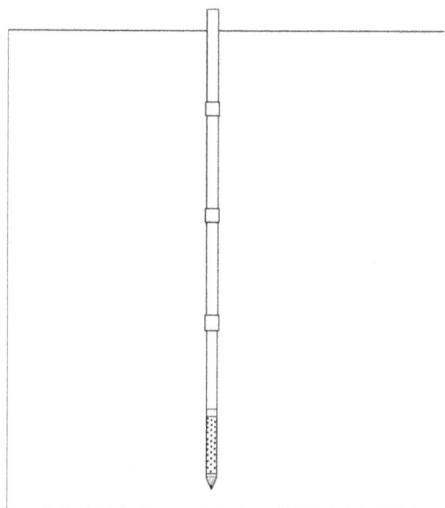

Remember to use the drive cap when adding the extension pipes.
Check couplings and remember to use Teflon tape.
You can use the plumb bob to try to keep things level and perpendicular to the ground. You are dealing with a long length of pipe. Do your best to send it straight down into the earth. Repeat till you reach the water table.
If you hit rock, don't try to break it with the well point. Depending on the depth, you can try to move the pipe side to side and to wiggle it to create some annular space around it. If unsuccessful, pull up the pipe and move to a new location. No use

Make sure that the new pipe goes straight into the coupling. Threaded pipes and fittings are prone to leaks if not straight and sealed.

destroying your well point.

5. Reaching the water table means that you are in water bearing sand. There are a couple of ways to test if you've reached the water bearing sand.

• When hitting water bearing sand, you will suddenly become aware that it is easier to drive your well point through this section.

• Also, listen for a variation in sound when you strike the cap. If you suddenly start to hear a hollow sound like made by a dinner gong, then you are probably in fine, water-bearing sand.

Water Table

• You can pour water into the top of the pipe. If it sinks down within a short period of time (2 mins), you are in the water table. If it stays at the top, it means that you are still in the soil layer.

If you sense that you have reached the water table, check your notes and compare with your local water table depth that you researched beforehand. Take a line with a small weight attached and drop it down the pipe. Measure how deep you are into the water table.

6. When you have reached the water table, continue for at least another 8-10 feet if possible. The deeper the better for you want the well screen to be totally submerged in water.

Water Table

8 feet

5 feet

3 feet

Remember that groundwater is replenished through rain. There are always seasonal variations in rainfall, which means that the level of the water table underground, will also rise and fall.

The deeper you go into the water table, the better off you'll be in the dry season.

7. Once you've reached the correct depth you can start to develop the well. This will improve the yield and also the longevity. You have to clean around the well screen, to remove the fine particles and to leave only the larger particles behind. The well screen will filter the larger particles. You can clean the well by using either a surging technique or jet washing it with a garden hose.

a.) **To surge**, place a long pole down the pipe till below the water level and push up and down to surge the water through the perforated point.

b.) You can push the garden hose all the way down the pipe **to jet** the particles out.

8. The next step is to attach a pump and a concrete apron at the top of the well. The apron should drain away from the well towards a storm drain.

To avoid well contamination during a flood scenario, you should try to keep your pump at least 3 feet off the ground. This applies to both hand pumps and electric pumps.

If your pump pipe diameter and the well pipe diameter don't match up, you can fit a reducer coupling to connect the two.

Operate the pump to further remove debris and particles from

Extracting Water From The Ground

around the well screen. This will take a while, but you have to do it till you see clear, clean water coming out the top of the well.

Remember that off-the-shelf hand pumps are mostly used for depths up to 20-25 feet. These pumps have to be primed to get the water from 20 feet down all the way up into the pump.
If you cannot or don't want to prime your pump, then you will need a check valve. This is an inlet valve that is positioned on the horizontal line leading to the pipe. It is a one-way valve that allows water to go up towards the pump, but not down and out. Having a check valve means that u don't constantly have to prime the hand pump. The result is that you always have water at the ready in the pump.

If you are close to an electrical source then you have an op-

Your pump should be installed a minimum of 3 feet above ground, to prevent contamination during a flood event.

---

tion of installing an electric Jet pump.

Conclusion

Using a well point is a very simple and straightforward method for water extraction. Try not to break the well point by forcing it through the rocky patches. Just move to a new location and start a new hole.

People tend to get excited once they hit water. Take your time and make sure that the well screen is completely submerged in the water. The deeper the better.

Be smart and do not drink water from the ground, except if you are 100% sure about the quality. It's always best to test your water before consumption.

All wells need a pump to transport the water to a place of storage. Tanks are perfect vessels for water storage.

Make sure you take a look at Chapter 5 where we take a closer look at holding tanks, and also at Chapter 7 where we discuss well pump basics.

How To Dig And Construct A Well

The most basic method for extracting water involves digging, with basic tools, through the dry, unsaturated zone. The depth of the water table will decide how deep you have to dig. You have to dig into the water table and line it with a porous material for clean water to enter the well. Line and seal the upper part of the well to prevent cave-ins and contamination. This is a very dangerous method that should be done with the aid of a professional.

Dug Wells

To dig a well by hand should be a last resort, for desperate times. This method is dangerous, slow, unpredictable and not feasible as a long-term solution. It is also open to contamination which is problematic, to say the least. A shallow water well should be at least 100 feet from any source of possible contamination. It is this writer's opinion that 150 feet (45m) is a safer distance, since we are experiencing more adverse weather conditions than ever before. There is an increase in floods in certain areas and floods are a well's biggest enemy. See the section on well maintenance at the end of this chapter. When selecting a location for your well, consider contamination, the soils, geology, and slope of the land. The well should be located uphill of septic systems, barnyards, livestock pastures, and fuel tanks, and at least 30 feet (10m) from streams and ponds. In addition, wells should not be located in extremely wet areas.

The following design will introduce the basics of well digging and it will give you an idea of all the dynamics at work. Dug wells work on a simple prin-

Well Drilling Glossary

Apron. A reinforced concrete floor all around the top of the well. It prevents contaminants from entering the well.

Caisson ring. A watertight retaining structure used on the foundations of a bridge pier, for the construction of a concrete dam, or for the repair of ships.

Concrete. A mixture of cement, sand and gravel.

Windlass. A type of winch used to lower buckets into and hoist them up from wells.

Well Digging Basics

Pump

Concrete apron

Clay and dirt

Water Table

**Gravel layers plug
the bottom of well.**

Fine gravel and sand

ciple:

• Find an aquifer close to the surface and dig a round hole that extends below the water table level. Never ever dig a square hole. It will cave-in!

• Remember to reinforce the well wall as you dig deeper and to remove dirt and debris from the hole. You can reinforce the well wall with bricks or with poured cement.

• Make sure you are below the water table, for this is where water will start to seep through the well wall and to accumulate in the bottom of the hole. Plug the bottom of the well with gravel to keep sediment and large particles out.

That's your well.

This method only works in areas with suitable soil like sand, clay or gravel. In rocky areas with boulders you can forget about it. On paper, it's definitely possible to use a shovel and pickax to dig a hole and to find water.

The width of the hole is determined by the soil conditions. Loose soil, smaller hole, firm soil wider hole.

Unfortunately, the whole process is not as simple as it sounds and it is not recommended doing this on your own. It is, at the very least, a five-man job that requires experience, lots of common sense, and a variety of tools. Basic well digging is a low cost method of well construction, but it is also considered very dangerous due to the possibility of cave-ins. Traditionally these wells for personal use are 4-5 feet in diameter and are dug by hand. Depending on the ground in your area, you can go anywhere from 8-20 feet deep. The method we are going to discuss is considered the easiest, safest and requires fairly simple tools and moving equipment. It

You will need:

• A shovel and pickax for digging.

• Simple waterproofing plaster.

• Lengths of rope or cable used to lower and haul equipment.

• A winch with head frame to haul heavy objects from well.

• Pulleys for simple lowering and hauling tasks.

• Bailing buckets for hauling

dug material from the well.

• Hammers, nails, wood.

• Hard hats.

• Level, plumb bob and plumb line.

• Ladder (rope or rigid).

• Eye protection.

• Medical kit.

Extracting Water From The Ground

involves reinforcing the inside of the well with a concrete well lining, also called a Caisson ring. If digging in unstable ground, you run the risk of the well wall collapsing.

The best and simplest method is to use precast concrete well rings as your well lining (Caisson rings). These are precast and are about 2″ (5cm) thick and 3-5 feet (90-150cm) in diameter. They are similar to the manhole cement rings we see on road construction sites. They should have joints that allow them to "fit" into place. You will need to construct a windlass (winch on tripod or head frame) above your well to assist with the moving of dirt, rocks, concrete rings and bailing of water.

Preparations

There are various ways to dig a well. The use of precast concrete rings has proven to be a very efficient method, but it does involve a fair amount of preparation.

• Prepare your concrete rings. You will have to do some research to see what's available in your area. Discuss in detail what you need and the implementation of the rings. They must be wide enough for a person to stand in. Around 4-5ft (1.2-1.5m) will do. Remember to determine the depth of the water table beforehand. This will give you an indication of how many rings you require. You will also

Dug wells should only be attempted as a last resort, when all options have been exhausted and only if it's a dire emergency.

need professional lifting equipment.

Do not attempt to move or lift a concrete ring without proper lifting equipment as prescribed by the manufacturer!

• These rings are heavy and it will be an arduous and a dangerous task to move them around. Each ring must be safely position over the well hole and to do this, you will need a forklift and a truck. There is no way around this. A standard ring has at least two "lifting holes" (through the side) which are used for hoisting and lowering. Make sure you get rings with lifting holes on the inside or with holes that go straight through the sides. Use the correct lifting straps and lifting keys/ hooks. Don't rig any ropes around or on the underside of the ring. Once your well is finished, remember to seal off all holes where potential contaminants can enter.

• You should have a sturdy platform constructed around the opening of the well hole. When you are ready to sink the first concrete ring, place two thick pieces of timber over the hole.

You can rest your first concrete ring on top. Once ready, lift the ring, remove the timber, and slowly lower the ring into the hole. This part of the process will require patience and teamwork. Make sure that safety is a first priority.

• You will need lifting equipment. Moving material in and out of the well is no simple task. Take care that your lifting equipment is not too heavy, for that can also cause the top of the well to collapse. Use a heavy-duty electric winch with head frame for heavy objects and a simple pulley system (or windlass) for buckets filled with dirt. It is not advisable to lower the cement rings by hand. The process of hauling and lowering material is a very dangerous one. This is where most accidents occur. The head frame can also act as windlass and should have a solid platform underneath (wood) to prevent objects from being knocked into the well hole.

• You will need waterproofing plaster to seal the top ten feet of the well. This is to prevent contaminants from entering the clean well water. It is not necessary to plaster the bottom section of the well. This part is submerged in the water-bearing sand of the water table and you want the water to enter through the openings between the concrete rings.

• Organize your well. Draw up a plan with the layout of the construction areas. This should include the dumping area, no-driving zone, no-contamination zone, washing area, rest area, tool storage, etc.

• You will have to prepare a dumping area well away from the well hole. This is where all the material taken from the well will be dumped. Calculate how much space you'll need by determining the volume of dirt that must be excavated from the well. Make sure that the daily routine of moving the dirt will not cause the well sides to collapse.

• Prepare storage space for construction tools. Tools should be locked away when not in use.

• Create a path system for workers to follow. This creates a safe environment with designated areas for work and rest.

• The construction team should be well trained and everybody should know his or her task(s) and what equipment they are responsible for. Use a system of hand signals when communicating with diggers inside the well.

How To

1. Start by digging a hole wide enough for you to stand in. Remember that your concrete ring has to fit inside this hole. Around 4-5ft (1.2-1.5m) will do. Keep the diameter of the hole in mind and leave the wall curves nice and smooth.

Extracting Water From The Ground

At this stage, nothing should be suspended or hanging above the digger.

4 feet / 1.2 m

2. Go down to about 3 feet (1m) and stop to inspect your hole. The first cutting ring should be able to fit snugly inside. Typically, the first well ring has a "cutting edge" to scrape away the dirt. Dig down to a depth that will allow the first well ring to sit level in the well.

CAUTION! When lowering these rings, no workers should be inside the well!

3. Once the ring has been lowered, a worker can be allowed to go down and to stand inside the hole. While standing inside the ring, start to excavate underneath it; as you remove the dirt, the ring's weight will allow it to sink deeper into the hole. Remove the soil gently and evenly from underneath the ring. This will allow the ring to slide in a level position down the well.

Just allow it to slide down a few inches. You have to leave the upper part of the ring exposed to join the second ring. Gently lower the second ring and make sure that the joints line up.

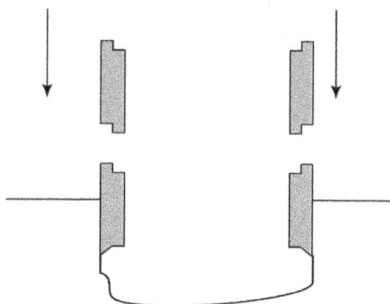

Remember that once the hole is completed, you will have to seal the upper joints of the well with waterproofing plaster!

4. The next step is very important. Connect the second ring to the first ring with metal rods or chains.

This can be achieved by placing a metal connection inside the "lifting eye" of the ring. This method will aid in sending the whole column of rings down evenly and in a rigid, straight line.

5. Level. Use a level or plumb-bob (a weight on a string) to check your progress and if you are digging in a straight line. Do this routinely as you go deeper. The stack of rings must slide evenly, at a ninety degree angle, down the hole.

6. Keep on stacking these rings on top of one another till you reach the water table. All the rings should be in a column, tightly fastened with rods or chains. This is no easy feat and you will have to pay close attention to the task at hand. At this stage, the help of an expert will come in very handy. For a novice, this can be considered as on-the-job training and it will require some perseverance.

Patience is key and it will undoubtedly take a qualified person to guide you through this process. Upon reaching the water table, you have to stop.

7. Pump or bail. Once you reach the water table, you can expect water to start seeping into the bottom of the well. This is where digging gets hard and where you will get wet. Try to go as deep as you can. At least 5 feet more. You will have to pump or bail the water from the well.

Extracting Water From The Ground

When using a pump and generator, take care that the generator is downwind and that it is not sending fumes down into your hole.

8. Gravel. Once you find that the flow rate of water into the well is faster than the bailout rate, then you have to stop. You are now truly under the water table. (You should aim to be at least 5 feet under the water table.) Fill the bottom of the well with gravel.

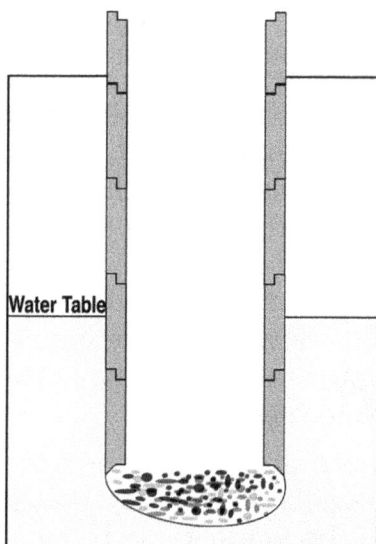

One foot of gravel will do nicely. Use coarse gravel as a top layer and fine gravel underneath. Fill it up properly to prevent clay and other sludgy material from entering the well. Clean water can penetrate into the well from the porous sides and from the bottom filled with gravel.

9. Protection. Seal the top 10ft (3m) of well rings on the inside with a waterproof concrete seal-

ant to create an effective seal against contaminants that might seep in through the adjacent soil on the outside.

11. Annular space. Fill any openings on the outside of the concrete ring casings (top 10 feet) with clay or concrete. This is to prevent surface water contamination. This is of great importance!

12. Seal the well. At the top of your well, you want the well lining to extend about 3 feet (1m) above ground. This is where you have to consider contamination. Make sure that no contaminants can seep into your well, whether through the well opening at the top or through the adjacent soil.

To seal your well top you can create an apron from reinforced concrete. Make sure that it runs downhill and that it drains water away from the well into a storm drain or another collection area. This apron should be reinforced, strong and wide (6 feet of space all around). This is where people walk and where water containers are filled. Cracks in the apron will cause contaminants to seep into your well.

13. Pumps. Install a hand pump at the top of your well. Remember that off-the-shelf hand pumps are mostly used for depths up to 20-25 feet. These pumps have to be primed to get the water from 20 feet down all the way up into the pump. If you don't want to prime your

pump, then you will need a foot valve. This is an inlet valve that is positioned at the bottom, suction end of the well pipe. It is a one-way valve that allows water to go up towards the pump, but not down and out. Having a foot valve means that u don't constantly have to prime the hand pump. The result is that you always have water at the ready in the pump. If you are close to an electrical source then you have an option of installing an electric Jet pump.

Options

You can consider alternative well casing support. The main issue is safety. In loose soil, the concrete ring method is best. This basic method allows water to enter the well from the bottom. However, once inside the water table, you have the following alternatives:

a.) There are porous concrete rings available that can be used within the water table to let water in. Tiny holes in the concrete wall will keep sediment out and let water in.

b.) Concrete rings with holes (slanted upwards) can also be used within the water table. The holes must be angled upwards from the outside in. This aids in keeping sediment out.

When concrete well casings are not an option, you can consider the following methods:

How to lower concrete rings in a level position?

• Digging method: When scraping the dirt away from underneath the ring, start by making four fist-sized holes in the 3, 6, 9, 12 o'clock positions. Next, make four holes in between the previous four created. Make eight holes in between the existing holes created. Your ring should start to slide down while doing this.

• Join the concrete rings together as you lay them on top of each other. This creates a unit of rings that slide down the wall in a straight line. You can join the rings with bolts, chains or lap joints.

• Clay bricks can be used in stable ground and at shallow depths. You have to dig as deep as possible before you start laying the bricks. This method requires stacking bricks from the bottom of the well (within the water table) and it means getting wet and bailing water by hand or with a pump. This method is for experts only.

• Various molds (Brit. moulds) can be used to pour concrete that can act as the well lining.

Dug Wells and Safety Concerns

• Place a fence around the well to keep ALL animals, no matter how big or small, out of the well. A scorpion or snake can kill you.

• Place a fence or barrier to keep people, especially children, out.

• During the construction period, place a lid on the well opening when the construction site is abandoned.

• Always leave a safety line in the well, in case someone were to fall in. This line should be a sturdy rope, twice as long as your planned well depth.

• Make sure that the digger wears a hardhat or helmet when in the hole.

• Check that all ropes are new and not worn.

• Check that bucket handles are secure and that the bottoms of the buckets have no cracks.

• Get a pair of steel-capped boots to protect your toes. Using shovels in a confined space increases the chance of accidents.

• Knots should be double-checked.

• Protect the top of the well by placing some wooden planks all along the edge of the well hole. This will prevent workers from wearing away the ground around the well.

• Always keep a safety kit on site.

• Toilets and washing areas should be 75 feet away from your well.

• Plan ahead where vehicles and forklifts will be allowed to drive. Do not disturb soil around your well's edge.

• When using generators, make sure that fumes are downwind of the well hole.

• The attitude of all workers should be professional and alert. Do not joke around a well site and do not allow alcohol or other mind-altering substances to be consumed while working.

You can dig down to around 10 feet, create a mold from wood or sheet (corrugated) metal, and then pour your concrete. The concrete will set in between the mold and the soil of the well wall. This will also require the help of an expert.

• In very stable soil, and with a fairly shallow well, you also have the option of digging the shaft first. Afterwards, you can slide the concrete rings down. This is also a dangerous method and not recommended. In stable soil and hard rock, the risk of a cave-in is lower.

Conclusion

Some of the biggest issues with wells of this nature is safety awareness and prevention of contamination. A deep, open hole has the potential to cause accidents, not just to workers, but to anybody who ventures

Part of being aware of safety and contamination is instructing the excavation foreman to implement strict excavation guidelines.

---

onto the construction site. Wherever humans and machines are involved, we find an immediate rise in pollution levels and also in contamination of the environment. Extra care must be taken to guarantee a safe, contaminant-free environment. Part of being aware of contamination is instructing the excavation foreman to implement excavation guidelines.

These guidelines will include work schedules, safety procedures, emergency procedures, waste disposal, workplace etiquette, etc.

Benefits of using precast concrete rings

• They are strong, durable and ideal for use as a well lining.

• Using concrete rings cuts down on manpower needed.

• They can be sealed with waterproofing plaster to prevent contaminated surface water from seeping in.

• They help to cut down on excavation time.

• They will not corrode or rust and will not contaminate the water in the well.

• They come in different sizes are considered safe to use by the industry.

• They are perfectly round, lock into place and provide good structural strength.

Summary

Having a well can be a very rewarding experience, but just how rewarding will depend on a couple of factors.

— Make sure that your well is fully developed. Once your well installation is complete, make sure that all cuttings and sediment are removed to ensure that water can freely enter the well.

— Make sure that your borehole has no stability issues. The well should be sealed and the well casing, screen and pump system should be made of quality material. Cracked pipes and screens normally means drilling a new well.

— Watch for over-pumping. This occurs when water is withdrawn at a faster rate than it can be replenished. It is a common problem with wells and it leads to premature well failure.

— Watch out for dissolved gas (nitrogen, methane), corrosive water and biofouling. Water saturated with oxygen can cause bacterial growth, which causes a biofilm to develop inside the well. This can mean reduced well yield and water quality.

Have a look at the discussions on holding tanks (Chapter 5) and well pump basics (Chapter 7).

My Checklist

√ I had my water tested to see if it is fit for human consumption.

√ I selected the correct well for my needs.

√ I have determined the use of my well water.

√ My well is at the perfect location. It is not affected by surface runoff water and in the vicinity of potential sources of contamination.

√ I checked with local government.

√ I am legally allowed to own a well.

√ I double-checked all installation requirements. Both plumbing and electrics were done (or checked) by a licensed well professional.

√ I know how to maintain my well water system.

√ My well has a well seal to prevent contaminants, and critters from entering.

√ I am not abusing the groundwater in my area.

√ I am only collecting for my basic needs.

√ My well does not pose a safety hazard to people or animals.

√ I have considered all worst-case scenarios. I have a backup plan.

The Basics of Wells And Water Pumps

Pumps are used to "pull" or "push" water from a water source to a holding tank or to directly feed the household plumbing. Typically, the water source can be a well, spring or a pond. Pump installations should be done by a licensed professional to make sure that you get the most out of your pump. A correctly installed pump will last long, use very little energy and deliver water with optimum flow rate and pressure.

Your well must be fully developed and pumped clean of large particles, debris and fine sand before you install the pump. No use clogging your pump or pipes with sediment or drill cuttings.

To select the appropriate pump for your water volume needs, you will have to consider the following:

a.) The water level of the water in the well.

b.) The diameter of your well pipe.

c.) The number of plumbing fixtures (water consuming appliances) that require water.

d.) The volume of water required in gallons per minute (gpm) during peak water demand.

e.) Your preferred power source. (Connected to the grid or solar.)

These are questions that every well owner should be knowledgeable about.

Different pumps are used for different applications and it's vital to select the correct pump for your needs.

Connecting An Electric Pump

A pump is used to draw water from the well and to move it to a new location. Selecting the right pump for your needs, will depend on the following:

1. The estimated volume of water you need for your property.

2. The power source you will connect to. Pumps can connect to the power grid, batteries, solar panels or generators.

3. The environment. A harsh environment with dry and dusty conditions will require a quality pump with screen and shield protection.

Pump Basics

Depending on the aforementioned conditions, you can consider looking at the following types of pumps:

• **Jet pumps** are, generally speaking, suitable for wells that are 3 inches or less in diameter.

- *Shallow well jet pumps* are often used for shallow water wells which are no deeper than 25 feet. The pump is located at surface level.

- *Deep well jet pumps* work well with wells as deeper as 80-100 feet. The jet is located inside the well, below the water level.

• **Submersible pumps** are long cylindrical pumps (with motor) around 2-3 feet long. They are used in wells 3 inches or more in diameter. Submersible pumps are very efficient pumps with high yield and high delivery pressure.

Check Valves And Foot Valves

One-way valves are a very important component of the pump system. The use of one-way valves prevents the water from flowing back down into the well and it ensures that the pump is primed.

• There are two options for jet pumps:

- Usually, a **foot valve** is placed at the end of the suction line, which is at the bottom-end of the well. They are mostly used in drilled wells.

Having the foot valve at the bottom of the well can be problematic, because it's hard to get to for maintenance purposes.

- A **check valve** is a good option (especially for driven wells) and can be installed in the feed line next to the pump. This assures that the pump line and pump is filled with water when the pump is switched off. If you put your check valve next to the pump, above ground, then you need an additional fitting above ground (at the top of the suction line) to prime the pump.

You can use 1¼ inch male PVC adapters with the valve.

• For submersible pumps we use check valves where needed. Usually submersible pumps come with a check valve pre-installed in the pump that you place at the bottom of the well. If your well is very deep, install a check valve for every 150 - 200 feet (45-60m) of pipe.

You should also have a check valve at surface level to ensure a steady flow of water to your distribution system.

Pressure Tanks

Pumps work very well in combination with pressure tanks.

The function of the pressure tank in a water well system is to create water pressure by using compressed air to push down on the water in the tank.

The pressure tank functions as a reservoir and holds enough pressure to flush a toilet in the house, without turning the pump on.

• The normal operating pressure ranges for pumps are 20/40, 30/50, 40/60 or even as high as 60/80 psi. This means that pressure is kept constant within a 20 psi range, which sets a boundary for starting and stopping the pump.

To measure the depth-to-water in a well, drop a line with a bobber (float) and a small weight down your well hole. Once the line is slack, (the bobber is floating) you have your measurement.

A 40/60 ratio is recommended since it's by far the best ratio to keep a constant shower stream. This pressure range indicates when the pump will turn on and off, and this function is controlled by a pressure switch device. This is the device that will turn your pump on and off automatically.

Example: If you have a 40/60 psi setting, the pump will turn on when the pressure in the pressure tank drops to around 40 psi and off when the pressure reaches 60 psi.

The relationship between the pressure switch, pressure tank and the pump is what allows water to flow through the pipes in your home. When selecting a pressure tank, you will need to know the performance of the pump in gallons per minute.

• We measure the volume of water required to serve a household, in gallons per minute (gpm). It is calculated by looking at the water consuming appliances in the house and also at the pump's flow rate in gpm.

The gpm of the pump must equal the total number of water consuming appliances.

Example:

5 faucets, 2 toilets, a shower and a washing machine would require 9 gpm.

• To determine the appropriate size of the tank, match the draw down of the tank to the capacity of the pump.

Another easy way to size a tank, is to take the gpm system requirement that you determined for your house, and to multiply it by 3 and then to go to the next largest tank size.

In our previous example:

9 (gpm) x 3 = 27.

Buy a 30 gallon or bigger pressure tank.

Usually, when it comes to pressure tanks, bigger is better. A larger pressure tank will not hurt your pump's performance, but it will give you a larger draw down capacity, which guarantees even more usable pressure in the plumbing system, before the pump needs to come on.

• **In general**, a ½ HP pump is enough for a small house with one bathroom and a couple of people.

For a larger house, you'll need a ¾ -1 HP pump.

• Take into consideration that a larger pump will affect your electricity bill and that it will also require a larger pressure tank.

• If you want a generator as a back-up power source, make sure that the generator can provide enough power to start the pump.

Pitless Adapters

In colder climates where water pipes should be protected from

---

Well Pump Glossary

Cavitation. The formation of bubbles in a liquid, typically by the movement of a propeller through it.

Check valve. A valve that closes to prevent backward flow of liquid.

Foot valve. A one-way valve at the inlet of a pipe or the base of a suction pump.

Pressure switch. A switch that automatically turns water on and off, depending on pressure settings.

Pressure tank. A tank in which a liquid or gas is stored under pressure greater than atmospheric.

This helps maintain water pressure to keep appliances running efficiently.

Depth to water. The distance

Pressure tank · Control box · Frostline · Discharge pipe · Pitless Adapter · Deep well drop pipe · Pump inside pump housing · Well casing

can be used with standard jet pumps, they are commonly used with submersible pumps, where the pressure tank is located in a pump house or basement.

This adapter consists of a special fitting that is installed 6-10 ft (2-3 m) below ground level for protection from frost. A hole is made in the well casing and the water coming up from the well is diverted horizontally at the adapter, and discharged into a water pipe that runs underground to the house or pump house.

The main benefit of these adapters are:

- These adapters are cheap and reduce the risk of contamination in your well.

- A pitless adapter makes it easy to access the well for routine maintenance or emergency service.

freezing,a pitless adapter is used to keep the water, pumped from your well, under the frost line and in a sanitary environment.

Installing a pitless adapter is a much better option than using the old well pits we still see in certain parts of the world today.

Although a pitless adapter

Well Pump Glossary

measured from the ground level to the water level in the well when the pump is not in operation.

Draw down. Amount of usable water we can get out of the water pressure tank before the pump has to turn on

Draw down water level. The distance from ground level to the water level inside the well,

while water is being pumped from the well.

Well capacity (gpm). The amount of water measured in gallons per minute that the well produces without the water level dropping.

Well total depth. The distance measured from the ground level down to the bottom of the well.

Typical shallow well jet pump setup

Prime with water

Jet pump

Check valve (option)

Foot valve (option)

Option A

Jet pump

Prime with water

Screw cap

Check valve (option)

Foot valve (option)

Option B

The Basics Of A Shallow Well Jet Pump

Depth: 10-25 feet

Expected life: 10 years

For a shallow water well you will need a simple jet pump. Jet pumps are relatively inexpensive and require little maintenance. Expect your jet pump to last an average of ten years. Some basic information about jet pumps:

• Simple, shallow well jet pumps can draw water up to 25 feet. They do not work with deeper wells. For a deeper well you will need a deep well jet pump.

• Jet pumps can also be used as booster pumps to improve the existing pressure to a higher level.

Mechanics

These pumps are easy to operate and basically "suck" the water out of the well. When we say suck, it actually means that the pressure from our atmosphere is pressing down on the water and pushing it up the well pipe.

When you turn on the pump, it creates suction in the well pipe and with the push from the atmosphere, the water is jetted up the pipe. Inside the pump, the impeller pushes water through a narrow jet which is a cone-shaped device which creates a vacuum with suction. This is the suction that draws water from the well into the pumping sys-

The Basics of Wells And Water Pumps

tem. The sudden decrease in diameter causes the water to shoot through the jet and eventually out the pump at end use.

You can install your pump at ground level, above or next to the well hole.

Installation and priming

Before you install your jet pump, make sure that your well is clean and ready to be connected to the pump.

Your well should have a sanitary seal on top of the suction (well) pipe. This should fit your well diameter.

You can also, if needed, make the well head area frost proof with a concrete containment area.

To prevent air pockets, make sure that the pipe slopes slightly downward from the pump to well.

Basic installation of a jet pump.

1. Make sure there's no debris and large particles in the well.

2. Assemble the pump as per manufacturer's instructions. Make sure that you follow the instructions to the letter.

3. Install a 1¼ inch foot valve at the bottom of the suction pipe if this is an option. This will suit wells that have easy access to the well pipe like a drilled well.

Another option, as seen with driven wells where the well casing is used as the suction pipe,

is to install a 1¼ inch check valve in the feed line. You can do it near the pump, in the horizontal or vertical position

Shallow water pumps generally need to be primed to work. This is the process of flushing and forcing water into the pump in order to create enough pressure for it to work.

1. Make sure that the pump is turned off.

2. Locate the priming plug and unscrew it.

3. Use a funnel and slowly pour water in. The pump head should be completely filled with water. The water primes and lubricates the pump. When priming, remember that you want the pump and suction pipe to be completely filled with water.

4. Replace the plug once the pump head is completely full.

5. Turn on the pump. Check for leaks.

6. Optionally, you can also give yourself the option of being able to prime the well pipe if needed. To connect the well pipe to the pump, use a Tee fitting with a threaded cap on top. This is where you can prime the pipe by filling it with water.

The Basics Of A Deep Well Jet Pump

Depth: 25-110 feet

Expected life: 10 years

Priming plug — Pressure switch

Well seal

Suction pipe

Pressure pipe

Injector

Foot valve

If your well's water level is deeper than 25 feet, you can look at a deep well jet pump to "push" your water to the surface.

Deep well jet pumps are slightly different from shallow well jet pumps in that they use two water lines in the well, instead of one.

Expect your jet pump to last an average of ten years.

Mechanics

This pump is not as complicat-

ed as it looks and uses a very simple method to extract water from a well.

A deep well jet pump works similar to a shallow well jet pump, but the main difference is that the jet is separated from the motor and placed at the bottom of the well. This pump uses a system of two pipes; the one pipe is mounted to the impeller housing and "pushes" water down into the well and into the jet body. The jet is located about 15 feet below the minimum water level.

On the output side of the jet body, the second pipe drives the water from the jet back up to the pump and on to a storage tank or to the household plumbing.

A foot valve is placed at the bottom of the well piping. This foot valve keeps the system primed and prevents draining of water from the pipes.

The jet uses suction and the impeller creates pressure. The combination of these two forces creates a simple application that can produce water lift from 25-110 feet deep.

The Basics Of A Submersible Deep Well Pump

Depth: 25-400 feet

Expected life: 25 years

Submersible pumps are placed

inside the well (or water source) and are used to "push" the water to the surface.

Pushing water takes up less energy than pulling water, especially in a deep well.

Mechanics

These are very effective pumps that consist of a pump motor and a series of impellers that are placed inside a cylindrical shape. When turned on, the impellers spin, and this causes the water to be pulled into the pump, which pushes the water to the surface for storage. The pump uses electrical wires that connect to a power source above ground. Note that a pump with

three wires plus a GROUND, is a single-phase pump and it requires a control box. The control box is matched to the pump motor. Two wire plus GROUND pump/motor assemblies do not require a control box. Submersible pumps are very reliable and all working parts are sealed within the cylinder. They do not need priming and deliver great volume and pressure. These pumps can deliver water at pretty much any working delivery rate, depending on well depth, pipe diameter and pump horsepower.

Submersible well pumps are typically seen with horsepower ratings of ½ HP, ¾ HP, 1 HP, and 1½ HP.

Pay attention to the following:

• Follow the instructions of the pump manufacturer. Make sure that you are installing the correct pump for your needs.

• When following the manufacturer's instructions, make sure that you get the correct diameter drop pipe to connect to your pipe. The pump's discharge rate in gpm, must match the diameter of the pipe.

Example: A 10 gpm pump can handle a 1" pipe up to 300 ft.

• All electrical wiring, connections and system grounding must comply with local codes and ordinances. If unsure, hire an electrician to assist with the electric installation.

• Submersible pumps should be

Disconnect switch and circuit breaker

Pressure tank

Control box

Pressure switch

Well sea

Check valve (option)

Submersible electric drop cable

Deep well drop pipe

Torque arrester

Check valve (option)

Water intake

Pump inside pump housing

Well casing

installed 5 feet or more from the bottom of the well.

• Make sure that you use the correct pipe size and material for the well depth, pump type and water quality.

• When cables are spliced and connected, make sure that they are water tight. Besides crimping the wires together, they can also be soldered for an even more secure connection.

• Pumps usually come with a built-in check valve.

For very deep wells, you will have to use a check valve every 150 - 200 feet (45-60m).

Check valves prevent water from flowing back down into the well when the pump shuts off. They also ensure immediate water flow into the tank when the pump starts up, which prevents unnecessary physical strain on the pump.

• When selecting a submersible pump, pay special attention to the hermetic seal that protects the electric motor from water.

• The pressure switch senses the pressure coming through from the well and automatically turns the pump on or off.

• Attach a poly safety rope to your pump. You do not want to loose it down the well hole.

• Another safety feature is a torque arrestor.

This is basically a rubber support that clamps to the outside of the pipe and the top of the

Always disconnect the power before servicing a water pump and ensure that the motor is properly grounded.

pump with hose clamps.

The torque arrestor protects the submerged system against the twisting force of the motor as it starts. This prevents unnecessary rotation of the pipe threads.

Absorbing the thrust of the motor also keeps the pump centered in the well casing.

Submersible pumps are great pumps, but remember that the pump must first be pulled from the casing for repairs.

These days the submersible pumps are of a high standard and very reliable.

Pumps can last for 25 years before requiring any form of maintenance.

Connecting A Solar Water Pump

Solar powered water pumps have become very popular as of late and are often used for agricultural operations where conventional power systems are absent. The modern solar energy appliances have been demonstrated to reliably produce electricity and are considered ideal for rural, off-grid scenarios that include irrigation,

Tank with float switch

The surface pump
works off the solar
energy and pumps
water into the holding
tank.

Well

Surface pump or
Submersible pump

livestock and domestic use. New technology is making this a very exciting field and the future is looking bright. When buying a new solar powered water pump, make sure that you understand what you are buying, how it works and how it can be modified to suit your needs. Solar powered pumps are different from the regular AC powered pumps in that they use DC power. DC powered pumps are a very good option and they do not require large bursts of power like AC pumps do. Very much like conventional pumps, we find that solar water pumps can be divided into two categories: Surface pumps and Submersible pumps.

• Surface pumps are installed on the outside of the water source (well, spring, pond) and rely on a suction pipe to "suck" the water to the pump and then to "push" the water to the holding tank.

• Submersible pumps are installed under water (well, spring, pond) and "push" the water up to the holding tank

When installing a solar powered pump system, keep in mind that it is an integrated system that consists of various components.

For best performance, buy compatible components from a supplier who is knowledgeable about the complete system set-up and the variables that need

Tank with float switch

Power Grid

Inverter

Battery Bank

Charge Controller

Well in remote location

Surface or Submersible pump

consideration.

In considering energy efficiency, remember that pumps are better at **pushing** than **sucking**, and always keep the distance between the pump and the water at end use as short as possible.

There are two options worth considering:

1. You can power your pump directly with energy obtained from your solar panels.
(See Solar Pump Basics 1)
This means that the pump will only work when the sun is shining. To make it a viable option, you can store your water (as you pump it) in a holding tank

and use it when needed. Use a float switch in your tank to shut off the pump when full, and to turn it on when the water drops below a certain level. This is a very simple and effective option.

2. You can store the energy obtained from the solar panels in a battery bank and then rely on the batteries to power your pump.
(See Solar Pump Basics 2)
Having a battery bank allows for additional pumping during the night or when there's no sunlight available. This is a more complicated option.

If your household relies on a tank to provide water to the plumbing system, then you can

Tank with float switch

Booster pump

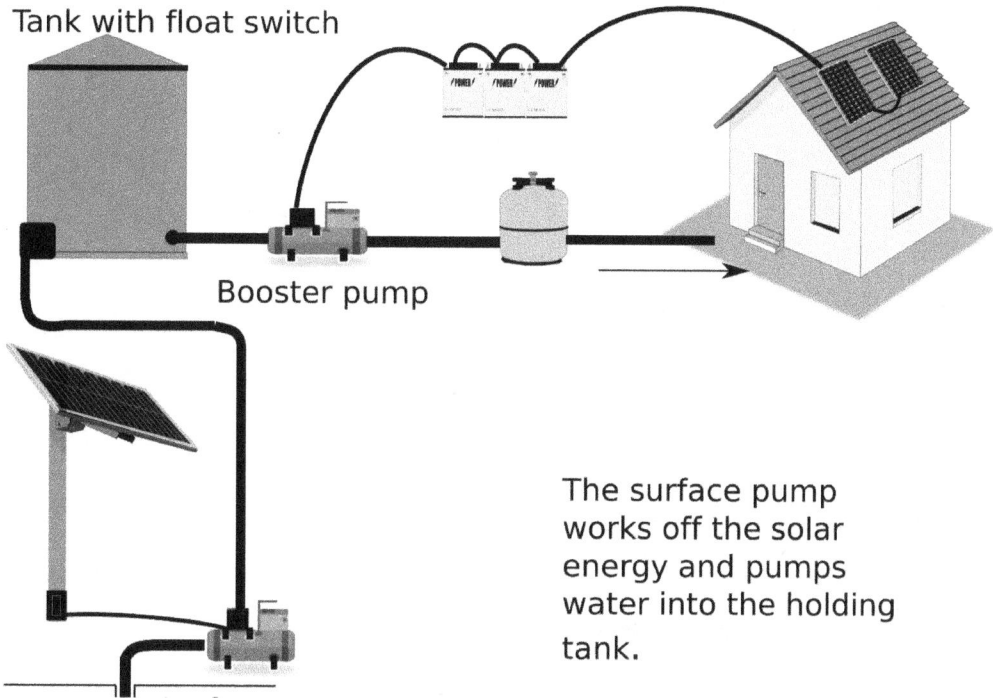

The surface pump works off the solar energy and pumps water into the holding tank.

---

consider the following options:

• **Booster pump.**
(See Solar Pump Basics 3)
Solar can still provide further solutions. A DC booster pump, powered by solar panels, can assist in providing pressurized water for your home. Booster pumps are to be installed after a storage tank in the water feed line. As mentioned earlier, if your pumping installation is not properly planned, you will not receive satisfactory water service.

• **Gravity feed.** This is a system where you rely on gravity to provide water pressure in your plumbing system. Basically, the higher your tank above

the outlets, the more pressure it supplies to the pipes. Gravity offers the advantage of using free energy to produce pressure, however, the tank must be elevated to a height that will deliver sufficient pressure. As a general rule, every foot of elevation provides 0.433 psi of pressure. This means that if the tank is 100 feet (30m) high, it will provide 43 psi of water pressure for your house (100' x 0.433 = 43.3 psi). That kind of elevation is not practical, but some elevation can be achieved by constructing a water tower or by placing the tank uphill of the house. Looking at the math side of things, it's obvious that gravity feed does

The pressure tank maintains the system pressure in the pipes.

The pump works off the solar energy and pumps water to the pressure tank.

Well

Surface pump or Submersible pump.

not offer a realistic solution for the modern home. It can still be used for irrigation and other agricultural purposes.

● **Pressure tank.**
(*See Solar Pump Basics 4*)
A pressure tank can also be utilized to provide water with enough pressure for your household. Water can be pumped directly from your well, with the solar powered pump, to a pressure tank where it is subsequently stored. The pressure tank is charged by the pump and this maintains pressure in the system, to the point of use in your home.

When buying your solar powered pump, you first have to calculate the lift required to get water out of your well, as well as the distance the water has to be pumped horizontally. This will determine which pump and which setup will provide the best, practical solution.

General Pump Maintenance

Always keep an eye on your well and your pump. Having a pump house, to keep your pump and well head protected from the elements, is a good option. Pay attention to the following:
● Surface pumps should be three feet above ground level to prevent contamination during flooding and in a location with ventilation and drainage. Pumps

should be allowed to breathe and not be covered in leaves or debris.

• Protect your pump and piping from freezing. If severe cold is forecast, drain your pump and remove it from the system.

• Get used to the sound of the pump motor as it pumps. A change in rhythm or unfamiliar hum may point to an issue.

• If possible, try to keep well screens clean and unclogged. This will ensure a steady flow of water and reduce friction and "laboring" in your pump.

• Make sure that your pump is securely fastened to its base. Fasten crews and make sure that there are no cracks in the surrounding cement or sealant. For submersible pumps, tether your pump to a safety rope.

• Keep all waste, chemicals and organic debris away from the system to prevent contamination.

• Be wary of any changes in water color, taste, or smell, as these and other signs may indicate a potentially dangerous issue.

• Only use galvanized steel and Schedule 40 PVC pipe and fittings for surface pumps.

• Electric pumps are not to be "experimented" with. Never tamper with the wiring of your pump. Only a licensed professional should do the work.

Conclusion

Keep things simple. Make sure that you are familiar with the operation of the pump and follow all maintenance and safety guidelines to increase the pump's longevity.

A simple and efficient pump setup will include a pump that feeds a storage tank with a floating switch. A second booster pump can be used to provide pressured water from the storage tank to the household plumbing.

Before installing a new pump, check the performance rating chart to make sure it can provide you with the pumping capacity and pressure that you require. Typically, 3-4 gpm is a minimum acceptable flow rate per outlet. Note that pumping capacity and pressure are inversely related. This means that when one goes up, the other goes down.

Example:
Under normal conditions, a pump can produce 10 gpm at 20 psi. If you are using two water consuming appliances, each will receive 5 gpm of water. If we increase the pressure to 30 psi, we might end up with only 6 gpm, which means 3 gpm per appliance. Conclusion: An increase in pressure, caused a lower flow rate in gpm at each water using appliance.

Sizing and installing a well pump can be a complex process and since pumps are not cheap it's best to consult a licensed professional who can guarantee the right pump for your needs.

Home Water Treatment Setup

Once you have a pump installed you can consider designing a complete home water treatment system. The main aim of such a system is:
- To feed the interior plumbing with water from your holding tank.
- To filter and purify incoming water for domestic needs.
- To provide a maintenance platform for your water's treatment.

Before you design such a system, you will have to determine your budget, how much energy (power) is available, and which contaminants need to be removed from your water.

Filters. You can use a system of pre- and post-filters to get rid of sediment and other contaminants. Filters come with either a mesh or a micron rating.

A wire mesh system indicates how many openings there are in one inch of screen. It can vary from inch to inch and is not very accurate.

A micron system is more accurate and represents the actual pore size of the filter; 1 micron (1μ) = 0.001 mm.

Filters calibrated in microns are intended to catch very fine particles of minute size. They are normally used at the end of the water line, before your water enters the indoor plumbing.

The main thing with filters is that they slow down the flow of the water as it moves though the water line. This puts pressure on your pump and all the other treatment systems. To alleviate the influence of filters, most domestic systems place the largest filters (big pore size) first in the water line and the smallest ones last.

In a standard setup, we find that the first filter is a filter with large pores which will catch larger particles. A simple spin down filter of 100 mesh will do. A 20 micron filter will work for a system dealing with finer particles. This pre-filter will need cleaning often.

You will need a **booster pump** to provide water to the appliances in your house. It should provide between 30 and 80 psi of pressure for optimum results. An automatic pressure sensor will regulate the on and off cycle of the pump.

A DC pump is very economical and only uses electricity when in use. These on-demand pumps are very energy-efficient and you can run it off a battery if needed.

An AC pump will also work, but uses more power.

Make sure that you have stop valves on entrance and exit points of your pump to allow for maintenance when needed.

The second filter catches slighter smaller particles and although the water is not potable yet, it should be clear of visible sediment. At this point in the feed line, the water can be

Basic Home Purifying System

Pump can work off a battery (DC) or be connected to the grid (AC).

Holding tank

Water

Pump

Pump

100 Mesh Filter

500 Mesh Filter

Pressure tank

1000 Mesh Filter

to house

UV light

Main system

Filter options
1. Standard 100/ 500/ 1000 mesh.
2. Fine 20/ 5/ <1 micron.

Main system options:
1. Ceramic candle filter
2. Reverse osmosis sytem
3. Carbon filter

diverted to showers, toilets and washing machines, except if you have known pathogens in your water that have to be removed.

Next in line is your pressure tank that will provide pressure to the indoor plumbing and minimize pump usage. Make sure you size your tank according to your pump specifications.

The third filter should be the final one that takes care of all sediment. The water should be clear of hard particles and only dissolved chemicals and pathogens will require removal from here on out.

You **main water treatment system** can be a ceramic candle filter, a reverse osmosis system or a specific filter for your indi-

vidual needs. It should render your water safe to drink and give you the peace of mind to use it on a daily basis with confidence.

Finally, a UV light can also be considered to get rid of viruses. When utilizing such a light, first make sure that all sediment has been removed, for pathogens can hide behind particles and bubbles causes by turbulence. If specific impurities like dissolved chemicals need to be removed, then specialized filters can be employed in the final stage the treatment process.

See Chapter 9 for more information on the various treatment systems available.

The Basics Of Managing A Well

Keep in mind that a well is an investment that can last for years if properly taken care of. From "day one" you will have to be involved in the whole process of creating a sustainable well with a healthy life-expectancy. Start with simple observations, measurements and calculations.

a.) While under construction keep notes of time of year, water table depth, soil quality and yield.

b.) Once your well is up and running keep records on productivity, seasonal fluctuations, water testing and general maintenance.

These basic observations will provide you with the information to keep contaminants out of your well and also to prevent your well from running dry due to over-pumping.

Managing your well means that you will also have to be prepared in case a flood event or an environmental disaster strikes your area.

These are unexpected events and they usually catch people off guard, but by simply being prepared, the impact on your water supply can be minimized.

The responsibility to manage a well lies squarely on the shoulders of the owner.

A well can cause problems on many levels not just for the owners, but also for members of the surrounding community.

Remember that your well uses the same local groundwater as your neighbors and that your actions will affect other groundwater users as well.

Managing Your Wel

No matter which method you used to create your well, you still have to manage and maintain the structure.

Well maintenance can protect your investment, prolong the life of your well and also protect you and your family against possible contaminants.

Protect Your Well

According to the Centers for Disease Control and Prevention (CDC), here are some steps you can take to help protect your well:

- Wells should be checked and tested ANNUALLY for mechanical problems, cleanliness, and the presence of certain contaminants, such as coliform bacteria, nitrates/nitrites, and any other contaminants of local concern, (for example, arsenic and radon).

- Well water should be tested more than once a year if there are recurrent incidents of gastrointestinal illness among household members or visitors and/or a change in taste, odor, or appearance of the well water.

- All hazardous materials, such as paint, fertilizer, pesticides, and motor oil, should be kept far away from your well.

- When mixing chemicals, do not put the hose inside the mixing container, as this can siphon chemicals into a household's water system.

- Consult a professional contractor to verify that there is proper separation between your well, home, waste systems, and chemical storage facilities.

- Always check the well cover or well cap to ensure it is intact. The top of the well should be at least one foot above the ground.

Call An Expert

Along with the points previously listed, the following are indicators of when a water well systems professional should be called to evaluate the condition of your well:

1. Anytime that the well cap or seal has to be removed to look inside the well.

2. If you experience taste or odor problems, then you should contact a professional to have your water tested

3. If you experience turbidity or cloudiness of water caused by presence of suspended matter

The Basics Of Managing A Well

("dirty" looking).

4. If there is a loss of capacity or pressure—the well is not producing as much water as previously produced, the pressure drops and surges, or the pump cycles on and off frequently.

5. If a test is positive for total coliforms, anaerobic bacteria, or any positive test results indicating a potential health concern. Contact a professional or your local or state regulatory agency if you experience any positive test results or believe your well has been contaminated. A water well systems professional should be hired to thoroughly clean and disinfect any well that has had a positive "anaerobic" bacterial test result, which should include removal of any pumping equipment and evacuation of the well to its bottom to be sure of maximum removal of anaerobic growth.

6. When you find defects with your wellhead, the wellhead area, or the overall water system during your routine inspections and find that you do not have the proper tools and/or knowledge to fix the issue(s). A mistake in self-servicing your well can cost you thousands of dollars, cause personal injury or death, damage personal property, and leave you and your family without water until a qualified contractor can be on-site to fix the issue(s).

Once your well has reached its serviceable life, have a licensed or certified water well driller and pump installer decommission the existing well and construct a new well. Never dispose of any chemicals or organic waste inside your old, decommissioned well.

Visual Inspections

According to the National Ground Water Association, to monitor your well's performance, you will have to carry out specific visual inspections:

- The Well Casing (pipe protruding from the ground) must be examined. Check the general condition and check if the casing extends at least 12 inches above ground. If not, hire a qualified professional to investigate remedial action.

- The Well Cap (cap on top of casing) must be present. Check the condition of the cap and any seals present, that it is securely attached, and that it will keep out insects and rodents. If not, hire a qualified professional to repair or replace the well cap.

- Survey the area above ground, surrounding the well. Check the location relative to potential sources of contamination, flooding, and physical dangers. Look for chemicals such as paint, fertilizer, pesticides, or motor oil. Remove all unwanted contaminants if possible.

- It is important to maintain at least 100 feet between the well and any kennels, pastures, feeding areas, or livestock operations. Ensure a proper distance is maintained from buildings, waste systems, or chemical storage areas (including fuel tanks)—a water well systems professional should know local codes and requirements. If there is any concern, contact your water well systems professional or your local health department.

- The ground surrounding the wellhead should slope away towards a storm-water drain. This is to divert any surface water run-off and to prevent contamination. If not, consider allowing for the ground to slope away from the well casing, while maintaining a proper height of the casing above the ground. A water well systems professional can extend the height of the casing if needed.

- You should have a concrete apron around your well casing. If there is no concrete pad surrounding the well casing, contact your local health department or regulatory

Annual Water Well Checkup

The National Ground Water Association suggests that at a minimum, wells should be evaluated annually by a licensed or certified water well systems professional.

An annual water well checkup should include:

- A flow test.
- A visual inspection.
- A water quality test for coliform and anaerobic bacteria, nitrates, and anything else of local concern.
- Checking of valves.
- Performing electrical testing.

A written report should be delivered to you following completion of an annual checkup. The report should include recommendations and all laboratory and other test results.

Keep this in a safe place with all other well reports.

agency to determine if one should be installed by a water well systems professional.

- If the well is equipped with a vented well cap, check for the presence of the vent screen in the well vent, and clear away any debris that has accumulated on the vent screen. Check the condition of the vent screen to ensure it can prevent insects and animals from entering.

- Any growth of weeds, trees, shrubs, or grasses with root systems within 10 feet of the well should be physically removed.

- Avoid the use of chemicals or herbicides near the wellhead.

- The well should not be in a roadway or driveway. If it is within close proximity to a roadway or driveway, it should be properly marked to avoid being hit by vehicles. You can protect your well by placing bollards or bump posts near the well's vulnerable position(s) to increase visibility.

- Special care should be observed if your well is located near a driveway and you live where it snows. Wells easily disappear below snow cover and are easily overlooked when pushing snow takes place.

- Be conscious of any other potential threats to the well-

You should have your well evaluated annually by a licensed professional to ensure that you get the most out of your investment.

head—garages, ATVs, sledding hills, debris, dirt, surface water, fuels and chemicals (including fertilizers), and runoff water from kennels, pastures, or feedlots.

- Keep the well out of dog runs or animal pens.

- If your well is located in a low-lying area prone to flooding, you should consider having your water well systems professional raise the well casing to at least 12 inches above the historic record flood level, properly sealing the wiring conduit and providing casing bump protection if floating debris is a concern. Another option is to construct a new well at a location outside the flood-prone area.

Disinfecting A Well

The Centers for Disease Control and Prevention (CDC) made the following guidelines available to the public, concerning well disinfection after an emergency. Don't forget that plugging or capping your well before a disaster is a great way of preventing or reducing contamination.

If extensive flooding has occurred or you suspect that the well may be contaminated, DO NOT drink the water. Use a safe water supply like bottled or treated water.

Safety Precautions

The following safety precautions must be followed before you can disinfect your well:

1. Inspect the area around the well. Remove suspected contaminants that are visible.

2. Turn off all electricity to the well. Don't attempt to fix any machinery if not qualified.

3. Clear hazards away from the well.

4. Do not enter the well pit. Gases and vapors can build up in well pits, creating a hazardous environment.

5. Wear protective goggles or a face shield when working with chlorine solutions.

6. When mixing and handling chlorine solutions, work in well-ventilated areas and avoid breathing vapors.

7. Warn users not to drink or bathe in water until all the well disinfection steps have been completed.

How To Disinfect A Well

To disinfect your well, follow these steps:

1. If the well is equipped with an electrical pump, turn off all electricity and clear debris from around the top of the well.

Repair the electrical system and pump if needed. Contact a qualified electrician, well contractor, or pump contractor if you are not experienced with this type of work.

2. Start the pump and run the water until it is clear. Use the outside faucet nearest to the well to drain the potentially contaminated water from the well and keep the unsafe well water out of the interior household plumbing. If no pump is installed, bail water from the well with a bucket or other device until the water is clear.

If the well is connected to interior home plumbing, close valves to any water softener units.

3. Use the Tables (Imperial and Metric) on the next page to determine the amount of liquid household bleach needed to disinfect the well. Use only unscented bleach.

4. Using a 5-gallon bucket, mix the bleach from the Table with 3-5 gallons of water (12-19L).

5. Remove the vent cap. Pour the bleach water mixture into the well using a funnel. Avoid all electrical connections. Attach a clean hose to the nearest hose bib and use it to circulate water back into the well for thorough mixing.

6. Rinse the inside of the well casing with a garden hose or bucket for 5-10 minutes.

7. Open all faucets inside the home and run the water until you notice a strong odor of chlorine (bleach) at each faucet. Turn off all faucets and allow the solution to remain in the well and plumbing for a minimum of 12 hours.

8. After at least 12 hours, attach a hose to an outside faucet and drain the chlorinated water onto a non-vegetated area such as a driveway or storm water drain. Continue draining until the chlorine odor disappears. Avoid draining into open sources of water (streams, ponds, etc.).

9. Turn on all indoor faucets and run water until the chlorine odor disappears.

10. Wait at least 7-10 days after disinfection, then have the water in your well sampled. Water sampling cannot be done until all traces of chlorine have been flushed from the system.

11. Sample the water for total coliform and either E. Coli or fecal coliform bacteria to confirm that the water is safe to drink.

If the results show no presence of total coliforms or fecal coliforms, the water can be considered safe to drink from a microbial standpoint.

Managing your well and routinely scheduling annual check-ups, is in the best interest of your family and of the whole community.

Follow up with two additional samples, one in the next 2 to 4 weeks and another in 3 to 4 months.

12. Check the safety of your water over the long term, continue to monitor bacterial quality at least twice per year or more often if you suspect any changes in your water quality.

If results show the presence of any coliform bacteria, repeat the well disinfection process and re-sample. If tests continue to show the presence of bacteria, contact your local health department for assistance.

Take note!

Fuel and other chemical releases and spills are common during flood events. If your water smells like fuel, has a chemical odor or if you live in an area where the potential for a release of fuels, pesticides, or chemicals is high, contact your local health department for advice. Water contaminated with chemicals will not be made safe by boiling or disinfection. Until you know the water is safe, use bottled water or some other safe supply of water.

Disinfecting A Drilled Or Driven Well (Imperial)

• Use only unscented household liquid chlorine bleach.

• Bleach concentrations are generally 5% - 8.25%.

• Quantities given in this table are approximate and are rounded to the nearest practical measurement.

• Amounts given are calculated in accordance with reaching a chlorine concentration of >100 mg/L.

Key to abbreviations:

1 cup = 8 fluid ounces = 16 tablespoons (tbsp)

1 gallon (gal) = 16 cups

Well Disinfection Table: Approximate Amount Of Bleach

Depth of water	Inside Diameter of Well casing (Inches)						
	2"	4"	6"	8"	10"	24"	36"
10 feet	¾ tbsp	3¼ tbsp	½ cup	¾ cups	1¼ cups	7 cups	1 gal
20 feet	1½ tbsp	6½ tbsp	1 cup	1½ cups	2½ cups	14 cups	2 gal
30 feet	2¼ tbsp	9¾ tbsp	1½ cups	2¼ cups	3¾ cups	1¼ gal	3 gal
40 feet	3 tbsp	13 tbsp	2 cups	3 cups	5 cups	1¾ gal	4 gal
50 feet	3¾ tbsp	1 cup	2½ cups	3¾ cups	6¼ cups	2¼ gal	5 gal
100	7½ tbsp	2 cups	5cups	7½ cups	12½ cups	4½ gal	10 gal

Disinfecting A Drilled Or Driven Well (Metric)

• Use only unscented household liquid chlorine bleach.

• Bleach concentrations are generally 5% - 8.25%.

• Quantities given in this table are approximate and are rounded to the nearest practical measurement.

• Amounts given are calculated in accordance with reaching a chlorine concentration of >100 mg/L.

Key to abbreviations:

1 meter (m) = 100 centimeters (cm)

1 liter (L) = 1000 milliliters (ml)

Well Disinfection Table: Approximate Amount Of Bleach

Depth of water	Inside Diameter of Well casing (Centimeters)						
	5cm	10cm	15cm	20cm	25cm	60cm	90cm
3 m	12 ml	48 ml	118 ml	177 ml	296ml	1.66 L	3.78 L
6 m	24 ml	96 ml	236 ml	354 ml	592ml	3.32 L	7.56 L
9 m	36 ml	144 ml	354 ml	531 ml	888ml	4.98 L	11.34 L
12 m	48 ml	192 ml	472 ml	708 ml	1.18 L	6.64 L	15.12 L
15 m	60 ml	240 ml	590 ml	885 ml	1.48 L	8.30 L	18.90 L
30 m	120 ml	480 ml	1.18L	1.77L	2.96 L	16.60 L	37.80 L

Disinfecting A Dug Well (Imperial)

• Use only unscented household liquid chlorine bleach.

• Bleach concentrations are generally 5% - 8.25%.

• Quantities given in this table are approximate and are rounded to the nearest practical measurement.

• Amounts given are calculated in accordance with reaching a chlorine concentration of >100 mg/L.

Key to abbreviations:

1 cup = 8 fluid ounces = 16 tablespoons (tbsp)

1 gallon (gal) = 16 cups

Well Disinfection Table: Approximate Amount Of Bleach

Depth of water	Inside Diameter of Well (Feet)					
	0.5'	1'	2'	3'	4'	5'
10 feet	½ cup	1¾ cups	7 cups	1 gal	1¾ gal	2¾ gal
20 feet	1 cup	3½ cups	14 cups	2 gal	3½ gal	5½ gal
30 feet	1½ cups	5¼ cups	1¼ gal	3 gal	5¼ gal	8¼ gal
40 feet	2 cups	7 cups	1¾ gal	4 gal	7 gal	11 gal
50 feet	2½ cups	8¾ cups	2¼ gal	5 gal	8¾ gal	13¾ gal

Disinfecting A Dug Well (Metric)

• Use only unscented household liquid chlorine bleach.

• Bleach concentrations are generally 5% - 8.25%.

• Quantities given in this table are approximate and are rounded to the nearest practical measurement.

• Amounts given are calculated in accordance with reaching a chlorine concentration of >100 mg/L.

Key to abbreviations:

1 meter (m) = 100 centimeters (cm)

1 liter (L) = 1000 milliliters (ml)

Well Disinfection Table: Approximate Amount Of Bleach

Depth of water	Inside Diameter of Well (Meters)					
	0.15 m	0.3 m	0.6 m	0.9 m	1.2 m	1.5 m
3 meters	118 ml	414 ml	166 L	3.78 L	6.62 L	10.41 L
6 meters	236 ml	828 ml	3.32 L	7.56 L	13.24 L	20.82 L
9 meters	354 ml	1.24 L	4.98 L	11.34 L	19.86 L	31.23 L
12 meters	472 ml	2.49 L	6.64 L	15.12 L	26.48 L	41.64 L
15 meters	590 ml	3.72 L	8.30 L	18.9 L	33.10 L	52.05L

Cleaning Water For Survival

Long gone are the days when we were able to take a swig from a bottle filled with clean water coming from a mountain stream or lake. Truth be told, these days you would actually have to travel very far to find drinkable surface water anywhere on this planet. A very large part of the earth's water supply is polluted and it's not a stretch to state that it's getting worse every year. Water contamination occurs through various means, but the result is always the same: Disease, and in more serious cases, even death. This is one aspect of self-sufficiency that you want to be very knowledgeable about.

As a general rule, when unsure about the quality of your water source, test your water and make a decision to rectify the problem. Under no circumstances should you take a chance with contaminated water.

When we start to look at our water, and the different ways to clean it, we have to make sure that we understand what type of contaminants we are dealing with. This requires clarity about what exactly needs to be removed from the water before we can drink it.

We can distinguish:

• Chemical contaminants.
• Bacteria and Protozoa.
• Viruses.

If you live in a remote, wilderness area surrounded by nature, chances are that your only issue with surface water will be biological contaminants. Keep in mind that water from a well, no matter how deep, can still contain various chemicals that occur naturally in the ground and that are harmful to human health.

Cleaning Your Water

We live in a period where, depending on your budget, technological advancements are providing us with a multitude of options to treat our water.

These days water can be purified to a degree of 99.999 percent, which pretty much guarantees potability.

If you happen to live near an urban population and near heavy industry, you will probably have to deal with biological and chemical contaminants. Sadly, most of our water supply has been contaminated with toxic chemicals found in pesticides, human waste, dumping of waste products, leaching, etc. If you are concerned that your area might have fallen victim to some of these issues, there is a possible solution at hand.

Almost every country has something that equates to the Environmental Protection Agency (EPA) or the Centers for Disease Control and Prevention (CDC). They will have information about local drinking water standards on their websites and also in print at your local water department office. They should have

Water Glossary

Adsorption. The adhesion of ions or molecules from a liquid, or dissolved solid to a surface. This process creates a film of the adsorbate on the surface of the adsorbent.

Desalination. The removal of salts and minerals from a target substance.

Filtration. Various mechanical, physical or biological operations that separate solids from fluids by adding a medium through which only the fluid can pass.

Halogens. A group of elements that contain the chemical disinfectants iodine and chlorine.

Ions. An atom or molecule with a net electric charge due to the loss or gain of one or more electrons.

Micro-filtration. A type of physical filtration process where a contaminated fluid is passed through a special pore-sized membrane to separate microorganisms and suspended particles from process liquid.

Ultra-filtration. A type of membrane filtration in which pressure forces a liquid up-to-date **annual water quality reports for your area** and this includes the following:

- The source of the drinking water. River, lake, aquifer, etc.
- A summary of the risk of contamination of the local water source.
- The regulated contaminants found in local drinking water.
- Potential health effects.
- Information on nitrate, arsenic and lead in areas of concern.
- Information on Cryptosporidium, a parasitic protozoan that causes disease.

Take note that, testing water at its source is necessary and a

First determine what is in your tap water, then decide on which method is best to get rid of the contaminants.

priority, but also testing it, as it exits your faucet, is even more important. Water is transported through water pipes, some which are remnants from days gone by. Pipes were still made from asbestos cement not too long ago. The earth expands and contracts and pipes crack. At end use people are finding harmful chemicals coming out of their faucets like lead, arsenic and asbestos. It all comes

Water Glossary

against a semipermeable membrane. Solids are retained, while water and low molecular weight solutes pass through the membrane.

Nano-filtration. A membrane filtration process used with water such as surface water and fresh groundwater, with the purpose of softening and removing organic and synthetic organic matter. Nanofiltration membranes have pore sizes smaller than that used in micro-filtration and ultra-filtration, but just larger than that in reverse

osmosis.

Pathogen. Bacterium, virus, or other microorganism that can cause disease.

Purification. Similar to filtration, but purified water is cleansed and purified through additional purification processes, typically reverse osmosis, distillation or deionization.

Polishing filter. Polishing filters purify pretreated water, by removing trace levels of any residual contaminants.

down to knowing your water source, how it's transported to your house and what potential contaminants are present in the water.

Have your water tested if unsure. Your local EPA website should have information on where to get your water tested. It is a painless and simple process that will give you the answers, which will ultimately determine how to treat your water.

You can also purchase an inexpensive home test kit to test your water periodically.

The simple solution to all of the above is to educate yourself and to know what you are dealing with.

Let's take a look at some effective water treatment options.

Filtration vs. Purification

There are various water "treatment" systems on the market these days. Some are marketed as "filters" and others as "purifiers". Sometimes it causes confusion when the two terms are used interchangeably, to describe the same process. They all claim to be very effective when it comes to removing dirt and chemical particles from our drinking water. They also guarantee the removal of microbes, both viruses and bacteria. Let's look at how the two systems differ.

• Filters

Filters work on a very simple principle. They allow water to

Make smart decisions

• Determine what kind of contaminants need to be removed.

• Decide which system is appropriate to remove said contaminants.

• Decide which system is appropriate for your water volume needs.

• Decide which system can accommodate your family with the most suitable flow-rate.

• Check the guarantee of the system.

• Consider quality. A cracked filter/ purifier is worthless.

• Only buy the appropriate filter or purifier once you have done your research.

• Check the guarantee of the system.

• Remember that you can engineer your own system. You can add a pre-filter (that filters out larger debris beforehand), UV light, silver dust, etc.

• Are filter cartridges replaceable? Do they require cleaning to unclog holes?

travel through a tiny hole (typically measured in microns) that determines which organisms can pass through. A micron system is very accurate and represents the actual pore size of the filter; 1 micron (1μ) = 0.001 mm.

Some filters use a mesh rating. A wire mesh system indicates how many openings there are in one inch of screen. It can vary from inch to inch and is not very accurate.

Membrane filters use thin sheets with precisely sized pores that prevent objects larger than the pore size from passing through.

Depth filters use thick porous materials such as carbon or ceramic to trap particles as water flows through the material.

These days there are filters that have the ability to remove viruses, bacteria and protozoa. When you see a product with a label that reads as "absolute pore size", it means that the size given is the absolute and definitive size. A product labeled as "mean pore size" means that the size given represents an average, and that some of the pores might be bigger and some might be smaller. The Centers for Disease Control and Prevention recommends buying **absolute pore size filters**, since they give you a definitive value.

Filters can consist of elements made from the following materials:

Problem Solving

When living close to nature, always be alert to suspected surface water contamination.

Evidence of contamination will be visible in vegetation and the sudden decline in animal life in your area.

Dead vegetation and animals (especially birds and frogs) are an indication that toxins are present in the ecosystem.

Granular-activated carbon, micro-porous ceramic, carbon block resin, sand, micro-filtration, ultra-filtration and nano-filtration membranes.

Filters can also use different processes (or a combination of) to remove particles:

Sieving, absorption, adsorption, ion exchange, biological metabolite transfer, cross flow membrane filtration, etc.

When buying a filter:

• Know the filter's size and what it's rated for.

• Know the pathogens and contaminants present in your area. This way you are guaranteed to get rid of the relevant unwanted microbes.

Example: If you are worried about Cholera in your water because of a suspected cholera outbreak, you will need a micro-filter with a particle size rating of 0.2-1.0 microns.

The modern filters are quite advanced and they can filter out almost anything. Filters are simple to operate and require no holding time. They add no unpleasant taste and may even improve the taste and appearance of water.

A known issue with filters is that they are not very effective when it comes to dealing with dissolved minerals or chemicals. If you suspect the presence of such elements, consider purifying your water.

Remember than filters should be cleaned and maintained on a regular basis. As a filter clogs, increasing pressure is required to drive the water through it; this increase in pressure can force micro-particles and organisms through the filter.

Pathogens

- **Protozoa** (Size: 1-15 micron)
  Example:
  Cryptosporidium, Giardia.

- **Bacteria** (Size: 0.1-5 micron)
  Example:
  Campylobacter, Salmonella, Shigella, E. coli, Cholera

- **Viruses** (Size: 0.004-0.1)
  Example:
  Enteric, Hepatitis A, Rotavirus, Norovirus

• Purifiers

Purifiers are similar to filters in that they also use micro-filtration, but on top of that they also utilize additional purifying processes like distillation, reverse osmosis, or deionization. Some also use chemical treatment like iodine or UV light to kill viruses.

Conclusion

As we've stated before:

Buy quality and avoid products from countries that are known for their cheap prices.

Stick to a brand that is known for its quality and that provides you with the following:

a.) A safety guarantee that's approved by government agencies. A typical safety guarantee we see on filters: "Tested to exceed NSF/ ANSI Standard 53 or 58 protocol."

This should also include a list of the contaminants that can be successfully removed.

b.) Clear guidelines on how to use and maintain their product which should include factors like flow rate, how often cartridges have to be replaced, ease of use, etc.

c.) A thorough explanation on how the cleaning mechanism works.

Select a brand with a reputation for integrity and quality. Companies should know when to label a product as a filter and when to label it as a purifier. If not, they are gambling with your health.

Make **cleanliness** of your water a first priority, and **taste**, a second priority. It boggles the mind how people complain about the taste of the water, but they haven't determined what's causing it. Many companies have learned that a charcoal filter does wonders for taste and they are investing heavily in these, but this is not the most important component in the "cleaning" process.

Comparing Treatment Options

When comparing different methods and systems, we have to realize that there is no perfect method out there, since it all comes down to the needs of the consumer. Some systems use electricity, some use gravity and others use solar power. Some will suit well owners, others will not. In the end, know that you do not need to be stuck with one single option, but that you can also combine different systems and methods.

1. Boiling Water

Boiling is very effective at killing microorganisms. It is actually still one of the safest methods out there and when in doubt, boil it!

Common sense dictates that boiling does not remove harmful chemicals. These chemicals are invisible to the naked eye and more often that not, their effects are only felt years later when they have entered and damaged internal tissue and cells. Do not drink water with suspected chemical toxins.

Boiling water is one of the simplest and most effective ways of purifying biologically contaminated water for drinking.

Mechanics. When boiling water, we need to use a container like a pot, can or pan. Any canister made of heavy glass or metal will do. Remember to wash your hands and to remove debris and sediment before you boil the water.

The following applies as a standard rule of thumb:

• 30 min of heating at 70C or 160F kills all pathogens.

• 10 min of boiling at +85C or 185F kills all pathogens.

• The best solution: Boil it at 100C or 212F for one minute.

Keep in mind that the boiling point of water varies according to the atmospheric pressure. This means that water boils at lower temperatures at higher altitude. At elevations above 6,500 feet, boil your water for 3 minutes.

Upside

• Boiling does not impart additional taste or color.

• It is a single step process that

inactivates all enteric pathogens.

• Efficiency is not compromised by contaminants or particles in the water as is the case with halogenation and filtration.

Downside

• Does not improve taste, smell or appearance of water.

• Fuel sources may be scarce, expensive, or unavailable.

• Does not prevent recontamination during storage.

2. Faucet/ Sink/ Desktop/ Pitcher Filters

These filters come in all shapes and sizes. Replacing these filter cartridges has become a big industry and the emphasis is on replacing, which means revenue.

Mechanics. There are different models out there.

- Some use simple gravity filters. As the water flows through different layers of filtration material, the unwanted particles are simply left behind.

- Similar products rely on water pressure to separate contaminants from the clean water.

- The most common household water filters utilize activated carbon granules. An individual charcoal particle has a very large internal surface area. This area is unique in that the surface is filled with nooks and crannies, that attract and trap

unwanted particles through a process called adsorption. This separation action provides clean water for your faucet.

These filters are often used in the city where the water coming out of your faucet has already been filtered and purified. If the water in your area has already been cleaned by the local water works, then chances are that you will not have high amounts of contaminants. Following this logic, it's very possible that these filters simply just make clean water, cleaner.

In a nutshell, these filters are effective at improving the taste of water, but are not considered a solution for someone looking at cleaning contaminated water from a well, river or rooftop. Do research before buying.

When buying any of these filters:

- Check which contaminants they remove from the water (usually lead, mercury and pesticides).

- See if they are certified by an independent water quality association like the WQA Gold Seal.

- Check how often you have to replace the cartridges.

- The predicted flow-rate.

Upside

• Filters are easy to replace.

• Provides basic filtration only.

• Water tastes better.

• Easy to store for emergencies.

Downside

- Predominantly slow when it comes to flow-rate.
- Expensive in the long run.
- Cartridges get easily clogged and have to be changed every 1-3 months.
- Only suitable for a small family of two.

3. Reverse Osmosis Filters

Reverse Osmosis Systems incorporate a 4-5 stage process of filtration and purification and is considered one of the best systems out there. This system is used world-wide by governments and industries to purify water for various purposes.

Mechanics. Pressure is applied to a contaminated solution of water. This pressure causes the water to pass through a membrane to the other side. When the contaminants hit the membrane they are held back and only the clean solution of water is allowed to pass. These systems rely on various pre- and post-filters that are used in conjunction with the reverse osmosis membrane. The filter material has a very small pore size of around 0.0001 micron. This is considered a very effective method of cleaning your drinking water.

Upside

- Effective at removing protozoa, bacteria, viruses and chemicals.

Problem Solving

When your main filtration system has a very small pore size, flow-rate can be a problem. One solution is to install a pre-filter on your line, that will get rid of sediment and larger particles. This will help with keeping your main filter unclogged and to speed up the general filtration process.

If you use well water with heavy sediment, you can install 3 pre-filters, all with different pore size ratings.

First in line should be a large 20 micron filter followed by a 10 micron filter and then a 5 micron filter. This helps with keeping the whole system balanced and reduces the need for constant filter replacements.

- Will reduce a greater percentage of Total Dissolved Solids (TDS), including up to 90% of fluoride. This is one benefit that sets it apart from most other systems.
- Cartridges last for months and do not easily get clogged.
- Suitable for a large family due to decent flow rate.
- Softens hard water which causes scale buildup.
- Improves taste.
- Can be easily combined with

other systems (UV light, polishing filter) to remove or kill all pathogenic waterborne microbes.

- Reverse osmosis also removes radioactive plutonium or strontium in drinking water. If you live near a nuclear power plant, this is the system to use to guarantee clean water.

Downside

- It's not cheap.
- The system wastes water.
- Removes wanted minerals from water.
- This system needs electricity.

4. Reservoirs & Removable Gravity-Fed Filters

These systems are becoming more and more popular by the day. The reservoirs are made from high grade stainless steel and come in a range of sizes. The filters are made from different media types that consist of millions of little micro-pores.

Different filter element options are available and the filters are easy to clean.

Mechanics. Several methodologies are utilized by these filters.

First, the contaminated water is manually poured on top into a reservoir, from where it travels through a system of gravity-fed filters. You can use a basic set-up of one filter, or you can use two or four filter combinations to remove specific chemicals (fluoride) from your water.

Contaminants are filtered, adsorbed and absorbed. Heavy metals ions (mineral molecules) are extracted through an Ion exchange process where they are essentially electrically bonded to the media.

Finally, the water is collected in the lower reservoir where it can be accessed via a faucet.

Upside

- No electricity needed.
- Portable system and easy to keep hygienically clean.
- Very decent flow-rate. Depending on filter setup, 3.5-7 gallons per hour.
- Filters are removable and they last fairly long (3000 gallons per filter).
- Effective at removing heavy metals, protozoa, bacteria, viruses (most) and chemicals like chlorine and volatile organic compounds (VOCs).
- You can combine different kinds of filters with these systems.
- They are very handy in that the containers come in different sizes and the gravity-fed filters are purpose built to cater for your filtration needs.
- It is a very visible process that works on simple, yet efficient, technology.
- Adds no unpleasant taste and often improves taste and appearance of water.
- This system brings you clos-

er to your water due to the fact that you can replace filters yourself and that you can decide which filters are necessary at any given period.

• Can be easily combined with other systems (UV light, chemical disinfectants) to remove or kill all pathogenic waterborne microbes.

Downside

• You have to manually refill the reservoir.

• Eventually filters clogs from suspended particulate matter and may require some maintenance.

• Fairly expensive.

5. Ceramic Multi Candle Filter

A filter option that has to be discussed is the multi candle replaceable filters. These are very reliable filters and can be used to service the whole household.

Mechanics. Up to 6 ceramic filters are connected to a filter holder module and placed inside a housing. The filter system is designed to be fitted to the main municipal water inlet to the home, to supply large volumes of clean water. Ceramic water filters work by simply allowing the water to filter through millions of tiny pores in the water cartridge surface. This process catches the particles that are too large to pass through, typically organic and inorganic compounds, and they subsequently

Don't underestimate the toxicity of chemicals. Most chemicals are carcinogenic and have the potential to cause cancer later on.

gather on the filter surface. As a second line of defense, the inner workings of the ceramic consists of an intricate maze with a complicated structure. This is where even smaller particles, that passed through the cartridge surface, are trapped. Certain ceramic filters also incorporate a compound made of colloidal silver into the ceramic, and this compound keeps the ceramic surface clean because it repels bacterial growth.

Upside

• Removes up to 99% of pathogenic bacteria including salmonella, cholera and E. Coli, as well as cysts like cryptosporidium and giardia, sediment, and various organic chemicals.

• High flow rate. Depending on brand, these filters offer superior flow rate of up to 520 gallons (2000 liters) per hour (8 gal per minute) at 45 PSI (3 bars).

• Filters come with a 0.9 microns absolute filtration rating with 99.99% efficiency.

• Considered one of the most efficient systems for cysts removal compared to any available alternative technologies such

Pathogen Distribution

Viruses spread primarily through animal and human fecal matter. They can survive for a long time, but can only reproduce once inside a host. Typical viruses found in water: Norovirus, Rotovirus and Hepatitis A.

Bacteria are found where nutrients and temperatures allow. There are three types of indicator bacteria to test for:

• **Total Coliform.** Commonly found in the environment and harmless if found on its own. Having this bacteria indicates that there is a gateway for bacteria to enter and the problem must be resolved by finding the source.

• **Fecal Coliform.** Commonly found in feces of animals and people. Indicates that fecal contamination is present and that the drinking water is at risk.

• **E.coli.** Most are harmless and present in the fecal matter of humans and animals. Some strains will cause serious illness. If found in drinking water, it means that there is a risk of harmful germs present. It indicates fecal contamination.

Protozoa are observed in freshwater and in marine environments. They can remain dormant as cysts in surface water for long periods of time. They are also found in animal and human waste.

as chlorine, ozone, UV, reverse osmosis, etc.

• Can provide whole house filtration where drinking water is desired.

• Suitable for homes drawing water from lakes, streams or micro-biologically contaminated wells.

• Small footprint for parallel installation for large volume safe drinking water.

• Can be easily combined with other systems (UV light, gravity filter, chemical disinfectants) to remove or kill all pathogenic waterborne microbes.

• Adds no unpleasant taste and often improves taste and appearance of water.

Downside

• Requires electricity for flow of water.

• You have to manually replace the filters.

• Eventually filters clogs from suspended particulate matter and may require some maintenance.

• Fairly expensive.

6. Carbon filters

Carbon filters are very popular filters and are often seen where municipal water is used. They can be used as a stand-alone filter or as a component in a reverse osmosis system. They are very effective when it comes to removing odors and bad taste from water. We distinguish two types:

Granulated activated carbon filters and Carbon block filters.

Mechanics. As mentioned before, an individual charcoal particle has a very large internal surface area. This area is unique in that the surface is filled with nooks and crannies, that attract and trap unwanted particles through a process called adsorption. Carbon filters are effective at removing the contaminants that bond to carbon. This separation action provides you with clean water where you need it. Some of the more advanced, modern carbon block filters also utilize a combination of nano-mesh technology (and sub-micron filtration) combined with the chemical adsorption process. If you are using a carbon filter in combination with a sediment filter, note that the sediment filter should be used first to get rid of the heavier particles that would otherwise clog up the carbon filter. Once the heavier particles are removed, the purer and cleaner water can move into the carbon filter where the remaining unwanted compounds will bond with the carbon and be removed as well.

Upside

• Modern, advanced carbon block filters remove most pathogens such as bacteria, viruses and parasites like Giardia and Cryptosporidium. They function not just as a filter, but also as a purifier.

• Removes chemicals like chlorine, pesticides, herbicides and heavy metals such as lead, copper, arsenic and mercury.

• Removes volatile organic compounds (VOC's).

• Very efficient at removing bad tastes and odors.

• Does not remove the healthy minerals found in water.

• An affordable option.

Downside

• Does not remove dissolved solids or inorganic compounds.

• Does not remove fluoride.

• Requires electricity.

7. Distillation Systems

Distillation systems are very popular for they can create potable water from almost any source. People use distilled water for drinking and also for maintenance of machinery.

Mechanics. First the water is heated which turns it into water vapor.

Then, as the vapor condenses, it turns back into a liquid.

Finally, it gets collected in a reservoir or collection vessel as distilled water.

This process allows only the vapor to escape, and the contaminants to remain behind.

Upside

• Distillation is a method that is effective at removing proto-

Water Sanitation

Viruses: E.g. enterovirus, hepatitis A, Norovirus, Rotavirus

Can cause the following:
Gastrointestinal illness (for example, diarrhea, vomiting, cramps), hepatitis, meningitis.

Sources of viruses in drinking water are:
Human and animal fecal waste.

Methods that may remove some or all of viruses from drinking water are:

• **Boiling.** Rolling boil for 3 minute minimum has a very high effectiveness in killing viruses;

• **Standard Filtration** is not effective in removing viruses. Modern Nanofiltration techniques can remove some viruses successfully.

• **Chemical disinfection with iodine** or chlorine has a high effectiveness in killing viruses;

• **Chemical disinfection with chlorine dioxide** has a high effectiveness in killing viruses;

• **Disinfection** has a high effectiveness in killing viruses when used with iodine, chlorine, or chlorine dioxide.

zoa, bacteria, viruses and most chemical contaminants.

• It is also effective at removing salt from saltwater.

•It removes the "hardness" of hard water.

Downside

• Some statistics consider distilled water to be too clean and void of essential minerals and ions. There are no definitive answers surrounding this issue.

• The process of distilling water with a DIY system is a slow one.

• The yield is considered minimal.

• They do require electricity which might be an issue in an emergency.

Buying a commercially available unit is money well spent.

See Chapter 12 for a complete explanation of how homemade distillation units are made.

8. Ultraviolet Treatment Systems

Another very simple method to purify your water is to use a short-wave ultraviolet light. Water flows in the one end of the cylinder, is treated with Ultraviolet rays, and flows out the other end.

The wavelength range of short-wave UV is between 2000-3000 Å and this is considered the most effective range for deactivating harmful pathogens. It does not get rid of the microorganisms, it just renders them harmless.

Short wave UV has to be produced through electricity, since it does not naturally occur in the environment around us. These UV units are very convenient and are usually mounted vertically against a wall.

Mechanics. UV Water Purification systems use special lamps that emit UV light that can disrupt the DNA of micro-organisms (pathogens). Specific wave lengths of light have the ability to affect specific organisms.

When organisms in clear water are exposed to UV light, their genetic code comes under attack and this eliminates the microorganism's ability to function and reproduce. A pathogen that cannot replicate, also cannot infect other organisms. This process inactivates a large percentage (up to 99%) of harmful microorganisms without adding any chemicals to the water.

Upside

• An ultraviolet light is very effective at deactivating all waterborne pathogens; protozoa, bacteria and viruses.

• Very simple installation and low maintenance. Just change the UV light bulb annually.

• Great addition to any existing filtration system. Extra doses of UV can be used for added assurance and with no side effects.

• Very reliable system that works 24/7.

• Adds no unpleasant taste.

• Does not waste any water.

• Can be easily combined with other systems (reverse osmosis, gravity filter, chemical disinfectants) to remove or kill all pathogenic waterborne microbes.

Downside

• It requires electricity, though not much.

• It only works with clear water.

• UV light degrades plastics and PVC. It's best to use non-PVC piping immediately before and after the UV system. Copper is best.

• It definitely has no effect on chemicals and toxins in your water supply.

Make sure that the water has no floating particles, since organisms can hide behind these. Turbid water will render the system useless. It is best to first use a pre-filter, to get rid of large particles, after which the water can be exposed to the ultraviolet light. A 5 micron pre-filter will do the job.

Some things to look for in a UV light.

- The length of the lamp. The longer the lamp, the longer the organisms are exposed to the UV waves.

- How often does one need to change the bulb inside?

- Does it have a protective casing and wall mount?

- Does it allow for accessories

Water Sanitation

Protozoa: E.g. Cryptosporidium & Giardia

Can cause the following: Gastrointestinal illness like diarrhea, vomiting, and cramps.

Sources of Protozoa in water: Human and animal fecal waste.

Methods that may remove some or all of Protozoa from drinking water are:

• **Boiling.** Rolling boil for 3 minutes is very effective.

• **Filtration** has a high effectiveness in removing Protozoa when using an absolute, less than or equal to 1 micron filter (NSF Standard 53 or 58 rated "cyst reduction / removal" filter).

• **Chemical disinfection with iodine** or chlorine has no effect on Crypto. It has a low to moderate effectiveness against Giardia. Chlorine dioxide has a low to moderate effectiveness in killing Cryptosporidium and a high effectiveness in killing Giardia.

• **Combination filtration and disinfection** has a very high effectiveness in removing and killing Protozoa when used with chlorine dioxide and an absolute, less than or equal to 1 micron filter (NSF Standard 53 or 58 rated "cyst reduction / removal" filter).

and control mechanisms like valves, monitors and alarms?

9. Ozone Purification

The use of ozone as a form of water purification has been around for more than a century. These days we find complete domestic ozone water treatment systems where people are concerned about the quality of their well or rain water. Ozone is effective as both a disinfectant and an oxidant and has become one of the most effective water treatment options available.

Mechanics. A typical ozone system has a UV ozone generator that creates tiny bubbles saturated with ozone. It is pumped into your water tank at a constant rate and circulates the contents of the tank. Ozone ($O3$) is a gas that consists of typical oxygen ($O2$) with one extra oxygen atom that's weakly attached. As the ozone aerates the water tank, the one extra oxygen atom attaches to any substance that can be oxidized. Once this (3rd) atom has been given up, the by-product is pure oxygen.

Upside

• Kills bacteria, viruses, spores and fungus.

• It is considered a replacement for chlorine and since it's not a chemical it leaves no residue or harmful by-products behind.

• It typically improves the odor and color of your water.

- It can oxidize metals like iron, hydrogen sulfide, manganese, and inactivates pesticides and organic material.
- It prevents the buildup of residue deposits in pipes.
- Can be easily combined with polishing filters to further remove unwanted chemical contaminants.

Downside

- Ozone will not remove nitrates, sulfates, fluoride, sodium or chlorides.
- Ozone does not last long once dissolved in water and must be pumped constantly into the water.
- These systems do require electricity (minimal).
- They are not cheap.

10. Water Softeners

We find different forms of minerals in our groundwater. These minerals are dissolved in the water, which means a standard filter will not be able to remove them. Typical symptoms of hard water is a residual buildup of scale on household appliances and also on the inside of pipes. It also prevents soap from lathering and just leaves it slimy and sticky.

Mechanics. A water softening device uses a process called "iron exchange" to remove minerals from water.

The process takes place within a tank full of negatively charged polystyrene beads. Due to the negative charge, the beads bond to the positively charged sodium ions. As the water passes past the beads, the sodium ions (+) are replaced with calcium and magnesium ions (-).

A typical water softening device will remove calcium and magnesium ions from your water and it will replace them with more desirable ions like sodium. The calcium and magnesium ions are the particles that cause the water to be "hard".

Upside

- Some advanced systems also remove heavy metals, nitrates, arsenic, chromium, selenium, sulfate, and even radioactivity.
- Water treated with a water softened system tend to be softer on appliances, laundry, hair and skin.

Downside

- Water softeners do not remove any bacteria, protozoa or viruses.
- These systems do require electricity (minimal).
- They are not cheap.

11. Land-Based Marine Filters

If you live close to the ocean and you are concerned about water availability, then you might look into installing a desalination system. They are often found on sailboats and yachts and are very effective

Water Sanitation

Bacteria: E.g. Campylobacter, Salmonella, Shigella, E. Coli

Can cause: Gastrointestinal illness like diarrhea, vomiting, and cramps.

Sources of bacteria in drinking water are:

Human and animal fecal waste.

Methods that may remove some or all of bacteria from drinking water are:

• **Boiling.** Rolling boil for 3 minute has a very high effectiveness in killing bacteria;

• **Filtration** has a moderate effectiveness in removing bacteria when using an absolute less than or equal to 0.3 micron filter;

• **Chemical disinfection with iodine** or chlorine has a high effectiveness in killing bacteria;

• **Chemical disinfection with chlorine** dioxide has a high effectiveness in killing bacteria;

• **Combination filtration and disinfection** has a very high effectiveness in removing and killing bacteria when used with iodine, chlorine, or chlorine dioxide and an absolute less than or equal to 0.3 micron filter (NSF Standard 53 or 58 rated "cyst reduction / removal" filter).

at making seawater potable for human consumption.

These days you can install a complete setup for your house or buy a portable unit. The small, portable units are hand pumped and are for emergencies only.

Mechanics. A desalination system sucks in the seawater with a pump, and then sends it through a range of pre-filters to get rid of larger sediment.

Next, the water flows through a reverse osmosis chamber that is specifically designed to remove the dissolved salt particles. This is done through high pressure filtering which sends the contaminated water through a very fine membrane at high pressure.

The residual particles are left behind on the membrane and the clean water is flushed out into a collection chamber.

Upside

• Provides safe water.

• Very reliable and membrane filters last for a long time.

• Can be used for freshwater or saltwater.

• Small units available.

Downside

• Expensive and requires contractor installation.

• The output is very small. About 15% of original water volume.

12. Solar Disinfection

In an emergency situation, water can be disinfected with sun-light. Solar disinfection (SODIS) has been proven to inactivate the waterborne microbial species (viruses, bacteria, and protozoa) that cause diarrheal diseases.

Mechanics. Users of SODIS fill 0.3-2.0 liter plastic PET soda bottles with low-turbidity water, shake them to oxygenate, and place the bottles on a roof, rack or reflective surface (such as aluminum foil) for 6 hours (if sunny) or 2 days (if cloudy).

The combined effect of thermal heating of solar light and UV radiation causes DNA damage and thermal inactivation. These germicidal properties can inactivate disease-causing organisms.

Upside

• Proven reduction of viruses, bacteria, and protozoa in contaminated water.

• Proven reduction of diarrheal disease incidence.

• Simplicity of use and acceptability.

• No cost if using recycled plastic bottles.

• Minimal change in taste of the water.

• Recontamination is low because water is served and stored in the small narrow necked bottles.

Downside

• Need to pretreat water of higher turbidity with straining or filtration.

• Limited volume of water that can be treated all at once.

• Length of time required to treat water.

• Large supply of clean, suitable plastic bottles required.

There are a few ways that the efficiency of the system can be enhanced:

• Paint the surface underneath your bottles black to enhance solar heating.

• Place your bottles (filled with water) on a reflective surface to boost the amount of sunlight absorbed.

• You can increase the initial levels of dissolved oxygen by shaking the bottle vigorously for 30 s before sealing.

• Filter the water before you start the process. Clear water will definitely provide better results.

• Glass can be considered, but not all types of glass allow for the transmission of UV rays. Plastic bottles have the potential to leach compounds into water after exposure to strong sunlight conditions. Take this into consideration when deciding how long and under what conditions you want to rely on this method.

Conclusion

When the time comes to make a decision about which water treatment system or method is best, you will have to consider the following:

- How many people will require

water.
- The quality of the water to be treated.
- The availability of energy or fuel.
- The available space to implement the treatment.
- The importance of taste.
- Flow rate.

No method is best. Boiling is by far the best option when worried about pathogens. Consider that filters sometimes do miss some of the viruses and that halogens (Chemical disinfectants) do not deactivate Cryptosporidium. This leads us to the conclusion that in most situations a 2- or 3-step process is preferred.

A typical solution (power source is needed) will look like this:

Step one. Look at your water quality and based on the evidence, make a decision as to what needs to be removed. If you are worried about chemicals like fluoride, chlorine or lead, then make sure that your main treatment method will take care of these.

Alternatively, if you are using well water and you are concerned about microbes, make sure that you select the appropriate treatment method that guarantees elimination of bacteria, protozoa and viruses.

Step two. Pretreat your water to get rid of contaminants at an early stage in the feed water.

This means that you have to get rid of contaminants (like sediment) that may later, down the line, affect purification equipment.

UV lights and reverse osmosis systems should not be used if your water is contaminated with sediment.

Pretreatment examples: sediment filters, carbon filters, and water softeners.

Step three. Use your main purification method.

Gravity-fed filters and ceramic multi candles are very effective.

A Reverse Osmosis system removes 90 to 99% of all the contaminants found in water and is often used as the main treatment method in homes served by well water. It effectively removes a broad range of contaminants. Don't forget to use a pressure tank for increased pressure in your plumbing system.

Step four. A polishing filter and/ or a UV light is a good option to finalize the process. The polishing filter acts as the last before water exits your faucet and it should have a small pore size that should filter out the absolute smallest of contaminants (dissolved chemicals).

Concerning filters, The Centers for Disease Control makes the following recommendations:

Protozoa

Micro-filtration has a very high effectiveness in removing protozoa. It has no effectiveness in removing bacteria, viruses or chemicals.

Examples	Required Product Type	Required Certification
• Cryptosporidium • Giardia	Micro-filtration Filter. Depending on brand, pore sizes range from: 0.1-5 micron	Tested to exceed NSF/ ANSI Standard 53 or 58 protocol.

Bacteria

Ultra-filtration has a very high effectiveness in removing protozoa and bacteria. It has a low effectiveness in removing chemicals and viruses.

Examples	Required Product Type	Required Certification
• E. Coli, • Salmonella • Cholera	Ultra-filtration Filter. Depending on brand, pore sizes range from: 0.01-0.1 micron	Tested to exceed NSF/ ANSI Standard 53 or 58 protocol.

Viruses

Nano-filtration has a very high effectiveness in removing protozoa, bacteria and some viruses. It has a moderate effectiveness in removing chemicals.

Examples	Required Product Type	Required Certification
• Rotavirus, • Norovirus, • Enteris, • Hepatitis A	Nano-filtration Filter. Depending on brand, pore sizes range from: 0.001-0.01 micron	Tested to exceed NSF/ ANSI Standard 53 or 58 protocol.

Disinfecting Water With Chemicals

We can disinfect water through various chemical processes which can deactivate or kill the unwanted pathogenic microorganisms. Examples of chemical disinfectants are found in a group of elements called Halogens, of which the most common are iodine and chlorine. These chemicals are specifically used in the treatment of water for safe drinking and they come in tablet and liquid form.

In this chapter we will focus on the following chemical disinfectants available:

• Iodine.

• Unscented chlorine bleach.

• Granular calcium hypochlorite.

• Water disinfection tablets.

When using these chemicals, you have to pay close attention to the following:

• Follow the instructions provided by the manufacturer of the disinfectant.

• Pay special attention to the percentages. When choosing household bleach or iodine, make sure that you know the percentages of the active ingredients which will determine the ratio for mixing.

• Clear water and murky, brown water differ in treatment process. Disinfection does not work as well when water is cloudy or colored. It's best to filter the water before you start the disinfection process.

• Pay special attention to the temperature. Specific temperatures are required for these chemical disinfectants to be effective.

The Chemical Treatment Of Water

In an emergency situation, we should pay special attention to the quality of our drinking water. Floods, hurricanes and earthquakes are known to disrupt water supply lines and in these situations it's best to stick to bottled, boiled or disinfected water. Bottled and boiled water is by far the best option and disinfecting your water with chemicals should be a last resort.

Water Disinfection

Take note. Chemicals, are toxic in large doses and can still have an adverse affect on your health when taken in small doses, no matter which authority tells you it's safe. It is this writer's opinion that chemicals should only be used as an absolute last resort, when boiling or filtration is not an option; when you are faced with a life or death situation.

Iodine

Iodine is a strong chemical that can penetrated the cell walls of microorganisms. Iodine can kill many of the most common pathogens in natural fresh water sources, but it provides no protection against Cryptosporidium. For iodine to be effective, we have to pay special attention to the following:

1. This is a strong chemical that is light sensitive and must be stored in a dark bottle.

2. Iodine works best for water that are over 66 F (21 C). In colder water the iodine will take longer to activate and it will also be less effective.

3. Note that some people are allergic to iodine. Pregnant women, women over 50 or people with thyroid problems should also consult their doctor before ingesting water with iodine.

4. Iodine should not be used to disinfect water over long periods of time as prolonged use can cause thyroid problems.

When talking about iodine, we often see the word tincture. Tincture defined: a medicine made by dissolving a drug in alcohol: a bottle containing tincture of iodine. **Iodine comes in tincture, tablet and crystal forms.**

When using iodine tablets or crystals, you will have to follow the instructions provided by the manufacturer.

For common household iodine (or "tincture of iodine")

you can follow the following steps:

1. Locate your iodine in your medicine cabinet or first aid kit.

2. Prepare a container that is clean and that has been disinfected. A one liter or quarter gallon container in perfect.

3. Fill the container with the contaminated water. Make sure that the water is settled and clear. You can filter it beforehand with a cotton cloth or coffee filter.

4. Add 5 drops of 2% tincture of iodine to each quart or liter of water that you are disinfecting. If the water is cloudy or colored, add twice the amount (10 drops) of iodine.

5. Stir and let the water stand for at least 30 minutes before use.

Some additional information:

• Whenever possible use warm water (66 F/ 21 C) and let it stand a minimum of 20 minutes after mixing and before drinking.

• When using cold water around 40-59F (5 - 15C) you can increase the waiting time after mixing to 40 minutes.

Chlorine Bleach

If you don't have safe bottled water and if boiling is not possible, you can make small quantities of filtered and settled water safer to drink by using a chemical disinfectant such as unscented household chlorine bleach.

According to the Centers for Disease Control and Prevention (CDC), chlorinating water will kill most micro-organisms like bacteria and viruses. Unfortunately it **provides low protection against protozoa.** Some rules for purifying water with chlorine bleach:

• Do NOT use scented bleaches, color-safe bleaches, or bleaches with "added cleaners" as these will contaminate your water.

• Check the expiration date as the effectiveness of chlorine bleach is just six months.

• Do NOT use pool chlorine. It's a much stronger constitute than laundry bleach!

• The disinfection action of bleach depends as much on the waiting time after mixing as to the amount used. The longer the water is left to stand after adding bleach, the more effective the disinfection process will be.

Disinfectants can kill most harmful or disease-causing viruses and bacteria, but are not as effective in controlling more resistant organisms, such as the parasites Cryptosporidium and Giardia. (Chlorine dioxide tablets can be effective against Cryptosporidium if the manufacturer's instructions are followed correctly.)

To disinfect water with unscented household liquid chlorine bleach you will first have to assess the quality of the water. If the water is cloudy and colored you will have to filter it through a clean cloth, paper towel, or coffee filter OR allow it to settle. Be patient, for clear water allows for a faster and more efficient disinfection process. Once the water has settled, you can draw off the clear water to be used for disinfecting.

Consult the table provided and follow these steps:

1. Follow the instructions for disinfecting drinking water that are written on the label of the bleach product container.

2. If the necessary instructions are not given, check the "Active Ingredient" part of the label to find the sodium hypochlorite percentage, and use the information in the table provided as a guide. Typically, unscented household liquid chlorine bleach will be 8.25% sodium hypochlorite, though concentrations can differ.

3. Using the table provided at the bottom of the page, add the appropriate amount of bleach using a medicine dropper, teaspoon, or metric measure (milliliters).

4. Stir the mixture well.

5. Let it stand for at least 30 minutes before you use it.

6. Store the disinfected water in clean, sanitized containers with tight covers.

If you don't have liquid bleach, consider the disinfection method described on the next page.

Disinfect water using household bleach

Volume of Container	Concentration Percentage of Sodium Hypochlorite present in bleach			
	1% concentration	4-6% concentration	8.25% concentration	unknown concentration
1 Quart/ 1 Liter	10 drops/ 0.5 ml/ ⅛ teaspoon	2 drops/ 0.1 ml	2 drops	10 drops/ 0.5 ml/ ⅛ teaspoon
1 Gallon/ 3.8 Liter	40 drops/ 2.5 ml/ ½ teaspoon	8 drops/ 0.5 ml	6 drops/ 0.5 ml	40 drops/ 2.5 ml/ ½ teaspoon
5 Gallons/ 18.9 Liter	200 drops/ 12.5 ml/ 2½ teaspoons	40 drops/ 2.5 ml/ ½ teaspoon	30 drops/ 2 ml/ $1/_3$ teaspoon	200 drops/ 12.5 ml/ 2½ teaspoons

Granular Calcium Hypochlorite

Water can also be disinfected with Granular Calcium Hypochlorite. You can buy it online under the name Shock Chlorination. Make sure that the percentage of Calcium Hypochlorite to inert ingredients is 68% or higher.

Many people prefer not to use bleach. Some of the reasons include:

a.) It takes up more storage space.

b.) It only has a shelf life of 6 months.

c.) It's hard to get in the correct concentration.

If you prefer to use Calcium Hypochlorite, then pay attention to the following steps:

1. You first have to prepare the chlorine solution that you will use to disinfect your water. For your safety, do it in a ventilated area and wear eye protection. Gather clean, sanitized containers and prepare a measuring aid.

2. Add one heaping teaspoon (approximately ¼ ounce or 7 grams) of high-test granular calcium hypochlorite to 2 gallons (7.5 L) of water and stir until the particles have dissolved. The mixture will produce a chlorine solution of approximately 500 milligrams per liter. This is your chlorine solution that you will use to treat the contaminated water.

3. To disinfect the contaminated water, add one part of the chlorine solution to each 100 parts of water you are treating. Let's do the math:

This is a ratio of 1:100.

This gives us 10 ml added to 1 liter of water, or ½ liter to 50 liters of water.

This is about the same as adding 1 pint (16 ounces) of the chlorine solution to 12.5 gallons of water.

4. Let the mixture sit for at least 40 minutes.

If the chlorine taste is too strong, pour the water from one clean container to another and let it stand for a few hours before use.

CAUTION: HTH is a very powerful oxidant. Follow the instructions on the label for safe handling and storage of this chemical. Make sure that you label the storage container as DANGEROUS and POISON. You do not want children to come into contact with it. Store the granules dry for long-term storage. When buying calcium hypochlorite, make sure that it is the plain product and that it does NOT contain any water clarifiers or anti-algae agents.

Disinfection Tablets

You can disinfect water with light-weight tablets that contain chlorine, iodine, chlorine dioxide, or other disinfecting agents. These tablets (or crystals, drops) are available online or at pharmacies and sporting goods stores. Follow the instructions on the product label as each product may have a different strength. Pay attention to the clarity of the water, since chemical disinfectants are more effective when used with clear water. If the water is cloudy and colored you will have to filter it through a clean cloth, paper towel, or coffee filter OR allow it to settle. Once the water has settled, you can draw off the clear water. This is the water that should be used for disinfecting. After treating the water, make sure not to wait too long before consuming it. The water can become active with pathogens after a period of time (30-40 hours) and it's advisable to drink the treated water within 24 hours.

● *Iodine based tablets*

Although not a perfect solution, iodine tablets can come in pretty handy out in the field when you need a light-weight solution to take with. Usually these tablets come with an additional Vitamin C (ascorbic acid) tablet to improve the taste of the iodine disinfected water. Add the Vitamin C only after the iodine has done its job of disinfecting the water. Follow the instructions of the manufacturer and pay special attention to the following:

- **Warning.** Not for persons with iodine allergies or restrictions like persons with thyroid prob-

lems, are on lithium, are allergic to shellfish (they may also be allergic to iodine), women over fifty and pregnant women should consult their physician prior to using iodine for purification.

- **Effectiveness.** Iodine kills bacteria and viruses before they mutate.

- **Treatment Time.** The waiting time prescribed is 30 minutes.

- **The shelf life.** The guaranteed shelf life is usually 4 years for an unopened bottle. Around one year for an opened container with exposure to air.

- **Storage instructions.** Product should be stored in a cool, dry place.

● *Iodine based crystals*

Iodine in crystal form is very easy to use and is a handy option to have. It's advisable to heat the water slightly before you add the crystals. Warm water aids in dissolving the crystals and thus increases its efficiency.

Follow the instructions of the manufacturer and pay special attention to the following:

- **Warning.** Keep away from children. Non-dissolved crystals can be deadly if consumed. Not for persons with iodine allergies or restrictions like persons with thyroid problems, are on lithium, are allergic to shellfish (they may also be allergic to iodine), women over fifty and pregnant women should consult their physician prior to using

Disinfecting Water With Chemicals

iodine for purification.

- Effectiveness. Iodine kills bacteria and viruses before they mutate.

- Treatment Time. The waiting time prescribed is usually 20-30 minutes. Warmer temperatures will increase the effectiveness of the crystals.

- Shelf life. Indefinite shelf life when bottle is kept tightly capped.

- Storage instructions. They should be properly sealed to avoid exposure to air.

- Extra. Limits radiation intake in case of a nuclear disaster.

• *Chlorine dioxide based tablets (or drops)*

This is a very popular option that consists of a concentrated oxidant that makes it hard for protozoa, bacteria and viruses to survive. This is considered more powerful than standard solutions (e.g. iodine and chlorine) as it removes colorations, odors and also unpleasant taste from the treated water.

- Warning. Keep away from children. Volatile and sensitive to sunlight: do not expose tablets to air, and use generated solutions rapidly.

- Effectiveness. Effective against viruses, bacteria, giardia and cryptosporidium. It's important to note that it will take approximately four hours to treat the water for Cryptosporidium and Giardia, so plan ahead!

- Treatment Time. The waiting time prescribed is 30 minutes to 4 hours.

- Shelf life. It is guaranteed 4 years, but can be much longer if sealed.

- Storage instructions. Usually each tablet comes sealed in its own compartment.

- Extra. No nasty taste or odors.

• *Chlorine based tablets*

Sodium dichloroisocyanurate or Troclosene Sodium (also shortened as NaDCC), is a form of chlorine used for disinfection. They are effervescent tablets which kill micro- organisms in water to prevent cholera, typhoid, dysentery and other water borne diseases. It is approved by the EPA for long term drinking water treatment.

- Warning. Chlorine should be used for persons with iodine allergies.

- Effectiveness. It is used for killing bacteria, cysts, algae, fungi, viruses and protozoa.

- Treatment Time. 30 Minutes.

- Shelf life. Guaranteed for 5 years. If opened they should be discarded after 3 months.

- Storage instructions. Usually each tablet comes sealed in its own compartment which is designed to keep out UV light and moisture.

- Extra. These capsules are effervescent, meaning they self-dissolve.

Designing Your Own Filtration System

Years ago, having a traditional homemade filtration system was considered a normal component of a healthy homestead and people relied on it to provide clean drinking water. It's safe to assume that the environment was in a better state back then and that the biggest concern was probably dealing with water-borne pathogens that caused diarrhea.

These days we have volatile compounds in our homes and infrastructures that can create all kinds of problems. Dissolved chemicals are very hard to remove from your water and therefore I recommend that a system based on the traditional model only be used when you are sure that your water source has not been contaminated with chemicals or radioactive material. You can build a simple gravity filter that relies on gravity and layers of natural filtering material. You do not need electricity and you do not need to buy any commercial filters. Note that the thicker the layers of filtering material, the longer it will take for the water to pass through. In theory this also means the cleaner the water will be. You can experiment with different layers of filtering material: fine sand, coarse sand, fine gravel, coarse gravel, activated charcoal granules and even clay.

You also have the option of assembling a specialized gravity filtration system.

These filters remove almost everything from your water and do not require electricity. The only downside is that they are expensive and have to be replaced.

How To Design And Build A Filtration System

During a rain event, the water falls to the earth and with the aid of gravity, it is filtered through layers of sand, clay, gravel and rock. The result is clean groundwater fit for consumption. Applying the same logic, we can mimic the earth's perfect filtration system by creating layers of filtering material that removes contaminants as the water passes through. This is all possible with the aid of gravity.

A Homemade Filtration System

If you find yourself in an emergency situation, where water and electricity are no longer readily available, then the following method of water filtration might come in very handy. This is obviously not a preferred method for water treatment, but when you run out of options, this application might just save your life.

A traditional filtration system consists of a large container, made of natural material, filled with different layers of filter media:

Fine sand, coarse sand, fine gravel, coarse gravel, activated charcoal granules and even clay. The media all differ in particle size and application. They have been proven to clear water of turbidity, certain pathogens and iron. The larger gravel-like pieces will filter out the thicker sediment and debris. The smaller, compacted sand-like particles will filter out the microscopic contaminants.

Activated charcoal has microscopic pores that trap contaminants. It also attracts negative ions to its surface and thus removes them from the flowing water.

Besides plastic, glass and steel, you can also experiment with clay containers. In water-starved regions of the world, porous clay pots are constructed by mixing and pressing indigenous clay with sawdust, which leaves behind a porous structure. The inside is painted with silver particles and it is allowed to seep into the pore structure. Water simply filters through and is purified as it passes through the tine pores and over the silver.

First let's look at a modern, yet basic, version of this filtering system. This method is based off a traditional method used in the early 1900's by land owners to clean their drinking water. Important to note that you should be familiar with the quality of your water source. This means that if your water comes from a well, you should have it tested before and after filtration. This will give you a clear picture of what kind of contaminants are present and how effective your filtration system is.

CAUTION: Once filtered you should still boil your water. Boiling is still the best method to get rid of pathogens.

How To

Making a filtration system is very simple. Just keep the concept of filtering in mind. Your water must flow through various layers that will catch particles and contaminants. You have the freedom to experiment with different media layers made up of different filtering material.

Traditionally, sand, gravel and activated charcoal are used. You can also use a combination of fine sand and a layer of coarse sand. The same goes for the gravel. Make sure that you wash and rinse the sand, gravel and charcoal before you use it. Separate the media and swish each around in a bucket filled with clean water. Repeat till all floating particles have been removed.

In the end, your water must pass through all the layers of filtration and be collected in a collection vessel. Make sure it's safe to drink by testing a number of samples. If the tests still indicate the presence of pathogens, then you should boil the water for at least three minutes. If the tests indicate the presence of dissolved chemicals, discard the water and look at

Material needed for a Homemade Filtration System

• 3 x large food grade (BPA free) plastic buckets with lids. The bigger the better. You can still get 5 gallons/19 liters from stores like bakeries. Only use plastic containers with the following numbers and letters:

1-PETE, 2-HDPE, 3-LDPE, 5-PP.

• Large bags of fine gravel and coarse gravel. Enough to fill two containers.

• Large bags of fine sand and coarse sand. Pool filter sand works well.

• Activated charcoal. You can buy activated charcoal from pet stores that sell aquariums.

• 1 x Spigot

• Large drill bit or hole saw.

• Threaded Plumber's fittings with O-rings.

• Fine screen material to keep the material from flowing into the next bucket.

another treatment option. Let's look at the basic setup.

• **Step 1. Planning.** Prepare the material that you will need. Place the three containers on top of one another.

Take a marker and mark where you want to drill the holes.

• **Step 2.** Drill the holes. Drill holes in the bottoms of buckets A and B. The plumber's fittings will connect the buckets through these holes and should fit snugly. Do not drill a hole in the bottom of bucket C.

You should also drill a hole in both the lids of buckets B and C. Make sure they line up nicely with the holes of the buckets sitting on top of each. Bucket A's lid does not need a

hole, except if you wish for it to serve as an inlet for an exterior water source.

• **Step 3.** The hole in bucket A connects to the hole in the lid of bucket B. Likewise, the hole in the bottom of bucket B, connects to the lid of bucket C.

The plumber's fitting that connects the buckets should be watertight.

• **Step 4.** The screen filter should be placed on the top part of the threaded plumber's fitting opening. This is the part that is exposed to the layer of sand or charcoal. It will prevent sediment from flowing into the next container. It's very important

Designing Your Own Filtration System

to pay attention to fittings and connections for this is where water leaks will ruin the project. Stretch it nice and tight over the opening and use a rubber band or O-ring fitting to hold it in place.

• **Step 5.** For the last bucket at

Spigot

the bottom you can drill a hole at the side near the bottom. Get a threaded spigot, or flow valve, and screw it into the side of the bucket. This functions as your outlet. From here you should have a container ready to fill when needed.

• **Step 6.** Fill your buckets. One option is to fill bucket A with coarse gravel on top, and fine gravel at the bottom. Fill bucket B with a thin layer of coarse sand on top and the thick layer of fine sand at the bottom. Put the charcoal in bucket C. Use charcoal that's been crushed into small pieces to be effective. If your water has visible particles floating at the surface, strain it through a thick cotton cloth or coffee filter be-

fore pouring it into your filtration system.

• **Step 7.** Test your water. Filtering is a basic method that will remove some microbes, but it will definitely not remove dissolved chemicals. Clean and rotate the system every 6 months and keep it away from household cleaners or other contaminants.

CAUTION. No matter which filtration method you use, remember to still boil your water before consumption.

Alternative: Biofilter

The above-mentioned system introduces us to the basics of a traditional filtration system.

These days many people avoid using plastic products when it comes to food and water needs. If you want a truly traditional homestead solution, you can consider substituting the plastic containers with one large oak barrel/ tub or even a large clay or concrete urn with a lid. You have to make sure that the lid closes properly to prevent contamination.

The aim will be to design a bio-filter which consists of a filtration system with various layers of media filter (created by you) and a layer of biofilm (created by nature), to deal with disease causing pathogens.

The filter media needed:

- Fine, graded sand, 0.15 mm effective size.

- Coarse, graded sand, 0.35 mm effective size.

- Fine, graded gravel.

- Coarse, graded gravel.

- Activated charcoal, crushed (Optional).

- Use a thick cotton strainer at the top to catch the obvious particles when dealing with especially turbid water.

All media should be as sterile as possible. You do not want any organic matter in your filter, for incoming microbes will feed on it. Buy sand from a supplier that adheres to NSF 061 and/or AWWA B100-01 standards.

Mechanics: Water is poured into the reservoir at the top where small perforations allow the water to gently trickle down to the first layer of filter media (sand). It will form a little pool of standing water (3-5cm). It's important that the sand remains covered with a layer of water which provides oxygen to the system, so don't fret over the water at

Contaminated water

Standing water — Biofilm — Fine sand — Coarse sand — Fine gravel — Coarse gravel — Outlet — 5cm — 60cm — 3cm — 5cm — 6cm

PVC pipes, side by side, with holes. Use plumber's fittings, Schedule 40.

the top.

After a period of 3-4 weeks a biofilm (*Schmutzdecke*) will develop in the standing water, on the top layer of sand. This is a thin, slimy film of bacteria that adheres to the surface of the sand. A biofilm will only form if your water used is contaminated with microbes. This might sound counter intuitive, but healthy microbes will gather at the top of the sand layer and they will aid in fighting incoming disease-causing pathogens. Start using the filter once the biofilm is present.

Caution! When you pour the water in at the top, try not to disturb the biofilm. To achieve this, design a container that will gently sprinkle water over your biofilm. This is basically a reservoir with numerous holes punched in the bottom. You can use a plastic bucket, stainless steel or clay pot with holes drilled in the bottom. Once water is poured in, the holes will sprinkle the water like a shower head and it will not displace the biofilm clusters.

Once the water moves through the biofilm layer, it continues to percolate through the different layers of filter media. This addresses turbidity, some pathogens and general contamination like iron. Important that you don't want any air pockets in the filter media. These pockets cause pathogen development and foul odors.

Once it reaches the bottom, it is siphoned through the outlet pipe to the outside where it should be collected in a collection vessel.

Thanks to air pressure, the position of the outlet nozzle will determine the standing water level inside the container.

You have the option of filtering the water through an activated charcoal filter or to send it through a UV light.

Your system will require maintenance when it becomes ineffective at filtering water. Clean your system when the flow rate drops down to a trickle (could take years). Replace all filter media with new material.

It's necessary to use coarse gravel at the bottom of this system. The outlet pipe is located at the bottom of your system and a layer of sand will clog the outlet in no time. The last layer of media is coarse gravel, which cannot clog or obstruct the outlet pipe.

CAUTION. No matter which natural filtration method you use, remember to still boil your water before consumption.

Gravity-Fed Filtration System

Using filters made from natural material is an inexpensive option that gives you access to fairly clean water, for as long as you want.

Following the same principles, we can also combine this meth-

Material needed for a Gravity-Fed System

• 2 x large food grade (BPA free) plastic buckets with lids. The bigger the better (5gallons/ 19liters). You can still get these from bakeries. Only use plastic containers with the following numbers and letters:
1-PETE, 2-HDPE, 3-LDPE, 5-PP

• Your gravity filter system. Select the brand that suits your needs. Remember to read the instructions beforehand. Many filters have to be "primed" before use.

• 1 x Spigot kit or Faucet system

• Drill bit

od by substituting the filtering media with modern commercial filters. There are many options available and some of the modern ceramic filter candles are actually classified as purifiers that take out all biological and chemical contaminants. This means that they can remove almost all of the contaminants, that we expect to find in polluted or contaminated water. These filters are very effective and we find that some are specifically designed to rid water of chemical elements such as arsenic and fluoride. Such filters should be used in areas with documented chemical contamination of this kind.

It is best to have your water tested before you buy a specific gravity-fed filter. Knowing exactly what needs to be removed from your water source will guarantee cleaner water. Although expensive, these gravity-fed candle filters are good for around 3000 gallons (11000 liters) before they have to be replaced.

How To

A great option for any home, whether for daily use or in case of an emergency, is to incorporate standard gravity-fed purification elements (ceramic filters) into your treatment system. Although there's a wide selection of manufacturers to choose from, you will be looking for something that filters bacteria, chemicals such as chlorine, herbicides, pesticides, pharmaceuticals, VOC's, and heavy metals. Look for a product that relies on micro-filtration technology with a good flow rate and that's been tested to exceed NSF/ ANSI Standard 53 or 58 protocol. Avoid the cheaper products from unknown manufacturers.

It's very easy to assemble this system. You can use one, two or even three filters. Utilizing multiple filters means an increase in flow rate and also guarantees longer usage before replacement is needed.

● **Step 1.** Drill holes in the bottom of the top bucket for the filters you will use.

Drill holes in the bottom

The holes must be the same diameter as the filter threads to allow for a snug fit.

● **Step 2.** Follow the instructions provided with the filter and place seals and O-rings where needed. You will definitely need a seal between the filter and the

Install both filters with seals

Designing Your Own Filtration System

bucket.
Make sure that the filters are sitting tight and flush against the bottom.

• **Step 3.** Drill holes in the lid of the bottom bucket and make sure that they line up with the holes in the top bucket. This allows the filter shafts to stick into the lid of the bottom bucket.

Drill holes in the lid of the bottom bucket.

• **Step 4.** Install a spigot or faucet about 2" (5cm) from the floor of the bottom bucket.

• **Step 5.** Fill the top bucket with water and watch as the drinkable, filtered water fill the bottom container.
Note that different companies will make different guarantees as to the safety of the water once it's been purified.If unsure about the water quality in your area, have it tested before you use a purifying system.

How to make activated charcoal

It is very hard to produce activated charcoal without a furnace and chemicals. In a dire emergency, consider the following method developed at Santa Clara University. Use coconut shells as your carbon source.

1. Put your material in a 55 gal steel drum and place it on a large bonfire. The container should have a hole at the top to allow air to escape. The wood will burn inside the container and as it carbonizes, gases will escape with noises and sparks. Let it burn for around 3-5 hours. Wait till the fire has completely burnt out, before touching the container. **It will be very hot.** Inspect the charcoal and select the pieces that have been fully carbonized. Avoid ash and hard pieces.

2. Next, take out your charcoal and mash it into a powder or into small granules.

3. In a ventilated area, place it in a solution made of water and 25% *table salt, for 24 hours. The salt helps in opening the pores of the charcoal.

4. Take it out and rinse thoroughly to get the salt off.

5. Finally, let it dry in the sun or in an oven for several hours.

Never use charcoal from the grill. It's saturated with toxins!

*Optional, instead of salt, you can also use Calcium Chloride (CaCl2) and natural hickory or oak as carbon source.

Designing A Distillation System

In an emergency situation you will be very grateful to have a distillation system in your home.

These days complete distillation machines for domestic use are readily available and you can buy them at select consumer outlets. Such a system is not cheap, but it can pretty much purify any water as it mimics nature's very own hydrological cycle that we discussed earlier in this book.

A typical distillation system is highly effective at removing bacteria, protozoa and viruses. It also removes chemical contaminants like arsenic, barium, cadmium, chromium, lead, nitrate, sodium, sulfate and various organic compounds. Such a system will of course also remove salt from seawater. There are claims from very credible authors in the scientific community that it can also clean radioactive water, but I have no way of testing that claim.

The critics of distilled water as a potable water source argue that it's too clean and that all minerals are removed, which has a negative impact on human health. The counter argument, used by proponents of distillation systems, is that we actually get most (95%) of our trace minerals from our food. They further suggest adding a pinch of salt (actual organic rock salt) to your distilled water to compensate for the loss in minerals. Whatever the case, having water will keep you alive longer than not having water.

Let's take a look at the various distillation options available.

How To Design And Build A Distillation System

A simple distillation system can be very helpful in an emergency situation. It is a simple system that needs heat for evaporation, lower temperature for condensation and a vessel to collect the water droplets in. The yield can be greatly improved by using large quantities of contaminated water (or brine) and to make the system vapor-tight. You will need an energy source to provide the desired amount of heat.

Distillation

A commercial distillation system is a good investment and a welcome addition to any home, but remember that it is still a machine and that it requires electricity. If you choose to purchase one of these systems, know that you should always have a backup generator at the ready, to supply you with electricity when the grid is down.

The knowledge of how to make your own system can be price-less, so let's look at two practical methods to distill water at home:

- One simple and cheap option involves filling a container with water, connecting it to a heat source and once steam is produced the droplets are collected in a collection vessel. This is a practical system you can assemble in your kitchen.

- If you want to be even more prepared, then you can look at constructing your very own outdoor solar still. This method requires more work, but is also a very efficient method that does not require a conventional heat source, since it uses energy

Distillation Glossary

Brine. Water impregnated with salt.

Condensation. Water that collects as droplets on a cold surface when humid air is in contact with it.

Evaporation. The process of a substance in a liquid state changing to a gaseous state due to an increase in temperature.

PVC board. Also known as Chevron board and Andy board, a board made of light weight, foamed PVC, which is lightweight, moisture and corrosion resistant.

Solar still. A solar still distills water, using the heat of the Sun to evaporate, cool then collect the water.

Tempered glass. A type of safety glass processed by

from the sun.

Note that we are dealing with water vapor and tiny droplets. This is a slow process and the output is especially slow. If you have a large family, it might be best to have one system available for every family member.

Distillation With A Heat Source

Basic distillation of water is a concept that we were all introduced to as students, in science class.

The process:

1. Heat water in a container and eventually vapor will start to rise from its surface. This is evaporation. The contaminants remain behind in the container.

2. Condensation occurs when we catch the vapor droplets against a cold surface.

3. Wait for the droplets to run down and to collect in a collection vessel.

The key ingredient in this experiment is heat. Heat speeds up the process and is the catalyst

for evaporation to take place.

Preparation

The concept of water distillation is a simple one. Keep the basics in mind and you'll be able to scale down or up, according to your needs. Avoid plastic or any material that can leach chemicals into your system. The main components are:

• **You need a heat source.**
This can cause some problems. Electricity or generators can provide ample energy for this task, but what if you do not have a readily available power source? You will have to invest in a simple wood stove, rocket

Distillation Glossary

controlled thermal or chemical treatments to increase its strength compared with normal glass.

Trough. A channel used to convey a liquid.

VOCs. Volatile organic compounds, (also called VOCs), are organic compounds that can easily become vapors or gases. Along with carbon, they

can also contain elements like hydrogen, oxygen, fluorine, chlorine, bromine, sulfur, or nitrogen.

Vapor. The gaseous state of a substance that is in a liquid or solid state at room temperature.

Yield. The amount or quantity that's obtained from a specific process or reaction.

stove (wood fuel), solar powered water heater or a gas burner.

• **A container.** Stainless steel or copper will do. Basically a clean container that produces steam and that can be sealed off to direct the steam into your copper tube. You can also use a pressure cooker. Pressure cookers work well because they seal the steam in the container and are vapor-tight.

• **Copper tubing.** Buy some 10-15 feet of copper tubing at your hardware store. The thickness will depend on the fittings you want to use (¼ or ½ inch).

If you want to use a pressure cooker, the hole in the top of the lid will be of a small diameter and you will have to decide what size fitting will work best. (A ¼ inch fitting seems to work well.) If you are using a copper boiler or kettle, then you will need a wider diameter tubing. Only buy the copper tubing once you know the corresponding fitting size.

You will also have to shape the tubing into a coil. Before you bend the tubing, fill it with water and then let it freeze in your freezer overnight. Get a long cylinder or PVC pipe (4-5") and then wrap the copper tubing around it. This method helps prevent cracks and kinks in your

Pressure Cooker Fittings

Assess the thickness of the metal lid of the pressure cooker and select the correct compression fitting (brass).

• If the metal is thick enough for a screw thread, then use a screw "tap" to make a thread in the metal. Just screw the fitting that you bought into the threaded hole.

• If the lid is too thin, then drill a hole through the lid (over the original hole).

Copper Tubing

Nut

Ferrule

Male Brass Pipe Coupling

Lid

Rubber washer

Stainless steel washer

• Use a Male brass compression coupling and screw it through the hole. Remember to add a rubber washer and also a stainless steel washer to make your cooker vapor-tight.

• You can also use a Tee- or Elbow fitting if you need the tubing to point in a specific direction.

Designing A Distillation System

tube. Shaping the copper tubing into a coil increases the efficiency of the system. When steam meets resistance, it condensates back to water. If the coil is straight, the steam will simply escape out the back end.

• **Fittings.** You will need brass or copper compression fittings. A male fitting will work well if you are using a pressure cooker. Ask for advice at your hardware store to see which fitting will do the job for the system you have planned. If you are not familiar with fittings and soldering, get some "push connect" fittings. They are easy to use and will work just fine.

A flexible coupling will also come in handy for large diameter pipes where an exact fitting is not available.

• **Corrugated copper tubing** (Optional). Having a flexible section of tubing at one end (or both) just makes life easier. It provides you with options in that you can fit or place your coil in different positions. This is to prevent kinks in your main coil. Use it if you feel it will improve the efficiency of your system.

• **A container or material to cool down the coil and to speed up condensation.** This can be a tricky one, because most of us want a system that does not use electricity. Let's look at the possibilities:

a) If you are connected to the grid, then you have electricity to cool water or to make ice.

Bring the water to a rolling boil before you put the lid on for distillation. This kills off all pathogens that might enter the tube.

Simply fill a large container with ice or ice water. You use the electricity to make the ice or ice water.

b) If you want a system that doesn't use electricity, and you live in an area with a cold climate, then you can use snow or cold water to cool down the coil. It can be any contaminated water, from a river, pond or lake, since its only function is to cool down the outside of the coil.

c) If you don't have electricity, then things become more complicated. Making ice or cold water without electricity is near impossible. To cool the coil to some degree, wrap a wet towel around it and place your whole system outside where it can receive some air flow. A solar powered fan will help as well. Not having a way to cool down the coil will slow down the process considerably. Remember, the reason we cool the coil is to speed up the condensation process.

d) If none of the above are available, just leave the coil as it is. It will just take much longer for the water droplets to condensate.

Copper coil

Pressure cooker

Bucket

• **A collection vessel.** Any container will do. Make sure that it is sterile and keep it as close as possible to the tubing opening, where the water flows out.

How To

Before you start, lay all the pieces out in front of you. All parts should be sterile and clean. Make sure that all the fittings are the right size and that the steam will be contained without any leaks. You want a vapor-tight system!

A system that leaks is a faulty system and will have a negative impact of the distillation process. This is a very important issue that deserves your full attention.

This system follows a very simple process.

1. Connect your tubing (with the correct fitting) to the container you selected. Make sure that your fittings are vapor-tight.
2. Submerge the tubing in the cold (ice) water at a downward angle. The droplets caused by the condensation inside the tubing will run downhill into your collection vessel.
3. Fill the container with the contaminated water. Start to heat the container.
4. When the water starts to boil, let the first few clouds of vapor out before you close the lid. This will get rid of some Volatile Organic Compounds (VOCs).
5. Constantly check for leaks during the distillation process.
6. Eventually the water will start to trickle out of the tubing into the collection vessel.

Discard the first 100 ml if the contaminated water had obvious impurities like acetone or gasoline.

Coil in ice water

Pressure cooker

You have the option of pouring the water through a charcoal filter at the end, which will get rid of unwanted odors.

Solar Still Distillation

These days many people prefer to rely on mother nature and to get their energy from the sun. If you are also leaning in this direction, then you might consider building a passive solar powered water distillation system. Note that although you require sunlight for maximum efficiency, you can still use a solar still in cloudy weather, but the yield will be about half of normal.

This method works on a simple principle:

1. Heat the water with the aid of the sun, this causes evaporation.
2. Allow it to condense, against a pane of glass.
3. Let it flow down and out into a collection vessel.

Preparation

Solar stills use very simple technology and depending on your budget and skill-set, you can ramp up the size as much as you desire.

CAUTION! Before you start this project, note that lifting and moving large panes of glass is very dangerous. Use suction cup lifters, gloves and protective eye wear. This is a two-man job.

For a basic still, you will need the following material:

• 1 x Tempered glass pane 30½" x 60". A thickness of ⅛ inch (3.175 mm) will do. This is placed on top of the still. You want a solid piece of glass that can rest safely on your still under all conditions. Make sure the surface is clean, smooth and even. This is important! Tempered glass can crack and chip easily. Keep metal tools away from the glass. (If looking for recycled, a sliding door's glass will do.)

• 1 x Tempered glass pane 28½" x 58½". The thickness of this pane is not crucial, since it is placed in the bottom of the still. These measurements are correct if used with ¾ inch PVC side-boards. Dark, tinted glass is best for heat absorption, but clear glass with black silicone

Solar Still Basics

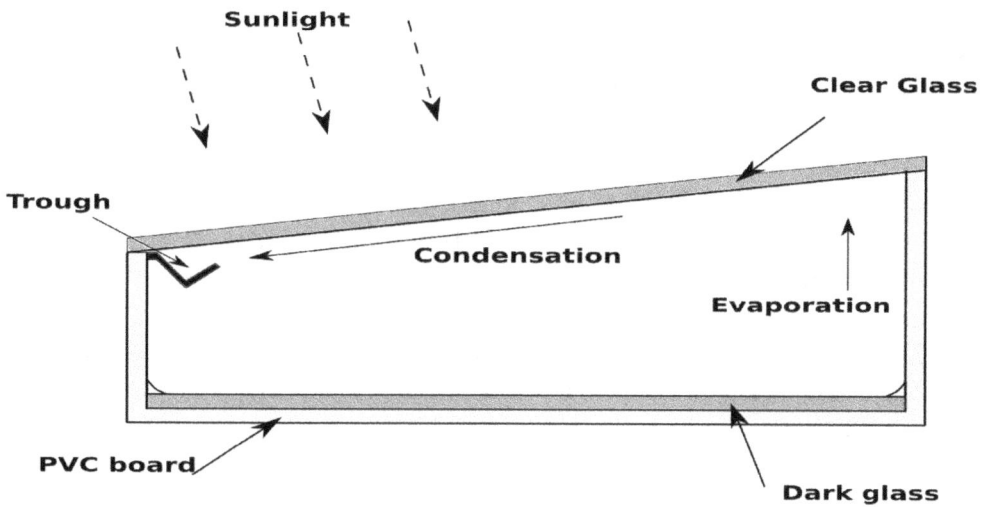

Sunlight

Clear Glass

Trough

Condensation

Evaporation

PVC board

Dark glass

underneath will also suffice.

• PVC board as needed for the construction of the still. A ¾ inch width should be thick enough.

• Silicone caulk as needed.

• PVC fittings. These are used for the inlet and outlet.

• PVC cement or a substitute to join the PVC boards.

• Wall anchors and screws to join the PVC boards.

• Aluminum angle strips. Use these strips at the bottom of the still to seal the pane of glass in place with silicone. Use ¾ - 1 inch angles.

• Trough material. Copper, stainless steel, aluminum or PVC pipe.

A couple of things to keep in mind before you start construction:

1. A bigger surface area will increase the yield. The bigger the better. Remember that you are dealing with glass. Too big and things get complicated. A 30" x 60" pane of glass is already a very large still. You will need an extra pair of hands (and suction cup lifters) to help with construction.

2. The angle of the Cover glass. You can experiment with different slope angles for your glass that will be placed on top of the still. Anything from 10°- 40° will do. In the end you will have to select a design that you are comfortable with. Personally, I think it's cheapest and easiest to start off with a low angle around 10°. Remember that the

angle will determine the width of the glass as well. A steep angle means quite an increase in cover glass size. At a 10° angle, the glass width is 30½ inches. At a 30° angle, the width increases to 34½ inches.

3. For maximum efficiency, the system must be vapor tight. This is crucial. Loss of water vapor causes less yield.

4. Use thin, tempered glass for the cover of the still. The sun will eventually crack the normal glass due to the constant fluctuation in temperature. Too thick cover glass will have a negative affect on the energy efficiency of the system.

5. You can use heat resistant, food grade silicone caulk. This material is safe to use and very little of it will be exposed to the water in the system. If you are absolutely against silicone, use the aluminum angle strips for the glass at the bottom of the sill.

6. The glass pane should be as close to the water as possible. This makes for a more efficient system and less vapor is lost during evaporation. Have the glass cut before you start. When you start building, remember that you will work off the measurements of the glass pane. It's always easier to cut wood than glass.

7. Water depth. A water depth of 1 cm of contaminated water is optimum. It is an energy efficient depth that requires minimal energy for evaporation.

Designing A Distillation System

8. Alternatives. Besides PVC board you can also use wood, but eventually it will rot from the exposure to heat and moisture. Remember that we are dealing with potable water for human consumption so avoid treated (sealant or oil) wood. If you do not have glass available to place at the bottom of the still, then simply cover and seal the whole inside of the still with black silicone caulk. Make sure that you get it as smooth and even as possible.

If you prefer not to use silicone, and you do not have glass available, then you can consider using a large, flat, black tray as the holding vessel for the contaminated water.

How To

Prepare the material needed to construct your still. Think carefully about the assembly and how complicated a design you want to create.

1. You should have the two precut panes of glass prepared and ready. Take the smaller of the two (tinted), the one that you want to put at the bottom of the still, and place it on a large piece of PVC board. We will call this the base-board. A board of 30" x 60" will do, but you can go smaller to suit your budget. Trace the outline of the glass on the base-board. Leave space all around the glass for the side-boards to be placed upright. If you are using ¾ inch

Comparison of inclination angles

Model A (10°) has a short distance between the bottom and top of the still. This allows for improved evaporation output, but due to the low inclination angle it causes slower speed of distilled water output.

Model B (30°) has a larger distance between the bottom and top of the still. This affects evaporation due to increase in distance, but the increase in inclination angle allows for faster distillation output. This model is more expensive due to the increase in size of material used.

In the end, the difference in yield between the two models is not huge. Design a still that you find practical in design and make sure that it's vapor-tight.

thick boards, then leave a ¾"
space all around the glass.

Remember when cutting or buying the clear cover glass pane,

that it is slightly wider (½") than
the PVC base-board. The cover
glass pane sits at an angle on
the still, and is therefore wider.
Example: If you used a 30" x
60" base-board, the top glass
cover should measure 30.5" x
60".

**2. You want the bottom of
the solar still to be black**. You
can do this by spreading black
silicone caulk over the base
board. This will function as the
bottom of your still.

Use a putty knife and spread it
evenly. Place the pane of tem-

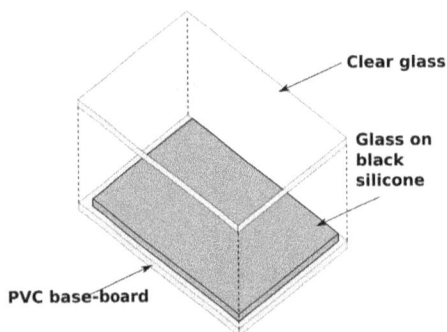

pered glass on top.

Clean the excess silicone and let
it dry.

**3. You will also need PVC
boards for the sides of the
structure.** We will call them the
side-boards.

Cut your boards according to

your measurements, but remember to cut the front and
back boards first. The back
board must be higher than the
front board. Remember to cut
both the front and back boards
at an angle to accommodate the
glass that will rest on top (*See
p. 195 for a comparison of inclination angles*).

• If you prefer a low angle of

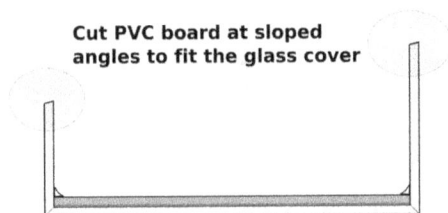

Cut PVC board at sloped
angles to fit the glass cover

10°, then a back board of 9" will
do. The front board is 3½" high.

Designing A Distillation System

• For an angle of 30°, a back board of 20" will do. The front board is 3½" high.

You should use wall anchors,

screws and PVC cement to fasten all boards and joints securely. Once assembled, the four side-boards should fit perfectly around the glass pane on top of the base board.

4. Once dry, take the assembled side-board frame and fit it on the base-board with the glass. The bottom will be quite heavy on account of the glass.

You now have a structure that

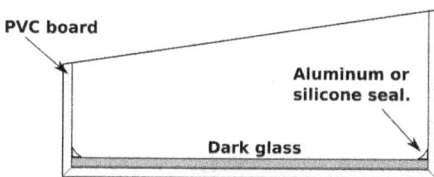

resembles an open box with a glass covered bottom.

Seal the glass with aluminum angle strips or just use silicone caulk.

5. Next comes the trough. To make the through you can use a piece of stainless steel, aluminum, copper or even PVC pipe (Eventually the PVC pipe will sag due to the heat, so best to put little supports underneath to prop it up. In general, you want to avoid anything that can leach chemicals into your water.).

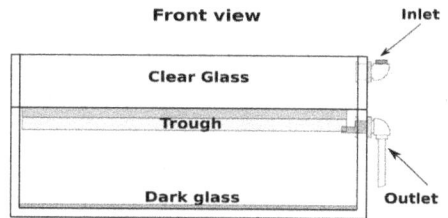

The trough should be long enough to cover the inside width of the still.

Bend the trough material in a shape that will allow it to rest on top of the front PVC board and also to form a tray for the water to run down. Use silicone and screws to fasten it to the front PVC board.

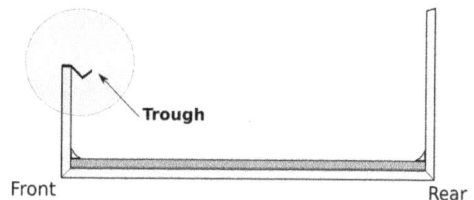

The trough should be slightly tilted to run downhill. To achieve this, make sure that you bend the trough, where the water flows, on a crease that runs at a slight angle.

6. Once the water runs down the trough, it runs into a small diameter PVC pipe that forms the outlet.

Remove 3/4 of top half of PVC pipe with hacksaw

Trough

Both the inlet and outlet are on the same side of the still.

Drill a hole through the PVC side-board where you want to place your PVC fittings. You should have about 1½" pipe that protrudes from out of the side board.

Use a hacksaw and remove three quarters of the top half section of the PVC pipe. Use PVC cement and connect it to the joint that sits on the outside. This section of pipe basically just provides space for the trough to rest on.

Alternative: For a simpler trough solution, just cut a section out of a piece of PVC pipe. This pipe should be long enough to run across the width of the still. One end connects to the PVC joint that flows into the collection vessel. The other end can go through the PVC side-board.

Make sure it's closed up and sealed with silicone.

Using a PVC trough

Cut the trough

Supports

PVC Board

From the trough and the PVC joint, the water runs down into a collection vessel.

Do not use any translucent piping or tubes since exposure to the sun will promote algal growth.

7. In a similar fashion you can create a filling inlet, to pour the contaminated water into your system.

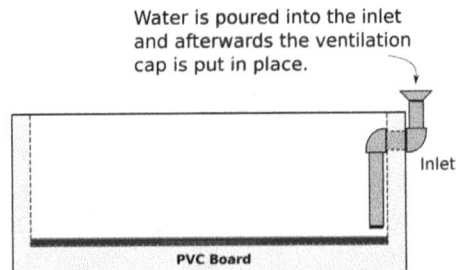

Water is poured into the inlet and afterwards the ventilation cap is put in place.

Inlet

PVC Board

Designing A Distillation System

You will have to drill a hole in the side-board, the same side as the outlet. Use plumber's fittings and add a down-pipe that almost touches the bottom of the still. On the outside, you can use a PVC pipe with a threaded end. This will allow you to place a cap on it when not in use, or to use a funnel when needed.

8. If your system is properly constructed, it will be almost vapor-tight. This means that when you fill the unit with water, air pressure will build up inside the still (from displaced air) and this will put stress on your joints. The solution is a ventilation outlet, that is basically just a cap with a tiny hole drilled in the middle, which will allow the air to escape. Glue a small piece of screen material to the inside of the cap, to keep ants out. Just place the cap on the inlet pipe when the still is in use.

Ventilation cap is placed on inlet when the still is used. Air is allowed to escape.

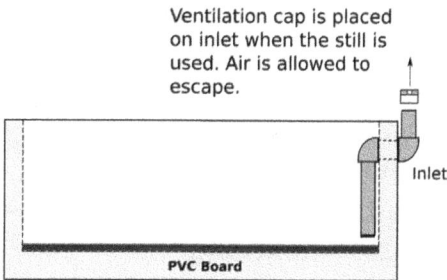

Inlet

PVC Board

All these fittings can be bought at your local hardware store. They consist of PVC pipes, elbows and caps of appropriate dimensions that fit snugly together. Remember to use PVC

cement where needed.

9. Once the inside of the still is done, and the trough is in place, you can place the glass cover on top of the still. This is the final piece of the puzzle as the glass cover will effectively seal the whole unit. Make sure that the water droplets will collect in the trough. If necessary, you can glue a thin strip of PVC onto the glass, just above the trough. This strip will **guide** the droplets to fall straight onto the trough.

There are no guarantees as to how much your yield will be. It all depends on your workmanship and how vapor-tight your still is. If you have a contaminated water solution with expected chemicals like hydrocarbons (acetone and gasoline) note that they will rise to the top, which means that you can discard the first 100ml of distilled water. This is considered unfit for drinking.

Sunlight

Clear Glass

Trough

Condensation

Evaporation

PVC board

Dark glass

Depending on weather conditions and quality of construction, a still that's 30" x 60" should be able to provide you with more than a gallon (3.785 L) of water a day.

Options

A basic solar still will come in real handy when you run out of water. Depending on your budget, you have quite a few options on how to improve on this design.

• **Pre-filter your water if possible.** A simple cotton cloth or coffee filter will do. Try to eliminate larger particles before you pour the contaminated water into the still. Once the water has been distilled, you can also use a home-made charcoal filter to improve the taste of the water.

• **Use waterproof aluminum duct tape.** This is optional, but it will definitely help with keeping heat in and also to make the whole system vapor-tight. Seal every joint and opening for added efficiency.

• **You can also add reflective material to your sill to concentrate the energy from the sun.** A reflective panel, like a mirror, can be placed above the back-board of the still. Angle it to reflect the sun's rays onto the glass top.

• **You can add a drain plug to drain excess water.** Having a drain hole means that you can flush the system to get rid of unwanted sludge.

• **Insulate your system.** This prevents heat loss inside the still. Go to a store that sells roof insulation and get the thinnest insulation material available. You should be able to find sheets around 1-1½ inch thick. The insulation material should be placed at the bottom and sides of the still. Insulating the whole system means that you will have to buy extra PVC board to "wrap" the insulation material in. Use a 2 x 4" timber wood frame with cross sections as a base frame to place your bottom section on. This will accommodate the combined weight of the structure.

• **Having access to the inside of your still might be good for maintenance and cleaning.** The big issue here is how the new design will affect the overall effectiveness of the still. Every little hole, gap or crack will cause precious water vapor to escape. This will have a huge effect on the still's water production capability. Adding hinges might seem like a good idea, but they will most definitely cause vapor loss.

A practical solution is to separate the still into a top section and a bottom section (See diagrams on next page).

Note that you will have to adjust your measurements of the top section, to allow for the width of the aluminum strips and silicone sealant used on the bottom section. There is no need to connect the two sections with screws, since the weight of the top section will be enough to

Designing A Distillation System

hold it in place. It should be a snug fit, and once the bottom of the still is filled, the actual water will seal the openings in between the two sections and this will prevent vapor loss.

Place handles on the sides of the top section to make it easier to lift it up. Use pop-rivets.

As mentioned earlier with the insulation discussion, you can use a 2 x 4" timber wood frame with cross sections as a base frame to place your bottom section on.

This information should provide you with the know-how to build a solar still that will suit your pocket and water needs. Keep in mind why we use solar stills; they can purify any water and they do not require a conventional energy source. This is a resource worth investing in.

I would like to thank a gentleman named Robert Howell, who lives on the coast of North Carolina. An expert at solar stills, his knowledge and creativity proved very useful in contributing to the design of this still.

In his own words, "I have built and used this type of water distiller for close to 20 years. In my opinion a more pure water for drinking can not be found. I have purified water from rivers, creeks, the ocean and more sources."

Creating a Top and Bottom

• You can make your still more versatile with an option of separating it into a top and bottom section.

Top section

Handle

1 x 1" Angled Aluminum

1/8"Tempered Glass sheet

1/2" Insulation foam

1/4" Plywood

2 x 4" Timber

PVC board   Bottom section

• The top section consists of the frame, the cover glass and handles on the sides.

Top section

1/8"Tempered Glass sheet

1/2" Insulation foam

2 x 4" Timber

Bottom section

• Once the bottom of the still is filled with water, it will be vapor-tight.

Top section

Water Level

2 x 4" Timber

Bottom section

Testing Water: Disease and Contamination

Testing for pathogens and contaminants are essential. The United States Environmental Protection Agency (EPA) recommends that, as the owner of an individual water system, it is up to you to make sure that your water is safe to drink.

As mentioned earlier, we have reached a point in human history where a very large part of our fresh water supply is contaminated with microbes, pollutants and toxins. The ever increasing need for population growth to feed the economy will do that to our environment. This already gives us reason to test our water, but if still not convinced, read on.

About four years after the Fukushima disaster in Japan, I found myself visiting the island nation of Taiwan, to the south of Japan. During this trip, I had the opportunity to speak to many Japanese citizens who had actually decided to leave Japan and to immigrate to Taiwan. In short, they felt that at the time of the incident, they had not been warned of the affect that the nuclear disaster would have on the environment and on humans; nobody had warned them that the radiation would eventually spread into the water and into the food chain, which it did. They had to take the initiative themselves, to do their own research and to make a decision to leave the area.

This is something we are starting to see more often. Large companies are reluctant to face responsibilities for their actions and major ecological disasters are almost always ignored and even dismissed as having "minor consequences".

Getting Your Water Tested

It's important to be aware of the potential dangers that your drinking water may pose for you and your family.

Be informed about:

- Why test?
- What to test for?
- When to test?
- Where to test your water?
- Water related diseases and contaminants in private wells.

Well owners have to pay special attention for a private well uses groundwater as its water source. There are many reasons why our groundwater can become contaminated. Here is a list of the most common sources of contaminants:

• Naturally occurring chemicals and minerals (for example, arsenic, radon, uranium)
• Land use practices in your area (fertilizers, pesticides, livestock, animal feeding operations, biosolids application)
• Manufacturing processes
• The overflow of sewers
• Faulty wastewater treatment systems (for example, nearby septic systems). This is an important one. Watch out for septic tanks!

You are responsible for testing your well water and making sure it is safe.

Visualize a province, state or county with surface water like rivers, lakes and dams. These water sources have a network of pipes that flow out of them and that connect with cities, suburbs and households all over the area. Any ecological disaster, like a sewerage spill or chemical disaster, near the source, will affect the millions of households down the line. The issue with large populations is, that the news of the spill will only reach us once the damage has been done. On top of that, damage might last for decades and for various reasons, the powers that be, might not even have reported it in the first case.

What To Test For?

According to the Centers for Disease Control and Prevention, if you are getting your water from a privately-owned well or from local surface water sources like streams, rivers or lakes, you should test for water quality indicators:

• **Total Coliforms**

Coliform bacteria are microbes found in the digestive systems of warm-blooded animals, in soil, on plants, and in surface water. These microbes typically do not make you sick; however, because microbes that do cause disease are hard to test for in the water, "total coliforms" are tested instead. If the total coliform count is high, then it is very possible that harmful germs like viruses, bacteria, and parasites might also be found in the water.

● Fecal Coliforms (E. Coli)

Fecal coliform bacteria are a specific kind of total coliform. The feces (or stool) and digestive systems of humans and warm-blooded animals contain millions of fecal coliforms. E. Coli is part of the fecal coliform group and may be tested for by itself. Fecal coliforms and E. Coli are usually harmless. However, a positive test may mean that feces and harmful germs have found their way into your water system. These harmful germs can cause diarrhea, dysentery, and hepatitis. It is important not to confuse the test for the common and usually harmless WQI E. Coli, with a test for the more dangerous germ E. Coli O157:H7.

● pH Level

The pH level tells you how acidic or basic your water is. The pH level of the water can change how your water looks and tastes.
If the pH of your water is too low or too high, it could damage your pipes, cause heavy metals like lead to leak out of the pipes into the water, and eventually make you sick. It's advisable to test pH levels often, since they

can be affected by various conditions.

When To Test?

The CDC recommends the following:

Wells

At a minimum, check your well every spring to make sure there are no mechanical problems; test it once each year for total coliform bacteria, nitrates, total dissolved solids, and pH levels. If you suspect other contaminants, you should test for those as well. However, spend time identifying potential problems as these tests can be expensive. The best way to start is to consult a local expert, such as the local health department, about local contaminants of concern. You should also have your well tested if:
● It is a new well and you want to document the water quality.
● There are known problems with well water in your area.
● You have experienced problems near your well (i.e., flooding, land disturbances, gas leakage, chemical spill, or discovered nearby waste disposal sites).
● You replace or repair any part of your well system.
● You notice a change in water quality (i.e., taste, color, odor).
● If someone in your household is pregnant, nursing an infant, or if there are unexplained illnesses in your family.

When To Test Your Water (EPA Guideline)

Conditions or nearby activities	Recommended Test
Recurrent gastro-intestinal illness.	Coliform bacteria.
Household plumbing contains lead.	pH, lead, copper.
Radon in indoor air or region is radon rich.	Radon.
Scaly residues, soaps don't lather.	Hardness.
Water softener needed to treat hardness.	Manganese, iron.
Stained plumbing fixtures, laundry.	Iron, copper, manganese.
Objectionable taste or smell.	Hydrogen sulfide, corrosion, metals.
Water appears cloudy, frothy or colored.	Color, detergents.
Corrosion of pipes, plumbing.	Corrosion, pH, lead.
Rapid wear of water treatment equipment.	pH, corrosion.
Nearby areas of intensive agriculture.	Nitrate, pesticides, coliform bacteria.
Coal or other mining operation nearby.	Metals, pH, corrosion.
Gas drilling operation nearby.	Chloride, sodium, barium, strontium.
Odor of gasoline or fuel oil, and near gas station or buried fuel tanks.	Volatile organic compounds (VOC).
Dump, junkyard, landfill, factory or dry-cleaning operation nearby.	VOC, Total disolved solids (TDS), pH, sulfate, chloride, metals.
Salty taste and seawater, or a heavily salted roadway nearby.	Chloride, TDS, sodium.

• As the well owner, you suspect there is something wrong with your water quality.

Public Water

If you do not own a well, you can still have your water tested. If you are purchasing water from a public water system, then your water is monitored, tested and the results reported to the federal, state or tribal drinking water agencies responsible for making sure it meets the National Primary Drinking Water Standards. Your water company must notify you when there are contaminants in the water they provide, that may cause illness or other problems. You can also have your water tested if:

• If you suspect lead (or other chemicals) may be in some of your household plumbing materials and water service lines.
• There are known problems with water in your area.
• You notice a change in water quality (i.e., taste, color, odor).
• If someone in your household is pregnant, nursing an infant, or if there are unexplained illnesses in your family.

Where To Test?

Local health or environmental departments often test for nitrates, total coliforms, fecal coliform, volatile organic compounds, and pH (see above). Health or environmental departments, or county governments should have a list of the certified (licensed) laboratories in your area that test for a variety of substances. They cover both city water and well water and will require you to send them a sample. They test for hundreds of target contaminants and should have you covered. Typically, the process looks like this:

1. Find a lab and call them.
2. Tell the lab the water tests you need based on the EPA guidelines.
3. Ask if they're certified to do all the tests or use another certified lab.
4. Wait for the water test kits to arrive in the mail. The kits include empty bottles, directions, and forms to fill out.
5. Read the directions, fill the bottles with tap water, and mail them back to the lab.
6. Watch for test results in the mail and compare whether your results fall within the safe limits on well testing.
7. Make adjustments to your system if needed.

Self-monitoring test kits can also be bought online, at large hardware stores (plumbing) and select home retail outlets. These test kits are easy to use. A basic test kit will test for bacteria, lead, copper, pesticides, nitrites/nitrates, chlorine, hardness, and pH. Kits are also available that test specifically for contaminants like arsenic, lead, radon, coliform bacteria, etc.

Kits include all test materials and no laboratory testing is necessary.

Testing Odors Or Colors In Your Water

Certain odors or colors can indicate the presence of contaminants in your water system. As a simple rule of thumb, follow these guidelines to determine the cause of the odor:

- Odor in all faucets -> Problem with main water supply, whether public or from a private well.

- Odor in some faucets -> Problem in plumbing system (pipes) nearest to the faucet with odor.

- If the odor disappears after a few minutes -> Problem in plumbing system.

- If the odor lingers indefinitely -> Problem with main water supply or plumbing system or combination.

For odors in the kitchen around the sink, fill a glass with water and move away from the sink. If your water does not smell, then the problem lies with the drain system.

Often we find that plumbing systems and water heaters are the main culprits when it comes to odors and colors. Public water is treated with chlorine and when organic matter gets trapped in your plumbing system, the reaction with chlorine can cause sulfurous odors.

When dealing with wells we find that surface water contamination and septic tank seepage are the main causes of a change in color or odor.

Colors with a residue (usually metals) will of course stain linen and clothes when washed with the contaminated water.

Test immediately if unsure about the source of the odor or color:

- **Sulfurous odor**

This is the rotten egg smell we sometimes find in drain pipes. This odor can be caused by a variety of problems and it's best to call in an expert plumber to do an assessment.

Cause: The smell may be due to hydrogen sulfide gas forming in the water heater itself, sulfur in the building water supply, bacteria in the drain pipes or in the water system, deteriorating water heater electrodes or dangerous sewer gas leaks. It can also be caused by decaying organic material underground, which causes hydrogen sulfide gas. The water picks up this gas underground and carries it to the surface where it is released again. To test for hydrogen sulfide gas, open both the hot and cold water faucets, to decide which faucets have the rotten egg odor.

- If the rotten egg odor is coming only from the hot water faucet, it means that the problem is probably in the water heater.

- If the odor is strongest when both the hot and cold faucets is first turned on, and then becomes weaker (or disappears) after the water has run for a while, the problem likely is sulfur bacteria in the well or plumbing system.

- If the smell is strongest when you first turn on both the hot and cold faucets and it stays constant and persists with use, the problem likely is hydrogen sulfide in the groundwater that supplies the well.

Solution: Have your water tested and call in an expert plumber to do an assessment.

• Chemical, chlorine odor

If you smell bleach or similar chemicals check for chlorine in your water system. Chlorine is not good for you, especially when you inhale it (showers).

Cause: The water treatment plants use chlorine for water disinfection.

Solution: If it persists, contact your water utility office or have it tested. Activated carbon filters, shower filters and reverse osmosis systems can remove chlorine.

• Petroleum odor

It's not often that you smell gasoline or petroleum in your water.

Cause: Anything that smells like gasoline, petroleum or turpentine indicates an external contaminant. This indicates that the source can be a chemical plant, gasoline tanks or runoff from neighboring areas. A known chemical found in gasoline is MTBE. Although not explicitly harmful, it's always best to avoid chemicals (especially used in gasoline) and to have your water tested.

Solution: Stop drinking the water and call in the help of an expert plumber. Have your water tested and check with your local water utility office to locate the source.

• Fishy, earthy or moldy odors

This smell can be caused by harmless bacteria or the presence of metal.

Cause: This can indicate decaying organic matter (bacteria) or pollution of well water from surface drainage. Another cause could be the presence of Barium or Cadmium. Barium is a metal that occurs naturally in nature. Cadmium can be caused by deteriorating galvanized plumbing.

Solution: Locate and test for the source of contamination. To remove Barium use: an Ion Exchange system, Reverse Osmosis, or a Water Softener system.

And for removing Cadmium: Filtration, Ion Exchange, Water Softener system, and/or Reverse Osmosis.

• Musty, unnatural odor

Cause: This usually indicates organic matter in the water supply. If you smell other familiar chemicals, remember that certain pesticides have a very distinct smell that can be easily identified.

Solution: Try to locate the source of the contamination. It can also indicate the presence of pesticides in your water. If you suspect the presence of pesticides, stop drinking the water and have it tested immediately.

• Methane gas

Cause: This can be caused by mining or oil drilling activities in the area. It is also found in wells located near swamps and marshes.

Solution: It's best to contact a certified well contractor in your area to see if a well vent or similar can solve the problem.

• Foam in your water. The presence of foam in your water is never a good sign, especially when accompanied by any odors.

Cause: This could be caused by a leaking septic tank close to a well. This is a very serious problem and the cause of the leakage will have to be investigated. Solution: Stop drinking the water and call in the help of an expert plumber to shock chlorinate your well.

• A blue or green color

This is a situation you sometimes find in homes with old plumbing systems.

Cause: This color indicates the presence of copper. There is copper in drinking water, but in small amounts.

Solution: If you suspect higher amounts in your water (usually well water), then stop drinking the water and have it tested. Anything higher that 30 ppm should be considered as problematic.

• A red or brown color

Sometimes you will see red stains in your sink and/ or an odor like sewerage, fuel, or cucumber.

Cause: These colors are indicative of iron or manganese. Ion is a common substance found inside the earth. It can dissolve in water and easily enter a home's water supply system. The red stains you see around drains and basins are deposits of either ionic ferrous iron, ferric iron, or "iron bacteria". Iron-bacteria are more commonly found in water from dug wells or shallow wells.

Solution: Ion or manganese filters and/ or water softeners can aid in removing the unwanted substances and calling an expert to disinfect your well (chlorine) can help in getting rid of the iron bacteria.

• Cloudy, milky white water

Sometimes water can appear milky white as it flows out the faucet.

Cause: One likely cause is tiny air bubbles in the water. A more serious problem can be surface water contamination.

Solution: Fill a clear glass with water and set it on the counter. If the water starts to clear at the bottom of the glass first, the cloudy, white appearance is trapped air. This is not a serious issue and might be caused by your well's pumping system. If it does not settle, then investigate for surface water contamination.

Water Related Diseases And Contaminants In Private Wells

As the owner of a private well, you are responsible for testing your water. Make sure that your house has a water treatment system installed if you are using your well as a source for drinking water. Certain unwanted pollutants can be routinely removed by a water treatment system. Depending on which contaminant is present, you can install sediment filters, a reverse osmosis system, ozone purifying system, etc.

If temporarily unable to find a treatment solution, then use the emergency solutions provided by the Centers for Disease Control and Prevention.

• Hepatitis A

Hepatitis A is a virus that can be found anywhere that human feces is present. This means that it can enter your well through the flow of storm-water runoff, septic tanks, sewerage overflow and contaminated waste water.

Immediate solutions:

1. Boil your water for 1 minute.

2. Disinfect your well. Chlorination kills the virus.

3. Remove the source of contamination.

4. Get advice from your local health department for recommended procedures.

• Giardia

Giardia is a parasite that causes diarrhea. It is found worldwide where humans live and defecate. This parasite can enter your well through the flow of storm-water runoff, septic tanks, sewerage overflow and contaminated waste water.

Immediate solutions:

1. Boil your water for 1 minute.

2. Install a reverse osmosis filtration system. It must have a pore size smaller than 1 micron. Tested and certified NSF Standard 53 for cyst removal and reduction.

• Campylobacter

Campylobacter is a bacteria we often see in the summer months. It causes diarrhea. It is found worldwide in human and animal feces. This bacteria can enter your well through the flow of storm-water runoff, septic tanks, sewerage overflow and contaminated wastewater.

Immediate solutions:

1. Boil your water for 1 minute.

2. Remove the source of contamination.

3. Get advice from your local health department for recommended procedures.

• Shigella

Shigella is a bacteria we often see in shallow wells after

an occurrence of flooding. It is a bacteria that causes a very contagious type of diarrhea. It is found worldwide in human and animal feces. This bacteria can enter your well through the flow of storm-water runoff, septic tanks, sewerage overflow and contaminated waste water.

Immediate solutions:

1. Boil your water for 1 minute.

2. An ultraviolet light device can be used.

3. In emergencies, use iodine tablets.

4. Get advice from your local health department for recommended procedures.

● Noroviruses

Noroviruses cause intestinal illness, or gastroenteritis, and have been associated with outbreaks on cruise ships and in communities, restaurants, camps, schools, institutions, and families. Noroviruses may be found in water sources, such as private wells, that have been contaminated with the feces of infected humans. Waste can enter the water through various ways, including sewage overflows, sewage systems that are not working properly, and polluted storm-water runoff. Wells may be more vulnerable to such contamination after flooding, particularly if the wells are shallow, have been dug or bored, or have been submerged by floodwater for long periods of time.

Solution:

1. Bring your water to a rolling boil for one minute (at elevations above 6,500 feet, boil for three minutes).

2. Water should then be allowed to cool, stored in a clean sanitized container with a tight cover, and refrigerated.

Because of the small size of the virus, using a traditional point-of-use filter will not remove it from your water.

● Rotaviruses

Rotaviruses are wheel-shaped ("rota-") viruses that cause intestinal illnesses and are the most common cause of severe diarrhea among infants and children. The virus may be found in water sources such as private wells that have been contaminated with the feces from infected humans. Waste can enter the water through different ways, including sewage overflows, sewage systems that are not working properly, and polluted storm-water runoff. Wells may be more vulnerable to such contamination after flooding, particularly if the wells are shallow, have been dug or bored, or have been submerged by floodwater for long periods of time.

Solution:

1. Bring your water to a rolling boil for one minute (at elevations above 6,500 feet, boil for three minutes) Water should then be allowed to cool, stored in a clean sanitized container

with a tight cover, and refrigerated. Because of the small size
of the virus, using a traditional
point-of-use filter will probably
not be effective at removing it
from your water.

- **E.Coli**

E. Coli is a bacteria that can
cause severe illness. One particular strain produces a very
powerful toxin that needs to be
avoided at all costs. This bacteria can enter your well through
the flow of storm-water runoff,
septic tanks, sewerage overflow
and contaminated waste water.

Solution:

1. Boil your water for 1 minute.

2. Disinfect your well. Chlorination kills the virus.

3. Remove the source of contamination.

4. Get advice from your local
health department for recommended procedures.

- **Cryptosporidium and Salmonella**

"Crypto" is a parasite that causes diarrhea. It is found worldwide where humans live and
defecate. This parasite can enter
your well through the flow of
storm-water runoff, septic tanks,
sewerage overflow and contaminated waste water.

Immediate solutions:

1. Boil your water for 1 minute.

2. Install a reverse osmosis
filtration system. It must have a
pore size smaller than 1 micron.

Tested and certified NSF Standard 53 for cyst removal and
reduction.

3. Consider an ultra-violet light
source or ozone as alternative
disinfection process.

4. Get advice from your local
health department for recommended procedures.

- **Arsenic**

Arsenic can enter a well through
industrial waste released into
the environment, the use of
arsenic containing fertilizers and
through the natural occurring
ground deposits found in the
earth.

Solutions:

1. Filter your water through reverse osmosis.

2. Ultra-filtration

3. Distillation.

4. Get advice from your local
health department for recommended procedures.

- **Nitrate**

Nitrate can occur naturally in
surface and groundwater at a
level that does not generally
cause health problems. High
levels of nitrate in well water
often result from improper well
construction, well location, over-
use of chemical fertilizers, or
improper disposal of human and
animal waste. Sources of nitrate
that can enter your well include
fertilizers, septic systems, animal feedlots, industrial waste,
and food processing waste.
Wells may be more vulnera-

ble to such contamination after flooding, particularly if the wells are shallow, have been dug or bored, or have been submerged by floodwater for long periods of time.

Solutions:

1. Treatment processes such as ion exchange,

2. Distillation

3. Reverse osmosis

Contact your local health department for recommended procedures.

Heating or boiling your water will not remove nitrate. Because some of the water will evaporate during the boiling process, the nitrate levels of water can actually increase slightly in concentration if the water is boiled. Mechanical filters or chemical disinfection, such as chlorination, DO NOT remove nitrate from water.

• Lead

Lead rarely occurs naturally in water; it usually gets into the water from the delivery system. Lead pipes are the main contributor to high lead levels in tap water. Other sources include parts of the water delivery system such as lead solder used to join copper pipes, brass in faucets, coolers, and valves. Although brass usually contains low lead levels, the lead can still dissolve into the water, especially when the fixtures are new. Private wells more than 20 years old may contain lead in the "packer" element that is used to help seal the well above the well screen. Some brands of older submersible pumps used in wells may also contain leaded-brass components. Corrosion of pipes and fixture parts can cause the lead to get into tap water.

Solutions:

1. First, try to identify and remove the lead source. If you have a private well, check both the well and the pump for potential lead sources.

2. Heating or boiling your water will not remove lead. Because some of the water evaporates during the boiling process, the lead concentration of the water can actually increase slightly as the water is boiled.

3. If it is not possible or cost-effective to remove the lead source, flushing the water system before using the water for drinking or cooking may be an option. Any time a particular faucet has not been used for several hours (approximately 6 or more), you can flush the system by running the water for about 1-2 minutes or until the water becomes as cold as it will get. Flush each faucet individually before using the water for drinking or cooking. You can use the water flushed from the tap to water plants, wash dishes or clothing, or clean. Avoid cooking with or drinking hot tap water because hot water dissolves lead more readily than cold water

does. Do not use hot tap water to make cereals, drinks or mix baby formula. You may draw cold water after flushing the tap and then heat it if needed.

4. You may also wish to consider water treatment methods such as reverse osmosis, distillation, and carbon filters specially designed to remove lead. Typically these methods are used to treat water at only one faucet.

Contact your local health department for recommended procedures.

• Radon

Radon is a colorless, tasteless, odorless, radioactive gas. It occurs naturally and is produced by the breakdown of uranium in soil, rock, and water. It can also dissolve into our water supply. High levels of dissolved radon are found in the groundwater in some areas flowing through granite or granitic sand and gravel formations. If you live in an area with high radon in groundwater it can get into your private well. Showering, washing dishes, and laundering can disturb the water and release radon gas into the air you breathe.

Solutions:

Radon can be removed from water by using one of two methods:

1. Aeration treatment - spraying water or mixing it with air and then venting the air from the water before use, or

2. GAC treatment - filtering water through granular activated carbon. Radon attaches to the carbon and leaves the water free of radon. Disposing of the carbon may require special handling if it is used at a high radon level or if it has been used for a long time.

In either treatment, it is important to treat the water where it enters your home (point-of-entry device) so that all the water will be treated. Point-of-use devices such as those installed on a tap or under the sink will only treat a small portion of your water and are not effective in reducing radon in your water. It is important to maintain home water treatment units properly because failure to do so can lead to other water contamination problems. Some homeowners use a service contract from the installer to provide carbon replacement and general system maintenance.

Remember to have your well water tested regularly, at least once a year, after installing a treatment system to make sure the problem is controlled.

• Fluoride

Fluoride is a mineral that occurs naturally and is released from rocks into the soil, water, and air. Various studies (some controversial) have been done to advocate for or against the fluoridation of drinking water.

For some reason, fluoride is always linked to tooth decay and there seems to be an obsession with the believe that it can and will prevent tooth decay.

It's interesting to note that only about 5% of the world population is fluoridated and more than 50% of these people live in North America. Fluoridation is rejected in most advanced societies including Germany, Austria, France, Denmark, Norway, Switzerland, Sweden, Japan and various others.

Decisions about adding fluoride to drinking water are made at the state or local level. The best way to find the fluoride level of your local public water system is to contact your water utility provider.

If you rely on well water you should have your water tested for fluoride. It is unusual to have the fluoride content of water be 4 mg/L or higher. If a laboratory report indicates that you have such a high fluoride content, you may want to consider alternate sources of water for drinking and cooking, or installing a device to remove the fluoride from your home water source. There are a variety of gravity-fed filters available that cater specifically for this need.

Conclusion

When reading through this list, it is obvious that the one issue that affects almost all wells is storm-water drains and run-offs. Failure to secure an effective storm-water drain runoff can be considered one of the main causes of well contamination. Storm-water runoff picks up all kinds of pollutants like pesticides, bacteria, and chemicals. It travels downhill at a rate that is too fast to be absorbed into the ground. When faced with floods, we are at mother nature's mercy, but with storm-water runoff we have options:

- Make sure that you storm-water drain is located away from your well, and also pay attention to the runoff direction of your water.

- Harvest the rain from your roof and make sure all gutters empty into downspouts that lead to tanks or barrels.

- Make sure that there are no potential contaminants in the vicinity of your well. Pay special attention to pesticides, compost manure piles, livestock areas and septic tanks.

- Consider permeable surfaces around your well to allow for water absorption. This includes investigating driveway paving, decks and lawns (bad).

- Get involved in the community. Make fellow community members aware of the importance of storm-water management.

How To Manage Waste

When disaster strikes and you run out of water, you will have to implement a water conservation plan. Water is responsible for our sanitation needs and without proper sanitation facilities, waste from infected individuals can contaminate a community's land and water, increasing the risk of infection for other individuals.

The absence of basic sanitation facilities can:

— Result in an unhealthy environment contaminated by human waste. Proper waste disposal can slow the infection cycle of many disease-causing agents.

— Contribute to the spread of many diseases and conditions that can cause widespread illness and death. Without proper sanitation facilities, people often have no choice but to live in, and drink water from, an environment contaminated with waste from infected individuals, thereby putting themselves at risk for future infection. Inadequate waste disposal drives the infection cycle of many agents that can be spread through contaminated soil, food, water, and insects such as flies.

Sanitation is an aspect of preparedness that the whole household should be aware of.

Basic hygiene when handling waste

• Wash hands with soap and water immediately after handling human waste or sewage.

• Avoid touching face, mouth, eyes, nose, or open sores and cuts while handling human waste or sewage.

• After handling human waste or sewage, wash your hands with soap and water before eating or drinking.

• After handling human waste or sewage, wash your hands with soap and water before and after using the toilet.

• Before eating, removed soiled work clothes and eat in designated areas away from human waste and sewage-handling activities.

• Do not smoke or chew tobacco or gum while handling human waste or sewage.

• Keep open sores, cuts, and wounds covered with clean, dry bandages.

• Gently flush eyes with safe water if human waste or sewage contacts eyes.

• Use waterproof gloves to prevent cuts and contact with human waste or sewage.

• Wear rubber boots at the work site and during transport of human waste or sewage.

• Remove rubber boots and work clothes before leaving work site.

The Need For Latrines And Toilets

Proper sanitation facilities (for example, toilets and latrines) promote health because they allow people to dispose of their waste appropriately. Make sure that you place your toilet away from area where food gets prepared or where people eat.

Keep toilets at least 100 feet away from water sources such as lakes, rivers, streams, and wells.

Make sure that people can wash their hands with soap, running water, and paper towels.

The emergency preparedness industry is rapidly expanding and these days emergency sanitation devices are readily available.

In an emergency, you can consider the following options:

- Emergency biodegradable bags

- Heavy-duty home refuse bags.

- Buckets

- A latrine trench

- An outhouse

1. Bags
Bags can be used on their own,

inside an empty toilet or in a container (bucket or portable toilet. We can use two kinds of bags:

1.) Special biodegradable waste bags (expensive).

2.) Heavy-duty home refuse bags (cheap).

1. Biodegradable bags

You can buy portable toilet waste bags for an easy solution to your toilet needs. They consist of an inner waste bag and a leak-proof outer carry bag.

A zip locking mechanism makes for a secure seal.

These bags come with a chemical disinfectant in powder or gel form.

These bags can be used with empty toilets, portable toilets or with buckets.

2. Heavy duty home refuse bags

An immediate (and very practical) solution for every individual in the household is to use heavy-duty home refuse bags. These bags typically are placed inside reusable buckets or empty toilets and when done, have to be buried or properly disposed of according to local health regulations.

You will need carbon material to cover the poo: A supply of sawdust, coffee husk chaff, finely shredded paper, kitty litter or coconut fiber.

Bags are very handy and can be a lifesaver in an emergency situation.

Upside:

- No infrastructure required.
- Lightweight and easy to transport
- May be used where space is severely limited or in flooded areas.

Downside:

- Active supply chain needed to provide approximately 1 bag, per person, per day.
- High costs of some types of bags.
- Need for disposal site and possibly collection services.
- Potential for bags to be discarded in open areas or areas posing risks to others.
- Requires intense hygiene campaign to educate the household on handling and disposal of bags.

2. Buckets

Bags work very well with 5 gallon (19L) plastic buckets. Buy two 5 gallon buckets with lids. One bucket will be the "pee" bucket, and the other will be the "poo" bucket. You can buy a snap-on toilet seat for both 5 gallon buckets and each unit will function as a toilet.

When dealing with waste we have to separate the fecal matter from the urine. Urine (of a healthy individual) is actually sterile and that's why it's better to separate it from the fecal matter. The harmful pathogens resides in the bucket with the fecal matter. Urine can later (wait a few days) be sprinkled on land as a fertilizer.

Prepare:

- Two 5 gallon plastic buckets.
- These days snap-on toilet seats are available for 5 gallon buckets.
- Carbon material to cover the poo: A supply of sawdust, coffee husk chaff, finely shredded paper, kitty litter, fireplace ash, or coconut fiber.

Pay attention to the following:

1. Make sure that you mark the two buckets as "pee" and "poo" (or similar).

2. Prepare a space that will provide some privacy and place the bag with carbon covering material nearby, along with a scoop or tongs.

3. Once it's time to clean the buckets, try not to mix the pee and poo. Once the pee and poo are mixed, the smell will be quite unpleasant.

4. After using the pee bucket, the user should put the toilet paper in the poo bucket. Then, remove the seat from the pee bucket and cover it with a lid that closes well.

5. After using the poo bucket, sprinkle as much carbon material as needed to completely cover the surface of the poo. This eliminates odors and keeps flies away.

6. Put the toilet seat back down on the poo bucket so it doesn't invite pests.

7. Sanitize your hands thoroughly!

3. Digging an emergency trench latrine

You can always buy a portable camp toilet to be used in an emergency. Eventually, if the disaster persists and you run out of bags and ways to dispose of them, you will have to consider digging a trench.

1. Choose a convenient site the minimum safe distance from water sources. Locate latrines and portable toilets at least 100 feet away from surface water bodies such as lakes, rivers, streams, and at least 150 feet downhill or away from any drinking water source (well or spring), home, apartment, or campsite.

2. Dig a trench 1 foot (0.3 m) wide by 3 feet (0.75 m) deep. The length of the trench will depend on the number of users ; about 3 feet (0.75 m) per user is enough.

3. Place boards along each side of the trench for people to stand on. Privacy can be improved by building a screen around the latrine. Use simple material.

4. Leave the dirt, obtained from digging the pit, in a pile near the trench with a shovel. Once used, each person covers over their feces with a shovelful of earth to keep away flies and reduce odors. Additionally, throw lime, mulch, sawdust, coffee husk chaff, finely shredded paper, kitty litter, or ash in the latrine to minimize odors and to keep flies, mosquitoes, and rodents away.

5. Store stacks of the traditional anal cleansing material used in the area close by, and top them up regularly. Old telephone books and Yellow Pages make excellent emergency toilet paper.

6. You can cover the latrine between use with plywood, or another material.

Close the trench when it is within 1 foot (0.3 m) of ground level. Cover it over with earth and pack it down tightly. The area should not be disturbed for two years.

4. Digging an outhouse

Make sure that you follow your local health regulations and the restrictions that apply to outhouses. Pay special attention to restrictions that apply to water sources, animal enclosures and domestic living areas. Design your outhouse to suit the weather and climate

Testing Water: Disease and Contamination

in your area. Give special attention to ventilation (vents), humidity (mold resistant paint), snow (insulation) and insects (screens). Important to note that you definitely want the soil around your outhouse to drain easily.

How to:

1. Dig a hole 4 ft deep, and 3.5 x 3.5 ft square. Make sure that the hole is square and that the walls are even and straight down.

2. You want to line the inside of the hole with wood. Keep the bottom of the hole open. This is where the waste will seep into the ground. Construct a "box" out of wood (2 x 4's with cross pieces) and wrap it in waterproof material like tar paper that construction workers use.

The tar paper will keep moisture out of the pit. The "box" should fit snug in the hole and the bottom and top sections should be left open.

3. Level out the area around the hole and create a square foundation for your outhouse with some 4 x 4's. You should have a square pit in front of you with the ground visible at the bottom and a nice frame of wood around the hole.

4. For the actual outhouse, you have two options:

a.) One option is to build a solid structure with four posts that

Keep small children away from the outhouse! Small kids should always be accompanied by an adult when using the outhouse!

can be set in concrete. Use a post hole digger to dig your post holes. This is a permanent fixture on your property and you can make it as sturdy as you desire.

b.) Another option is to make it a temporary structure that can be mobile when needed. Build the structure, but keep in mind that you will relocate it at a later stage.

For both construction options you can use plywood and timber posts. The corner posts should be timber (4 x 4's) and you can use ½" plywood for the floor, roof, and seat. Use ¼" plywood for the walls. The roof should be sturdy enough to keep rain and/ or snow out. Depending on climate, you can use shingles, roof panels or sheet metal.

You will also need a vent pipe. The vent pipe should be venting from as high as possible in the chamber, since hot air rises. One option is to use 4" PVC pipe (with holes) that runs from the seat all the way up through the roof. You can place a pipe cap on top to keep water out.

Another option is to run the vent pipe on the outside of the building, all the way up to the top next to the roof. Use black pipe and place it on the sunny side so that the sun-heated black pipe will draw the air by convection. This avoids having to put a hole in the roof as well.

Some tips to keep in mind:

- Use brass screws or coated screws to avoid rust.

- Waterproof the area around and underneath the toilet seat. You can use a plastic sealant. You can do this anywhere you think moisture might be an issue.

- If you live in a cold area you should definitely try to insulate the building.

- Paint the inside of the structure with mold resistant paint.

- Put screens on all pipe holes, vents and window openings to keep the bugs and critters out.

- Set your door so that it opens inwards.

You will need to keep carbon material in your outhouse to sprinkle over the waste when done. Store stacks of the traditional anal cleansing material used in the outhouse, and top them up regularly. Old telephone books and Yellow Pages make excellent emergency toilet paper.

Important! Do not put bleach, chemicals, pesticides, trash, cigarettes, or anything non-biodegradable down the hole. Keep things simple and try to live with the odors that will escape from time to time.

Small children should never be allowed near an outhouse. If you have small children in the house, consider locking the outhouse door with a simple combination lock.

What to do with a filled up outhouse?

This is something that should only happen when there is a sudden increase in users. For a normal family, a standard outhouse should last for decades. If, for whatever reason, your outhouse has reached the end of its holding capacity, you can consider moving it to a new location.

How to:

1. Prepare a new location. Dig a new hole.

2. Move the outhouse to the new location.

3. Fill up the old hole with saw dust, ash and natural organic matter. Use the dirt from the new hole to completely fill up the old hole.

4. Plant some trees, shrubs or flowers over the hole. This indicates where the old hole was. Do not disturb the area for at least two years.

Discussing Waterborne Diseases

As the name suggests, waterborne diseases facilitate their journey of contamination through the medium of water. When we have unnatural high rainfall, we see an increase in floods, overflowing rivers, stagnant pools and also rotten organic matter. This creates a perfect environment for these diseases to spread and ultimately, to infect human populations. Waterborne diseases are caused by pathogenic microbes that can be directly spread through contaminated water. Most waterborne diseases cause diarrheal illness. Eighty-eight percent of diarrhea cases worldwide are linked to unsafe water, inadequate sanitation or insufficient hygiene. These cases result in 1.5 million deaths each year, mostly in young children. The usual cause of death is dehydration.

The best way to avoid a waterborne disease is to be aware of proper hygiene and to avoid coming into contact with contaminated water. As living organisms ourselves, we can rely on our immune systems and supportive care to recover from a waterborne disease. In some cases, depending on the pathogen and also the infected person's ability to fight an infection, some people may require antibiotics or other forms of treatment. In most cases, restricting the patient to clear fluids and avoiding solid food for a period of time will do the trick. However, other symptoms in combination with diarrhea can be a sign of something more serious lurking underneath. Keep an eye open for the following additional symptoms:

• Fever greater than 101 F or 38.3 C.
• Blood in stool.
• Severe vomiting.
• Major intestinal pain.
• Severe dehydration.
• Diarrhea lasting longer than 3 days.

When we leave diarrheal illnesses untreated, we eventually end up with a state of dehydration. Since the human body consists of mostly (75%) water, it is no surprise that a loss of fluids causes severe discomfort and can lead eventually to death.

There are three stages of dehydration:

1. Mild dehydration. Loss of 0-5% of body water (weight). Symptoms:

- Anxiety.

- Loss of appetite.

- Dry, sticky mouth.

- Tiredness, and feeling less active than usual.

- Thirst

- Darker, concentrated urine.
- Dry skin
- Headache
- Dizziness or lightheadedness

2. Moderate dehydration.
Loss of 5-10% of body water (weight).
Symptoms:
- Nausea and vomiting.
- Dizziness.
- Fatigue.
- Mood swings.

3. Severe dehydration. Loss of 10% or more of body water (weight).
Symptoms:
- Patient becomes delirious and
- confused.
- Loss of coordination.
- Little or no urine output.

The best and easiest way to treat dehydration is by preventing it altogether.

Re-hydration

Oral re-hydration is the first step in managing diarrheal dehydration. Special care should be taken with the young and the old.

Consider the following methods:

• Over the counter re-hydration packets are available and contain vital minerals that need to be replaced in the patient.

• Clear fluids are readily absorbed by the body and can be considered when symptoms are less severe.

• You can also manufacture your own home-made re-hydration drink.
Take one liter of water and add:
- 1 teaspoon of salt
- 6 teaspoons of sugar.
- ½ teaspoon of baking soda.
- The patient should drink as much as possible.
As the patient improves, they can progress to thin cereals, congee (watery rice), broths and juice.

• For children the BRAT diet works well to treat dehydration:
- Bananas
- Rice
- Applesauce
- Toast or crackers.
This diet is effective at slowing down the movements of the intestines and thus it gives the body more time to absorb fluids and it slows down water loss.

• Alternatively, consider natural remedies like ginger tea, hot water with raw honey, a teaspoon of apple-cider vinegar in a glass of water, bananas and yogurt.

• As a last resort, consider antibiotic medication to treat your diarrhea. This will hopefully provide your body with an opportunity to rehydrate. Your personal physician should be able to give you some advice in this regard.
Caution! Check all expiry dates before using any medication.

Treating Water-borne Diseases

The following section is to be used as a guide to be consulted when needed. The information is provided by the Centers For Disease Control And Prevention (CDC) and is aimed at informing citizens of the dangers present in untreated water.

In an emergency, people are often forced to consume food and water from unknown sources. The disruption of power and water lines can cause sanitation problems and neglecting the treatment and proper disposal of human waste can have catastrophic consequences. As mentioned earlier, most waterborne diseases cause diarrheal illness. The majority of diarrhea cases are linked to unsafe water, inadequate sanitation or insufficient personal hygiene. If untreated, diarrhea leads to dehydration and in severe cases, to death.

Pathogens are extremely versatile and can survive in a variety of environments, but they especially flourish in areas with contaminated water. These pathogens that we find in water, all pose a potential threat to human health.

When it comes to waterborne diseases, the CDC recommends paying special attention to the following list:

- Cholera
- Giardiasis
- Shigellosis
- Amebiasis
- E. Coli
- Typhoid
- Hepatitis A
- Leptospirosis

These are serious pathogens that can cause severe illness.

Make sure that you are familiar with the symptoms of each.

CAUTION. Although most waterborne diseases cause symptoms that resemble food-poisoning, it's also important to be aware of the fact that anti-diarrheal medication is not to be administered to treat the symptoms. Only administer medication once the illness has been positively diagnosed by a healthcare professional.

A big problem with diarrhea is the waste that it creates. Waste, especially fecal matter, is highly contagious and should be disposed of according to local health regulations.

This is a serious issue that should never be neglected.

(See p.217 for advice on waste management.)

Cholera

Description

Cholera is an acute, diarrheal illness caused by infection of the intestine with the bacterium Vibrio cholerae. An estimated 3-5 million cases and over 100,000 deaths occur each year around the world. The infection is often mild or without symptoms, but can sometimes be severe. Approximately one in 10 (5-10%) infected persons will have severe disease characterized by profuse watery diarrhea, vomiting, and leg cramps. In these people, rapid loss of body fluids leads to dehydration and shock. Without treatment, death can occur within hours. The cholera bacterium is usually found in water or food sources that have been contaminated by feces (poop) from a person infected with cholera. Cholera is usually found in the aftermath of natural disasters like floods and hurricanes.
The cholera bacterium may also live in the environment in brackish rivers and coastal waters.

Symptoms

Cholera infection is often mild or without symptoms, but can sometimes be severe. Approximately one in ten (5-10%) infected persons will have severe disease characterized by
• Profuse watery diarrhea
• Vomiting
• Leg cramps
 In these people, rapid loss of body fluids leads to dehydration, shock and coma. Without treatment, death can occur within hours.

Treatment

Cholera can be simply and successfully treated by immediate replacement of the fluid and salts lost through diarrhea. Patients can be treated with oral re-hydration solution, a prepackaged mixture of sugar and salts to be mixed with water and drunk in large amounts. This solution is used throughout the world to treat diarrhea. Severe cases also require intravenous fluid replacement. With prompt re-hydration, fewer than 1% of cholera patients die.
Antibiotics shorten the course and diminish the severity of the illness, but they are not as important as receiving re-hydration. Persons who develop severe diarrhea and vomiting in countries where cholera occurs should seek medical attention promptly.

Testing Water: Disease and Contamination

Giardiasis

Description

Giardia is a microscopic parasite that causes the diarrheal illness known as giardiasis. Giardia (also known as Giardia intestinalis, Giardia lamblia, or Giardia duodenalis) is found on surfaces or in soil, food, or water that has been contaminated with feces (poop) from infected humans or animals. Giardia is protected by an outer shell that allows it to survive outside the body for long periods of time and makes it tolerant to chlorine disinfection. While the parasite can be spread in different ways, water (drinking water and recreational water) is the most common mode of transmission.

Symptoms

Giardiasis is the most frequently diagnosed intestinal parasitic disease in the United States and among travelers with chronic diarrhea. Signs and symptoms may vary and can last for 1 to 2 weeks or longer. In some cases, people infected with Giardia have no symptoms.
Acute symptoms include:
• Diarrhea
• Gas
• Greasy stools that tend to float
• Stomach or abdominal cramps
• Upset stomach or nausea/vomiting
• Dehydration (loss of fluids)
• Other, less common symptoms include itchy skin, hives, and swelling of the eye and joints. Sometimes, the symptoms of giardiasis might seem to resolve, only to come back again after several days or weeks. Giardiasis can cause weight loss and failure to absorb fat, lactose, vitamin A and vitamin B12 2,4,9-12.

Treatment

Several drugs can be used to treat Giardia infection. Effective treatments include metronidazole, tinidazole, and nitazoxanide. Alternatives to these medications include paromomycin, quinacrine, and furazolidone. Some of these drugs may not be routinely available. Different factors may shape how effective a drug regimen will be, including medical history, nutritional status, and condition of the immune system. Therefore, it is important to discuss treatment options with a healthcare provider.

Shigellosis (Bacillary dysentery)

Description

Shigellosis is a diarrheal disease caused by a group of bacteria called Shigella. Shigella causes about 500,000 cases of diarrhea in the United States annually. Shigella germs are present in the stools of infected persons while they have diarrhea and for up to a week or two after the diarrhea has gone away. Shigella is very contagious; exposure to even a tiny amount of contaminated fecal matter, too small to see, can cause infection. Transmission of Shigella occurs when people put something in their mouths or swallow something that has come into contact with stool of a person infected with Shigella. To prevent Shigella, wash your hands with soap and water for a minimum of 20 seconds. If people do not have soap and water, they can use alcohol-based hand sanitizer with at least 70 percent alcohol.

Symptoms

Symptoms of shigellosis typically start 1–2 days after exposure and include:
• Diarrhea (sometimes bloody)
• Fever
• Abdominal pain
• Tenesmus (a painful sensation of needing to pass stools even when bowels are empty)

Treatment

Diarrhea caused by Shigella usually resolves without antibiotic treatment in 5 to 7 days. People with mild shigellosis may need only fluids and rest. Bismuth subsalicylate (e.g., Pepto-Bismol) may be helpful, but medications that cause the gut to slow down, such as loperamide (e.g., Imodium) or diphenoxylate with atropine (e.g., Lomotil), should be avoided. Antibiotics are useful for severe cases of Shigellosis because they can reduce the duration of symptoms. However, Shigella is often resistant to antibiotics. If you require antibiotic treatment for shigellosis, your healthcare provider can culture your stool and determine which antibiotics are likely to work. Tell your healthcare provider if you do not get better within a couple of days after starting antibiotics. He or she can do additional tests to learn whether your strain of Shigella is resistant to the antibiotic you are taking.

Amebiasis (Amoebic dysentery)

Description

Amebiasis is a disease caused by a one-celled protozoan parasite called Entamoeba histolytica. Although anyone can have this disease, it is more common in people who live in tropical areas with poor sanitary conditions. E. histolytica infection can occur when a person:

Puts anything into their mouth that has touched the feces (poop) of a person who is infected with E. histolytica.

• Swallows something, such as water or food, that is contaminated with E. histolytica.

• Swallows E. histolytica cysts (eggs) picked up from contaminated surfaces or fingers.

Symptoms

Only about 10% to 20% of people who are infected with E. histolytica become sick from the infection. The symptoms are often quite mild and can include:
• Loose feces (poop)
• Stomach pain
• Stomach cramping
• Weight loss

Amebic dysentery is a severe form of amebiasis associated with:
• Stomach pain
• Bloody stools (poop)
• Fever

Rarely, E. histolytica invades the liver and forms an abscess (a collection of pus).
In a small number of instances, it has been shown to spread to other parts of the body, such as the lungs or brain, but this is very uncommon.

Treatment

For symptomatic intestinal infection and extra-intestinal disease, treatment with metronidazole or tinidazole should be followed by treatment with iodoquinol or paromomycin. Asymptomatic patients infected with E. histolytica should also be treated with iodoquinol or paromomycin, because they can infect others and because 4%–10% develop disease within a year if left untreated.

E.Coli

Description

Escherichia coli (E. Coli) bacteria normally live in the intestines of people and animals. Most E. Coli are harmless. However, some E. Coli are pathogenic, meaning they can cause illness, either diarrhea or illness outside of the intestinal tract. The types of E. Coli that can cause diarrhea can be transmitted through contaminated water, food, or through contact with animals or persons. Six pathotypes are associated with diarrhea and collectively are referred to as diarrheagenic E. Coli.

• Shiga toxin-producing E. Coli (STEC) also referred to as Verocytotoxin-producing E. Coli (VTEC) or enterohemorrhagic E. Coli (EHEC). This pathotype is the one most commonly heard about in the news in association with food-borne outbreaks.
• Enterotoxigenic E. Coli (ETEC)
• Enteropathogenic E. Coli (EPEC)
• Enteroaggregative E. Coli (EAEC)
• Enteroinvasive E. Coli (EIEC)
• Diffusely adherent E. Coli (DAEC)

Symptoms

The symptoms of STEC infections vary for each person but include severe stomach cramps, diarrhea (often bloody), and vomiting. If there is fever, it usually is not very high (less than 101°F/less than 38.5°C). Most people get better within 5–7 days. Some infections are very mild, but others are severe. Around 5–10% of those who are diagnosed with STEC infection develop a potentially life-threatening complication known as hemolytic uremic syndrome (HUS). Clues that a person is developing HUS include decreased frequency of urination, feeling very tired, and losing pink color in cheeks and inside the lower eyelids. Persons with HUS should be hospitalized because their kidneys may stop working. Most persons with HUS recover within a few weeks, but some suffer permanent damage or die.

Treatment

Non-specific supportive therapy, including hydration, is important. Antibiotics should not be used to treat this infection. There is no evidence that treatment with antibiotics is helpful, and taking antibiotics may increase the risk of HUS. Anti-diarrheal agents like Imodium may also increase that risk.

Typhoid

Description

Typhoid fever is a life-threatening illness caused by the bacterium Salmonella Typhi. Salmonella Typhi lives only in humans. Persons with typhoid fever carry the bacteria in their bloodstream and intestinal tract. In addition, a small number of persons, called carriers, recover from typhoid fever but continue to carry the bacteria. Both ill persons and carriers shed Salmonella Typhi in their feces (stool). You can get typhoid fever if you eat food or drink beverages that have been handled by a person who is shedding Salmonella Typhi or if sewage contaminated with Salmonella Typhi bacteria gets into the water you use for drinking or washing food. Therefore, typhoid fever is more common in areas of the world where hand washing is less frequent and water is likely to be contaminated with sewage.

If you drink water, buy it bottled or bring it to a rolling boil for 1 minute before you drink it.

Eat foods that have been thoroughly cooked and that are still hot and steaming.

Avoid raw vegetables and fruits that cannot be peeled.

Symptoms

Persons with typhoid fever usually have a sustained fever as high as 103° to 104° F (39° to 40° C). They may also feel weak, or have stomach pains, headache, or loss of appetite. In some cases, patients have a rash of flat, rose-colored spots. The only way to know for sure if an illness is typhoid fever is to have samples of stool or blood tested for the presence of Salmonella Typhi.

Treatment

Typhoid fever is treated with antibiotics. Resistance to multiple antibiotics is increasing among Salmonella that cause typhoid fever. Reduced susceptibility to fluoroquinolones (e.g., ciprofloxacin) and the emergence of multidrug-resistance has complicated treatment of infections, especially those acquired in South Asia. Antibiotic susceptibility testing may help guide appropriate therapy. Choices for antibiotic therapy include fluoroquinolones (for susceptible infections), ceftriaxone, and azithromycin. Persons who do not get treatment may continue to have fever for weeks or months, and as many as 20% may die from complications of the infection.

Hepatitis A

Description

Hepatitis A is a contagious liver disease that results from infection with the Hepatitis A virus. It can range in severity from a mild illness lasting a few weeks to a severe illness lasting several months. Hepatitis A is usually spread when a person ingests the virus from contact with objects, food, WATER or drinks contaminated by feces or stool from an infected person. A person can get Hepatitis A through:

Person to person contact when an infected person does not wash his or her hands properly after going to the bathroom and touches other objects or food

Hepatitis A can be spread by eating or drinking food or water contaminated with the virus. (This can include frozen or undercooked food.) The food and drinks most likely to be contaminated are fruits, vegetables, shellfish, ice, and WATER. In the United States, chlorination of water kills Hepatitis A virus that enters the water supply.

Symptoms

Some people with Hepatitis A do not have any symptoms. If you do have symptoms, they may include the following:
- Fever
- Fatigue
- Loss of appetite
- Nausea
- Vomiting
- Abdominal pain
- Dark urine
- Clay-colored bowel movements
- Joint pain
- Jaundice (a yellowing of the skin or eyes)

Treatment

There are no special treatments for Hepatitis A. Most people with Hepatitis A will feel sick for a few months before they begin to feel better. A few people will need to be hospitalized. During this time, doctors usually recommend rest, adequate nutrition, and fluids. People with Hepatitis A should check with a health professional before taking any prescription pills, supplements, or over-the-counter medications, which can potentially damage the liver. Alcohol should be avoided.

Leptospirosis

Description

Leptospirosis is a bacterial disease that affects humans and animals. It is caused by bacteria of the genus Leptospira and are spread through the urine of infected animals, which can get into water or soil and can survive there for weeks to months. Many different kinds of animals carry the bacterium. These can include, but are not limited to: Cattle, pigs, horses, dogs, rodents, and wild animals. When these animals are infected, they may have no symptoms of the disease. Humans can become infected through:
• Contact with urine from infected animals.
• Contact with water, soil, or food contaminated with the urine of infected animals.

Symptoms

In humans, Leptospirosis can cause these symptoms:

• High fever
• Headache
• Chills
• Muscle aches
• Vomiting

• Jaundice (yellow skin or eyes)
• Red eyes
• Abdominal pain
• Diarrhea
• Rash

The time between a person's exposure to a contaminated source and becoming sick is 2 days to 4 weeks. Illness usually begins abruptly with fever and other symptoms. Leptospirosis may occur in two phases:

• After the first phase (with fever, chills, headache, muscle aches, vomiting, or diarrhea) the patient may recover for a time but become ill again.

• If a second phase occurs, it is more severe; the person may have kidney or liver failure or meningitis. This phase is also called Weil's disease.
The illness lasts from a few days to 3 weeks or longer. Without treatment, recovery may take several months.

Treatment

Leptospirosis is treated with antibiotics, such as doxycycline or penicillin, which should be given early in the course of the disease.
Intravenous antibiotics may be required for persons with more severe symptoms. Persons with symptoms suggestive of leptospirosis should contact a health care provider.

Resources

Water. Why it's an issue.
http://www.worldbank.org/en/
topic/water/publication/high-and-
dry-climate-change-water-and-
the-economy

Understanding The Origins Of
Water

http://en.unesco.org/news/
water-action-cop22-address-cli-
mate-challenges

http://environment.nationalgeo-
graphic.com/environment/fresh-
water/water-conservation-tips/

Weather Patterns And Systems

http://www.ucmp.berkeley.edu/
education/dynamic/session4/
sess4_hydroatmo3.htm

http://earthobservatory.nasa.gov/
Features/LaNina/la_nina_2.php

https://en.wikipedia.org/wiki/Wa-
ter#Law.2C_politics.2C_and_crisis

https://en.wikipedia.org/wiki/Wa-
ter_right

Storing Water For An Emergency

http://naturalsociety.com/re-
cycling-symbols-numbers-plas-
tic-bottles-meaning/

http://edition.cnn.
com/2016/02/01/health/bpa-free-
alternatives-may-not-be-safe/

Collection And Storage Of Rainwater

https://en.wikipedia.org/wiki/Rain-
water_harvesting

https://en.wikipedia.org/wiki/
Pump

http://www.s1expeditions.
com/2014/08/161-solar-power-
off-grid-on-grid.html

Extracting Water From The
Ground

http://drillyourownwell.com/index.
htm

http://www.waterencyclopedia.
com

http://www.waterencyclopedia.
com/Ge-Hy/Groundwater.html

http://www.nzdl.org/gsdlm-
od?a=p&p=home&l=en&w=utf-8

http://siteresources.worldbank.
org/INTPHILIPPINES/Resources/
RWSVolIDesignManual.pdf

http://siteresources.worldbank.
org/INTWRD/864188-1171045933
145/21215368/33b.pdf

http://www.sswm.info/sites/de-
fault/files/reference_attachments/
ABBOT%204000%20Hand%20
Dug%20Well%20Manual.pdf

Designing Your Own Filtration
System

https://en.wikipedia.org/wiki/Bio-
film

https://en.wikipedia.org/wiki/Bio-
sand_filter

http://www.shared-source-initia-
tive.com/biosand_filter/complete_
biosand_new.html

http://ojs.library.queensu.ca/
index.php/ijsle/article/view-

File/4244/4344

Cleaning Water For Survival

https://en.wikipedia.org/wiki/Portable_water_purification

https://www.brita.com/?locale=us

http://www.bigberkeywaterfilters.com/berkey-water-filters.html?___SID=U

http://doultonusa.com/Pop%20up%20products%20desriptions/Ultracarb%20Water%20Filter%20Elements.htm

http://doultonusa.com/doulton_water_filters/Whole-house-ceramic-water-filter.php

https://www.espwaterproducts.com/about-reverse-osmosis/

https://www.espwaterproducts.com/uv-water-purification/

http://www.ozonepurewater.com

http://www.pelicanwater.com/whole-house-water-filter.php

http://www.culligan.com/home/water-softening

http://www.h2olabs.com

http://www.echotecwatermakers.com/beach_house_desalination_systems.htm

How to manage waste

https://en.wikipedia.org/wiki/Pit_latrine

https://www.unicef.org/cholera/Annexes/Supporting_Resources/Annex_9/WHO-tn7_waste_mangt_en.pdf

Centers for Disease Control and Prevention

http://www.cdc.gov/healthywater/disease/az.html

http://wwwnc.cdc.gov/travel/yellowbook/2016/the-pre-travel-consultation/water-disinfection-for-travelers

http://www.cdc.gov/healthywater/drinking/travel/backcountry_water_treatment.html

http://www.cdc.gov/ExtremeHeat/

http://www.cdc.gov/healthywater/emergency/drinking/making-water-safe.html

http://www.cdc.gov/healthywater/drinking/private/wells/maintenance.html

United States Environmental Protection Agency

https://www.epa.gov/privatewells/protect-your-homes-water

www.epa.gov/safewater/mcl.html

www.epa.gov/safewater/sdwa/sdwa.htm

World Health Organization

http://www.who.int/water_sanitation_health/emergencies/fs3_2/en/

http://www.who.int/water_sanitation_health/diseases-risks/diseases/diseasefact/en/

Index

Y

Notes

Notes

About The Author

Daniel Schoeman is a scholar and researcher of languages, cultures, carpentry, plumbing, construction, agriculture and how to live off the land. He first started traveling the planet in 1997 and worked as a willing worker on organic farms in Australia. His journey has since taken him to a variety of locales all over the world and given him the privilege to see how different cultures live and deal with their respective environments.

His motivation stems from an aspiration to create a world where self-sufficient, off the grid living is endorsed, and where housing can be affordable to all humans with the will and determination to work for it.

His latest endeavor is researching and writing how-to articles on hydroponics and cob house building techniques.

This is his third resource guide on water management.

www.ingramcontent.com/pod-product-compliance
Lightning Source LLC
Chambersburg PA
CBHW080246030426
42334CB00023BA/2724